An Insider's (

Toronto "The |

MW00570722

First Edition

Published by Aleron Publications Ltd.

73 Thornridge Drive, Thornhill
Ontario, Canada L4J 1C7

National Library of Canada Cataloguing in Publication

Weigel, Walter, 1958-
    An insider's guidebook to Toronto : the meeting place /
Walter Weigel. -- 1st ed.

Includes index.
ISBN 0-9731145-0-9

    1. Toronto (Ont.)--Guidebooks.

FC3097.18.W43 2002   917.13'541044
C2002-902739-X
F1059.5.T683W43 2002

Printed in Canada on recycled paper by Porter Fine Printing Ltd, Richmond Hill, ON
Photographs and maps by Walter Weigel (cover image – courtesy of Corel Draw)

Comments, suggestions, and error corrections are welcome and can be provided by contacting the Publisher at the address noted above or via the Internet at
www.insidersguidetoronto.com

MAPS

Please note that the maps are not to scale, nor do they include all roads or attractions. The orientation of all of them is north at the top and south at the bottom of the map. They are meant to provide you with a sense of where you are heading, some key roads to keep an eye out for, and where key attractions are. The map below is of downtown Toronto where, like most great tourist-friendly European cities, most of the action is.

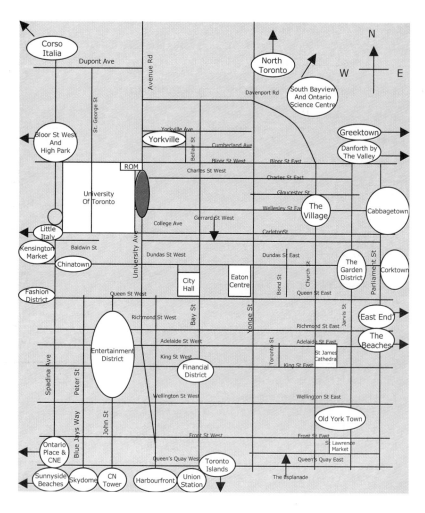

The map covers an area of about 2 miles east/west by 3 miles north/south.

MAP OF TTC SUBWAY ROUTES
in the Downtown Core

See "Getting Around Within Toronto" for further information on using the Toronto Transit Commission.

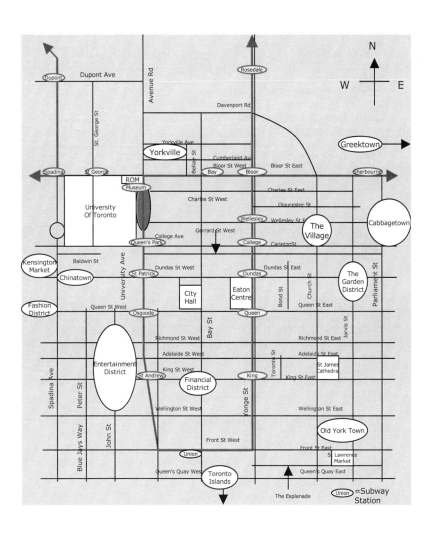

TABLE OF CONTENTS

INTRODUCTION

Why this Guidebook?

This guidebook provides a single, handy reference for you to easily carry around Toronto and enjoy great things to do that many Torontonians are not aware of. To assist you plan and get the most from your vacation, this guidebook includes detailed tour and trail maps, guidance on getting to Toronto and back through US Customs, Tours that ensure you won't miss those hidden but marvelous gems "around the corner", Sections on major interests (examples include Attractions, Hollywood North, Festivals, and African-Canadians) to enable you to customize your vacation plan to *your* preferences, scores of great things to do FREE, and lots of useful website addresses. Americans in particular will learn, and should be proud, of their substantial contributions to the great city of Toronto.

There is *lots* of information not provided in any other guidebook or promotional tourist material (and certainly not in one handy source). You get information on what a point of interest is *really* like, rather than the picture perfect claims of many marketing brochures. No fees or freebies of any kind were requested or accepted by me from any person or organization identified in the book. Nor did I proclaim my presence and purpose at the attractions, hotels, restaurants, or shops before checking them out. I have done every tour, hike, and bike trip, and most of the festivals, attractions, shops, and restaurants – I know and can help you with where most of the good stuff, FREE stuff, and hidden gems are.

Lastly, for those families looking to get even more for their money, I suggest you consider the "Entertainment" coupon book for the Toronto area. Savings of up to 50% on fine and casual dining, hotels, attractions, car rentals, and sports. Pays back its US$27 price in just one or two uses. (800) 374-4464, www.entertainment.com. See www.attractions.on.ca for coupons to Toronto.

Symbols used in the Guidebook

Items highlighted in **BOLD** are attractions and points of interest further described under "ATTRACTIONS" and "SPORTS and ACTIVITIES".

 Indicates a significant American involvement or history in a given attraction or point of interest.

Items highlighted in RED are eating establishments: those highlighted in bold **RED** are further described under "DINING".

Items highlighted in TURQUOISE are stores or shopping malls: those highlighted in bold **TURQUOISE** are further described under "SHOPPING".

Items highlighted in GREEN are parks or parkettes: those highlighted in bold **GREEN** are further described under "ATTRACTIONS, General".

Items of architectural or historical interest are marked in *italics* and further described under "ARCHITECTURE".

 Indicates an attraction or activity the author believes will offer the tourist an experience over and beyond the usual.

 Indicates a better than usual value for your money.

Toronto, Eh?

I have been lucky enough to travel throughout the US, Canada, Europe, and the South Pacific and yet I consider Toronto to be one of the best places to visit (and live in). It has come a long way from the 600 person burg the Americans captured in 1813 (see "In the Beginning") and from the view expressed by the US based *Columbian Centinel*, which wrote on May 20, 1812 just prior to the War of 1812:

"And will you spend thousands of millions in conquering a province which, were it made a present to us, would not be worth accepting?"

Even today some consider Canada generally as a land of beer drinking, toque-wearing hockey players or lumberjacks in a land of snow, polar bears, back-bacon, and the redcoats of the Royal Canadian Mounted Police. Hollywood likes to portray Canada this way, as "That 70's Show" did with its episode in 2001 on the boys heading off to Canada to buy beer, and with movies like "Canadian Bacon". Okay, while there is *some* merit to these views, many people don't realize that Canada's largest city, Toronto, is today one of the world's most vibrant, cosmopolitan cities with over 4 million people in the Metropolitan census area.

Toronto today is a superb destination with an overwhelming mix of things for visitors to do. Toronto offers a relatively easy and safe way to get a taste for the world's foreign cultures all in one vibrant and exciting city. Toronto has the theatres and nightlife of New York or Chicago, the film industry of Los Angeles, the cleanliness and safety of Smalltown USA, big-league sports including the Toronto Raptors and Toronto Maple Leafs, and the attractions of several cities combined. All close together and easy to get to in an amazing downtown. Toronto also offers the foreign country experience of a livable and walkable downtown similar to the "Centrums" or City Centres of Europe, different laws, different holidays (like Queen Victoria's birthday on May 24 and Boxing Day on Dec 26, but no Memorial Day), a cultural diversity represented by 170 countries of peoples and 100 languages and dialects including French, a "clothing-optional beach", colorful money, and much more. A small sample of districts include **Little Italy**, **Corso Italia**, **Chinatown** (two), Greektown, **Gerrard India Bazaar**, Portugal Village, **Caribana** (North America's largest black celebration festival), The Village and its Gay Pride Week (among North America's largest gay festivals), and **Caravan** (with 20+ pavilions of different countries where you can taste exotic foods and see ethnic dances). There are more festivals, parades, city celebrations, parties, outdoor cafes, art shows, dance shows, book readings, clubs, and so on than one can partake in as a city resident, let alone a visitor.

Americans may be interested to note that they represent about 90% of the 48.6 million visitors to Canada. Toronto is the most visited city in Canada with 10.9 million trips in 1999, far exceeding second place Montreal's 6.9 million trips! For Americans, it is a relatively inexpensive holiday as Toronto prices are nominally comparable to what you would see in the US, except that they are in Canadian dollars worth 63 US cents!! (Britons too, will find Toronto much less expensive than London!).

Which other vibrant worldclass city can you easily drive to (for Americans and Canadians), be safe, see and do hundreds of fantastic things, experience the cultural diversity of 170 countries, go to the beach, and do so inexpensively?

TRAVEL BASICS

Getting Here by Car

Most American visitors to Canada are from the States of New York, Michigan, California, Washington, Ohio, and Pennsylvania. 82% came by car. With the September 11, 2001 terrorist attack on New York, more people may choose to drive instead of fly. It's also often less expensive for a family to drive than fly.

The common routes into Toronto from the US are: 1) through Detroit, Michigan and 4.5 hours northeast along Highway (Hwy) 401; 2) through Buffalo, New York and 2 hours along the Queen Elizabeth Way (QEW); and 3) through Syracuse and Watertown New York, north along Interstate 81, and 3 hours west along Hwy 401. These highways have minimum 2 lanes in each direction and go straight to Toronto. The only tricky point is between Buffalo and Toronto. Stay to the left on the QEW after you cross over the Burlington Skyway (bridge) near Hamilton in order to get to Toronto. The right lanes and exit here are for Hwy 403 that looks like it is going east toward Toronto, but curves back and heads due west toward London!

For detailed information on road conditions throughout Canada and links to provincial government websites, see Trransport Canada's www.tc.gc.ca or the Canadian Automobile Association's (CAA) website www.caa.ca. The CAA is affiliated with AAA, and AAA coverage applies in Canada. Branch offices are generally open from Mon - Fri at 9 am - 6 pm, and Sat at 9:30 am - 4:30 pm. The downtown Toronto CAA branch is located at 461 Yonge St just north of Carleton St. Call (416) 221-4300 for assistance or see www.central.on.caa.ca.

Drivers should note:

-Ontario has the second safest roads in North America, second only to Massachusetts, as measured by the fatality rate per 10,000 licensed drivers.

-Seat belt use is mandatory for all passengers.

-Child car seats must be used for children under 40 pounds.

-Driving under the influence of alcohol is a serious offence with heavy penalties including the confiscation of one's driver license.

-The major highway speed limit is 100 kilometres (km) per hour or 62 miles an hour (0.62 miles per km). The fine for driving 120 km per hour (75 mph) is $100, and for driving 140 km per horr (87 mph) is $295!

-Speeding fines in the city of Toronto are:
-10 km/hour over costs	$40.00
-20 km/hour over costs	$100.00
-30 km/hour over costs	$142.50

For those of you who think you can skip paying by leaving the country, beware! Ontario has reciprocal agreements with the States of New York and Maine whereby you will be legally responsible for paying the ticket (and having it put on your record). Agreements with Michigan, Ohio, Pennsylvania, and Minnesota are imminent. And, yes, radar detectors are illegal and can be confiscated.

-Watch for tow away times, generally 3:30 pm or 4 pm on major streets leaving the downtown core!

-Helmets are mandatory for motorcycle drivers and passengers.

-A US driver's license and US vehicle insurance is acceptable in Canada, as long as the person is a tourist.

-Regular unleaded gas in Canada at time of publication is approximately $0.70 per litre, which is about US$1.97 per gallon.

-Canadians drive on the right side of the road despite our British heritage!

-Call 911 in emergencies, or call AAA/CAA for roadside car assistance.

-US citizens may also want to look at the US Government's "Consular Information Sheet" for Canada (www.travel.state.gov/canada.html).

Roadside Stops

If you're driving the roughly 100 miles to Toronto through Buffalo via the QEW highway, you may be surprised by how urbanized the "Golden Horseshoe" or the stretch from Fort Erie to Toronto is. Because of this, there are many *off* highway roadside stops and no on-highway stops (the only significant "empty" stretch is the 15 miles from Fort Erie north to Niagara Falls – this stretch can also be more treacherous in winter due to its proximity to Buffalo's renowed snow belt). One spot that's about ½ way between Fort Erie and Toronto in Grimsby offers food and a superior view across the lake. Get off at Casablanca Blvd exit and turn north (right) for about 100 yards. Turn left on Niagara Regional Rd 9 and left again on Windward Dr. There is a Swiss Chalet BBQ chicken restaurant, a Harvey's burger place, a Subway sandwich shop, a 24 hour ATM machine, and a Tim Horton's coffee shop. The road leads to a dead end a few hundred yards north on Lake Ontario's shore. One is afforded a rare easily accessible and beautiful view of the western end of Lake Ontario and the cities hugging its shores. On crystal clear days, you will be rewarded with a superlative view of Toronto's skyline.

If you're driving to Toronto through Detroit d along Hwy 401, make sure you have enough gas as there are few highway facilities or towns between Windsor and London. Eastbound roadside stops and their *approximate* distance from the border include:

1. 26 miles to Tilbury. Gas, Tim Horton's coffee shop, and Kentucky Fried Chicken.
2. 76 miles to Dutton. Gas, Wendy's, and Mr. Sub.
3. 126 miles to Woodstock. Gas, Wendy's, and Mr. Sub.

4. 196 miles to Mississauga. Gas, Wendy's, and Tim Horton's coffee shop.

If you're driving to Toronto through The Thousand Islands (via US Hwy 81) and west along Hwy 401, there are the following westbound roadside stops and their approximate distance from the border:

1. 32 miles to Odessa. Gas, Tim Horton's coffee shop, and Kentucky Fried Chicken.
2. 107 miles to Port Hope. Gas, Wendy's, Tim Horton's, and Mr. Sub.

See AAA/CAA for a trip-tik, or visit www.mto.gov.on.ca/english/traveller to plan your road trip. This site has useful tips like the Border Wait Times update, and Winter Conditions section.

Getting Here by Commercial Airliner

The September 11, 2001 events in the US made people more nervous about flying. There's an informative website for these people, www.airsafe.com, that provides interesting safety and other information by airline carrier, and airplane make. For those of you undeterred to fly (like me), you will land at Toronto's Pearson International Airport about 16 miles of urban mass from downtown Toronto. There are several ways to get from the airport to downtown (see the "Getting Here" section of the airport's website, www.ibpia.toronto.on.ca, for details and latest updates).

Airport limos and taxis (must be licensed) are on a fixed fee schedule based on where your destination is. The cost to most of downtown is $43 or $44.

Airport Express buses ((905) 564-6333, www.airportexpress.com) pick up on the Arrivals Level of all terminals around the clock. All buses are wheelchair accessible. Cost is $14.25/person or $24.50 return. Students and seniors receive a 10% discount on one-way fares. The buses stop at several convenient downtown hotels like the Royal York and Colony Hotels.

Rental cars from the normal rental agencies you would see at an American airport are also available at the Toronto airport. Once you have your rental, exit the airport and look for Hwy 427 south. Stay on Hwy 427 as it heads south and OVER the 16-lane Hwy 401, until you reach Queen Elizabeth Way (QEW) highway going left or east into Toronto. Follow the QEW, which will change names (but nothing else) to the Gardiner Expressway. If you see a highway sign that says "Hamilton" or "Niagara Falls" or even "London", you're going the wrong way. Assuming you are going the right way on the QEW, continue eastward until you reach Yonge St or whatever other highway exit street is closest to your hotel. The Yonge St exit is central to most of the downtown hotels. Look for the CN Tower, which at 1,815 feet high is hard to miss: it won't be far to your hotel if you're staying in the downtown core.

You can also get on Hwy 409 east to Hwy 401 east to Yonge St south if you would like to experience a 12-lane highway normally packed with vehicles! The drive south on Yonge St will take about 25 minutes for only 8 miles, but you'll see why Yonge St is the backbone of Toronto.

Public transportation into Toronto is via the Toronto Transit Commission (TTC) (www.city.toronto.on.ca/ttc) or GO Transit (www.gotransit.com). Use GO Transit or Mississauga Transit (www.city.mississauga.on.ca/transit) if you are heading into the suburbs (largest is Mississauga). TTC routes and schedules identified in this book are current at time of publication but may be subject to change. Call the TTC at (416) 393-INFO for the latest information.

TTC express bus 192 picks passengers up at the Arrivals Level of both Terminals 2 and 3 and costs $2.25 cash/adult. Bus 192 runs every 45 minutes from the start times below and will drop you off at the Kipling Subway Station in about 20 minutes. Grab a transfer from the bus driver when you pay and you won't have to pay again to get on the subway.

First and Last Trip Times	Mon - Sat & Holidays	Sunday
Kipling Stn.	5:40 am	8:40 am
Pearson Airport	5:59 am	8:59 am
Kipling Station	12:25 am	12:25 am
Pearson Airport	12:43 am	12:43 am

The subway here only goes east, as Kipling is the furthest west station. The trip to the Yonge/Bloor Station will take about 30 minutes. Transfer to the southbound Yonge line and get off at the stop closest to your destination.

If you arrive well past midnight, but would like to take public transportation, TTC bus 307 EGLINTON WEST, part of the Blue Night Network, provides overnight service between Eglinton Station on the Yonge Subway Line and Terminal 2 at Toronto Pearson Airport. Buses run every 30 minutes, from approximately 1:30 am - 5 am, seven days a week. One-way travel time is approximately 45 minutes.

GO buses cost $3.10/adult and will drop you off at Yorkdale or York Mills Subway Stations. You will have to pay for the subway separately - $2.25 cash/adult or $9 for 5 tokens.

Getting Here by Train

VIA Rail trains are available for long distance travel across Canada. Call (416) 236-2029 , your travel agent, or see www.viatrain.ca. Bookings can be made via www.Travelocity.com as well. For information on Amtrak trains coming into Toronto, visit www.amtrak.com or call (800) USA-Rail. Amtrak's "Maple Leaf" train runs from Washington D.C. to Toronto (Union Station, a few blocks from most hotels downtown) through Baltimore, New York City, Albany, Syracuse, Buffalo and many towns in between.

Getting Here by Bus

Greyhound Bus Lines travel to Toronto. The downtown bus terminal is on 610 Bay St, one short block north of Dundas St West and just one block away from the Eaton Centre. Call (800) 229-9424 or visit www.greyhound.com for detailed schedules and rates.

Can you get into Canada?

US citizens and persons lawfully admitted to the US for permanent residence (passport, Green card or other evidence of permanent residence) do not have to have a visa or passport to visit Canada for six months or less. Without a passport, Canada Customs may require a birth certificate along with a driver's license (with photo) or a certificate of citizenship to prove US citizenship.

Canada participates in a program to prevent child abduction. Custom officers may require documentary evidence that a child is yours and/or has travel permission of the parent not present.

Canada Customs (see www.cic.gc.ca) may deny entry to persons who intend to stay or work in Canada without proper authorization, have insufficient funds to cover their costs while traveling within Canada, are in poor health, and/or have a criminal record.

Medical Coverage in Canada

According to the US State Department's Bureau of Consular Affairs, **U.S. Medicare and Medicaid programs do not provide payment for medical services outside the United States.** Nor are visitors to Canada eligible for provincial health coverage. You should ensure you have suitable medical insurance for travel in Canada that covers hospitalization and, if necessary, medical evacuation to the US. It is important to determine whether the insurance will pay for services required upfront or whether they require you to pay first and then seek reimbursement. Blue Cross is one organization that offers travel insurance. See www.bluecares.com/healthtravel/worldwide.html.

Information on medical emergencies abroad, including overseas insurance programs, is provided in the Department of State's Bureau of Consular Affairs brochure, *Medical Information for Americans Traveling Abroad* (see www.travel.state.gov/medical.html).

Staying Here

Like any large, world-class city, Toronto has accommodation in all ranges to suit almost any traveler. Most hotels are in downtown Toronto or at Pearson International Airport (see "ACCOMMODATIONS"). One of my family's favourites is the downtown **Sheraton Hotel** on Queen St West. It has a superb location across from City Hall, reasonable prices, great huge indoor/outdoor pool (open even in the winter!), and a link to Toronto's underground "**PATH**" mall.

Crime and Safety

September 11, 2001 has made virtually everyone more conscious of safety. Toronto is a very safe city, both from crime and from natural hazards such as earthquakes and tornadoes. It is quite safe to walk most streets at day or night, and it is actually desirable to be in downtown after dusk.

Toronto has a lower murder rate than New York, Philadelphia, Pittsburgh, Rochester, Detroit, or even Honolulu and about the same number of murders in total as Flint, Michigan, a city of 132,000! About 75% of murders are solved and the perpetrators brought to justice. And, for most tourists, the best news is that the predominant downtown tourist areas account for less than 10% of the city's already very low murder rate.

Toronto's break and enter rate is the lowest of any city in Canada, and its motor vehicle theft rate is the 2nd lowest in Canada. The subway, buses, and streetcars are safe, clean, and well-maintained. The Toronto Transit Commission (TTC) bills itself as "...one of the safest transit systems in the world." Women may wish to avail themselves of the TTC's "Request Stop Program" allowing women traveling alone from 9 pm – 5 pm to request the driver to let them off at locations along the route other than normal stops.

Toronto has some homeless people in the main streets. "Squeegee kids" (named for their practice of washing your car windshield for a voluntary donation) sometimes work their trade on Lakeshore Blvd at Bay, Yonge, or Jarvis Streets. There is also a "Tent City" that has sprung up in the last couple of years, near Lakeshore Blvd and Cherry St. Both the homeless and the squeegee kids are generally not dangerous or bothersome to visitors.

Natural disasters are rare: the last was Hurricane Hazel in 1954!

Getting Around Within Toronto

Toronto is blessed with a superb public transportation system. Tourists should become familiar with the TTC's streetcars, buses, and subway. Most streets in Toronto run east-west or south-north, and so do the buses, streetcars, and subways. An easy way to know which is which once you're on the street is to look at the street sign: if it has a blue background, it signifies water (i.e. Lake Ontario) and runs south-north; if it has a yellow background, it signifies sun (rising and setting) and runs east-west!

The buses, streetcars, and subways are all clean, safe, economical, and run frequently. Musicians, who auditioned to earn the right, entertain at several different locations. Save yourself the hassle of finding parking downtown – ride the "Red Rocket", as the TTC is known locally. A single adult ride one-way, including transfers and irrespective of distance, is $2.25 for adults, $1.50 for seniors/students with ID, and $0.50 for kids. Make sure you ask for a transfer (a small paper ticket) when *entering* the subway, bus, or streetcar.

 An "All Day" family pass, good for unlimited TTC travel Monday to Friday after 9:30 am and all day Saturday/Sunday and holidays, costs $7.50/day. There is also an after-hours service, from 1:30 am - 5 am on many routes throughout the city, including Queen St, College St, Yonge St, and Bloor St. There is a great map of TTC routes/times at www.city.toronto.on.ca/ttc/schedules.

If you want to use your car, or a rental car, it's a wise choice as well if you want to check out some of the slightly further apart attractions. Toronto is relatively easy to get around in and to park in, but parking in most cases is CDN$1.50 per hour and up. Parking fines are generally $15-$20 if you pay voluntarily. Before deciding, please consider that Toronto's downtown is more like European downtowns than American downtowns: most things tourists like to see and do are contained within a few square miles and can be easily walked *to* in most cases. For those who insist on a car, see "Parking".

Rental Cars

All major rental car companies offer cars in Toronto. The major site is Pearson International Airport. Base rates generally are $30-$75 per day with unlimited mileage. Thrifty's (www.thrifty.com) downtown rental sites include Royal York Hotel (416-947-1385) and **Eaton Centre** (Parkade, 5th floor south, (416-591-0861)). Hertz's (www.hertz.com) downtown rental sites include 330 Front St near the Skydome (416-979-7119), and 44 Gerrard St West at Bay (416-979-

1178). Avis's downtown rental sites include Bay and Front Streets (416-777-2847, www.avis.com). Discount's downtown rental sites include 134 Jarvis St at Queen St East (416-864-0550, www.discountcar.com). Budget's downtown rental sites include 141 Bay at Front St (416-364-7104, www.budget.com). The Budget at 1128 Yonge St, north of Bloor St, offers exotic car rentals: Audi, Mercedes, BMW, Jaguar, and Porsche starting from $125 per day and $0.55/km over 50 km. You must be 25 years of age and be able to leave a $5,000 credit card deposit (416-964-7202). Dollar's downtown rental sites include 140 Carleton St east of Yonge St (416-921-1346, www.dollar.com).

Parking

There's lots of parking downtown. Street parking is $1.00-$2.00 per hour with a two-three hour maximum. In most cases there is one 7 foot tall green meter that you buy your ticket from (cash/credit card) and display in your window dash. Municipal parking lots are identified by a green circle with a "P" in the centre. Rates are $1.25-$1.75/half hour, to a maximum $8 from 7 am - 6 pm, or to a maximum $5 from 6 pm – 7 am. Locations include:

Financial and Entertainment Districts
1. 110 Queen St West under **Nathan Phillips Square** (underground).
2. 40 York St at University Ave and Front St (underground – best to approach via southbound University Ave in the right lane).

Yorkville, Yonge/Bloor, and the **Royal Ontario Museum**
3. 37 Yorkville Ave west of Yonge St and east of Bay St.
4. 9 Bedford Rd, just north of Bloor St West.

Old York
5. 1A Church St at The Esplanade. There are also entrances just east of Yonge St and at the foot of Market St.

Church/Wellesley and Garden District
6. 15 Wellesley St, 30 yards east of Yonge.

Bloor St West
7. 365 Lippincott, just south of Bloor St West and east of Bathurst.

The Beaches
8. 10 Lee Ave, just north of Queen St East.

I have found almost all to be well-situated, clean, well lit, and safe. Near the popular **Harbourfront** area, one of your best bets is the seven story-high parking garage at 200 Queen's Quay West. The garage is north across the street from Harbourfront. It is not part of the municipal parking lots, rates are a bit higher on weekends, and payment is by cash only. The entrance is off of Lower Simcoe St.

Taxis

Taxis are plentiful, clean, and safe. Rates are $2.50 to get in the car, plus $1 per kilometer (0.6 miles), plus $0.25 for every 33 seconds stopped in traffic, plus tax plus tip plus a fee for handling baggage. Taxis are available if their roof light is on. Major taxi companies include Co-op (416-504-2667), Metro (416-504-8294), Diamond (416-366-6868), and Yellow (416-504-4141).

Trains

Government of Ontario (GO) trains leave from Union Station frequently to several suburbs. Should you have the urge or necessity to travel to the suburbs, contact GO for detailed timetables and rates at (416) 869-3200, (888) 438-6646, or see www.gotransit.com.

Weather

Toronto has so many things to do indoors that for some visitors, weather will be a small consideration. Toronto's weather is very similar to that of the Great Lake states, except that Toronto generally gets less snow than cities like Cleveland and Buffalo on the south side of the Great Lakes.

Toronto gets about 32 inches of precipitation per annum, relatively spread out over each month. July and August are the warmest months with average high temperatures in the mid 70° F range. January and February are the coldest months with average high temperatures around 30° F or –2°C. June and September can be the nicest months with the best balance of sun, warmth, humidity, and bugs (lack of).

Languages

The predominant language is English, with small differences with Americans in pronunciation, accent, and use of words. Many Americans, especially those flying into Toronto with Air Canada or watching Prime Minister Jean Chretien, assume all Canadians can speak and understand French. Only about 1.5% of the Toronto population list French or French and English as their mother tongue. Montreal on the other hand has 68% of the population list French or French and English as their mother tongue.

There are 100 other languages and dialects spoken in Toronto, making Toronto one of the world's most ethnically and culturally diverse cities.

Taxes and Tax Refunds

You may get a bit of "sticker shock" when you receive your bill. The reason is taxes: the 8% provincial sales tax (PST) and the 7% goods and services tax (GST) added to the price of most goods and services, including your hotel. On the bright side, just remember those Canadian dollar prices will cost about $0.63 in US dollars for Americans and even less for Britons!

You may be able to get some relief as the Canada Customs and Revenue Agency (CCRA) offers qualifying visitors a refund of the GST on qualifying purchases if you meet the following conditions:

- You are not a resident of Canada;
- You purchased eligible goods, short-term accommodation, or both;
- You paid GST on these purchases;
- You have original receipts (original receipts for purchases of goods have to be validated, depending on how you travel when leaving Canada);
- For eligible goods, each receipt shows a minimum purchase amount (before taxes) of CDN$50; and
- Your purchase amounts (before taxes) total at least CDN$200 for eligible goods and short-term accommodation.

"Eligible goods" for GST refunds generally include goods you bought and will bring to and use outside Canada within 60 days. Unfortunately, GST is not refundable on purchased items such as meals and alcohol, tobacco, car rentals, or on air/train/bus tickets.

Original receipts must be included in the one page refund application form, which can be obtained at major hotels, at Customs, at duty free shops at the border or Pearson International Airport, and at CCRA's helpful website at www.ccra-adrc.gc.ca/tax/non-residents/visitors/tax_e.html. You can call CCRA toll FREE from the US at (800) 267-5177 for help. There is no processing fee. If you feel uncomfortable sending original credit card receipts and other papers with your personal data in the mail, the following are duty free shops that can process your refund application on the spot for up to $500 cash.

Buffalo/Fort Erie and Niagara Falls

Peninsula Duty Free Shops Ltd.
Queenston-Lewiston Bridge
Highway 405
Queenston, Ontario
(905) 262-5363

Niagara Duty Free Shops Inc
5726 Falls Avenue
Rainbow Bridge
Niagara Falls, Ontario
(905) 374-3700

Ogdensburg/Prescott

Sault Ste. Marie

Johnstown Duty Free Shop Inc.
Highway 416
Ogdensburg/Prescott International Bridge
Prescott, Ontario
(613) 262-5363

Sault Ste. Marie Duty Free Shop
127 Huron Street
International Bridge Plaza
Sault Ste. Marie, Ontario
(705) 759-6333

Detroit/Windsor

The Windsor-Detroit Tunnel
   Duty Free Shop Inc.
465 Goyeau Street
Windsor, Ontario
(519) 977-9100

Ambassador Duty Free Shop
707 Patricia Street
Windsor, Ontario
(519) 977-9100

There are several companies that will process your application on your behalf for a fee. "National Tax Refund Service" charges 20% of the refund, with a minimum CDN$12 charge, plus taxes. You provide the original receipts and information, sign an agreement to allow them to claim, process, and receive your refund on your behalf, and they take care of the rest. Their brochure is available at several hotel and tourist sites, or see www.nationaltaxrefund.com. They offer instant cash back at their kiosk on the 2nd floor in the southwest corner of the Toronto **Eaton Centre** (enter via Queen St).

"International Tax Refund Services Inc" offers the same service for the greater of US$7.50 or 15-18% of the refund, plus a "payment processing fee", plus taxes. Their brochure and application form is available at several hotel/tourist sites, or via www.itrs.com. "Canada Sales Tax Refunds" charges the greater of CDN$10 or 20% of the refund, plus CDN$2 postage and handling, plus taxes. "Premiere Tax-Free Services, Canada Inc" has brochures available at the airport, Terminal 2, if you missed picking a form up downtown.

In any event, you must have the goods' receipts validated by Canada Customs if you are making a refund claim even via the noted companies. Plus you will then have to mail your completed application with original receipts from the US to one of the companies. Given this, and how easy the CCRA's one page form is, I would process my claim at the border offices identified above and pocket the full refund. If you're flying out of Pearson International Airport, go to the Canada Customs Information Centre in either Terminal 1, 2, or 3.

The Province of Ontario also has a program to facilitate refunds of the 8% retail (provincial) sales tax on goods (not accommodation, not services) purchased by visitors and taken back permanently to the US within 30 days of the date of purchase. Unfortunately, one must have paid at least CDN$50 of retail sales tax per purchase (meaning individual purchases of over $625)! If you fall into this category, call (905) 432-3509 collect or (800) 615-2757 or see www.rev.gov.on.ca/images/rsie0298.pdf for the easy to complete form with instructions. The National Tax Refund Service handles retail sales tax refunds as part of its service of collecting the GST refund.

Accessing Cash and Foreign Exchange

All prices/costs in this guidebook are in Canadian dollars, unless specificallly identified otherwise. There are many banks with ATM bank machines open around the clock every day. They'll dispense Canadian dollars and you'll be charged a transaction fee, as well as the foreign exchange.

I find little need to carry much cash on vacation. You can bring traveller's cheques denominated in Canadian dollars with you, plus some cash for fast food restaurants, hot dog stands, etc.. Most other costs, including street parking, can be paid with a credit card that will bill you in your own currency. Or you can convert your money into Canadian dollars at any bank (although the hours aren't great), at a foreign exchange specialist like Thomas Cook at 10 King St. East (east of Yonge St), or at the venue you are spending your money at. I don't recommend the latter as you'll often get a poorer exchange rate. One retailer I saw was accepting US dollars at par!

Statutory Holidays

Jan 1: New Year's Day
Mar 29: Good Friday
Apr 1: Easter Sunday
May 20: Queen Victoria Day
Jul 1: Canada Day
Aug 7: Simcoe Day
Sep 2: Labour Day
Oct 14: Thanksgiving Day (note: not in November as in the US)
Dec 25: Christmas Day
Dec 26: Boxing Day

Canada does not have a Memorial Day holiday.

Getting Back into the US.

US Customs will require you to declare everything you bring back that you did not take with you when you left the US, including:

- Items you purchased abroad and are carrying with you upon return to the US, including items bought in "Duty Free" shops, gifts for others, and/or items to be used or sold in your business.
- Items you received as gifts and/or inheritances.
- Repairs or alterations to any items you took abroad and then brought back, even if the repairs/alterations were performed free of charge.

Because the onus of proof is on you that an item was yours before the trip, you may wish to consider getting and completing Customs Form 4457 for key items you owned before your trip and took along on your trip (eg. laptop computer, video camera). This form, known as the Certificate of Registration, must be certified by US Customs before you leave the country. This can be done at the airport of departure, for example. The value you will have to declare is what you actually paid, including taxes. You'll have to declare the estimated fair market value of gifts you received.

Now comes the real complex matter – what duty is payable, if any, on the declared items! Fortunately, US Customs offers a duty free exemption of US$400 per person (children and infants included, but they can't use it for liquor) on goods from your visit to Canada if:

- The items are with you upon your return to the US and are for your personal or household use.
- The items are not prohibited or restricted. One such item is Cuban cigars purchased in Canada! Other items include but are not restricted to cars, firearms, drug paraphernalia, cultural art and artifacts of national importance, fish and wildlife, and plants.
- The items are declared to Customs.
- You are returning from a stay abroad of at least 48 hours.
- You have not used your exemption, or any part of it, in the past 30 days. You can claim a US$200 exemption if you were not out of the country for at least 48 hours or if you've used up your US$400 exemption.

Family members who live in the same home and return together to the United States may combine their personal exemptions via a "joint declaration".

The duty payable is determined by adding up the value of declared items, subtracting the claimed duty exemption, and then applying a flat rate of duty of 3% on the first US$1,000 (since January 1, 2002). Any amount of declared item value thereafter is subject to duty rates as set out in the North American Free Trade Agreement (NAFTA).

To ensure you have the latest US requirements, contact the US Customs Agency at www.customs.ustreas.gov/ for further guidance. If nuclear rocket science is child's play to you, try www.dataweb.usitc.gov or www.usitc.gov for information on duties payable for various items. Or call the Buffalo Customs office at (716) 646-3400, the Detroit Customs office at (313) 442-0368, the Ogdensburg Customs office at (315) 393-0660, the Port Huron Customs office at (810) 985-7125, or the Sault Ste. Marie Customs office at (906) 632-7221.

U.S. Consulate

The U.S. Consulate is at 360 University Ave, just north of Queen St. Hours of service are Mon – Fri, 8:30 am - 1 pm, excluding US and Canadian holidays.

The U.S. Consulate provides services for US citizens such as passports, voting information, tax forms, reports of birth, foreign country travel information, and assistance in emergency situations (eg. death or arrest of US citizens).

Extensive information is available at http://www.usembassycanada.gov/. From Canada, you may call (800) 529-4410 for detailed recorded information and forms on a full range of topics in English and French. Call (416) 595-1700 or (416) 201-4100 for after hours emergencies.

EMERGENCIES

The 24 hour emergency room at Toronto General Hospital is at 200 Elizabeth St. (416) 340-3948 or dial 911 for emergencies.

A 24 hour Shopper's Drug Mart is at 700 Bay St. (416) 979-2424.

"Dental Emergency Service" is open 7 days a week from 8 am - midnight. 1650 Yonge St, 2 ½ blocks north of St Clair St on the west side (about 10 minutes north of Yonge and Queen Streets). (416) 485-7121.

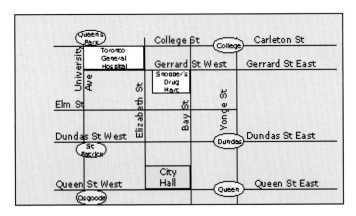

In the "Beginning"

Beaver furs were a huge part of Canada well before it became a country. The French and English fur traders used two key routes to get to the beaver-rich upper Great Lakes and beyond: via the Ottawa River, and via Lake Ontario, Humber River (in present day Toronto), and Lake Simcoe. The French built **Fort Rouille** in 1750-51 near present day **Fort York** to enable trading along the second route with native people, primarily the Mississaugas. A few years later the French burned the fort to the ground and left the area after the British defeated the French in North America.

Americans Help Found Ontario and Toronto!

Even before Ontario (then Upper Canada) was founded, the Americans had a hand in setting its future. The 1783 peace settlement between the Americans and British resulted in an international border drawn from the St. Lawrence River through the lakes Ontario, Erie, St. Clair, Huron, and Superior. In the 1770s and 1780s, Americans loyal to Great Britain during the American Revolution, called United Empire Loyalists, sought refuge in Canada. The Loyalists were persona non grata in the US during and immediately after the American Revolution and many fled to the Maritime Provinces and Quebec. Those who fled to Quebec posed a problem for the Canadian Governor who saw potential trouble in mixing so many Protestant English-speaking Loyalists, with Catholic French-speaking Canadians. The Governor encouraged Loyalists to head to the very sparsely populated land west of Montreal along the St. Lawrence River and on Lakes Ontario and Erie. In 1784, as many as 5,000 Loyalists traveled to Upper Canada (now Ontario) to be the first white settlers, but none went to the uninhabited Toronto area.

To facilitate settlement in the Toronto area, the British "bought" 250,808 acres of land between the Don and Humber Rivers from the Mississaugas on Sept 23, 1787. The challenge was then to persuade people to settle here.

 The communities the Loyalists founded grew rapidly, resulting in the colonies of Upper Canada and Lower Canada (now Quebec) being created as a result of the Constitutional Act of 1791. Thus, Ontario was born in large part thanks to the Americans! A British Colonel, John Graves Simcoe, who fought against the Americans in the Revolutionary War as Commander of the famous Queen's Rangers, was then appointed to be the first Lt. Governor of Upper Canada in 1791. Simcoe enticed many Americans to come to Ontario, especially from Pennsylvania.

Toronto was born, in large part thanks to Americans. The U.S. attacked Canada before in 1775, during the Revolutionary War, and there was increasing conflict with the Americans thereafter. Upper Canada's capital, Newark (now Niagara-on-the-Lake), was just a few miles from the US border near Niagara Falls, New York. Simcoe sought a new capital of Upper Canada and was instructed to choose Toronto for its distance from the US border, and its natural and defensible harbour. As Toronto was his second choice behind present day London, Ontario, Simcoe wrote in a letter to a friend: "I shall console myself – excellent salmon."

<u>1793-1812</u>

On July 19, 1793, Simcoe sent a hundred of the Queen's Rangers to Toronto to begin building and fortifying a new fort, a new town of several blocks clustered around today's Front and Sherbourne Streets (see Tour 9), and roads like Yonge (the world's longest street at 1,856 km) and Dundas Streets. **St. James Cathedral** and **St. Lawrence Market** stand on the same land set aside for a church and market in the original 1793 town plan and survey!

 Yonge St, most of York Township, and York town's first expansion were surveyed in the 1790s by Augusta Jones, a Loyalist.

 Once Toronto was founded and Yonge St partially built in 1793, many Americans settled in or near Toronto in communities such as Willowdale (James Davies, a Loyalist, in 1792, and Jakob Kummer from Pennsylvania, in 1797), Hogg's Hollow (Thomas Mercer, a Loyalist, in 1796), Ashbridge's Bay (the Ashbridge family from Pennsylvania in 1793), and Markham (William von Berczy and Germans and Dutch who left Pulteney settlement in the Genesee River area of New York State, in 1796).

Simcoe, his wife Elizabeth, and their three children arrived in Toronto bay on July 30, 1793. Unfortunately, one of Simcoe's children, 15 month old Katherine Simcoe, was the first internment at *Toronto's first burying ground* near Fort York at present day Niagara and Portland Streets.

 Americans burn Toronto to the ground. The White House was burned in retaliation, and the Stars and Stripes Anthem was born.

US President James Madison (1807-1817) declared war on Great Britain on June 18, 1812. Sure, US President Andrew Jackson became President in 1829 in part due to his stunning victory over the British/Canadians in the Battle of

New Orleans in 1815. The US Navy excelled in taking on and often besting the world's premier navy of the time. But the primary battlegrounds were the current province of Ontario (then Upper Canada), and the current states of New York, Pennsylvania, and Michigan, and the Americans did not do well.

The general American strategy was to attack Upper Canada (Ontario) both to divert attention away from the key objectives of Montreal and Quebec City, and because Upper Canada had a small population of mostly Americans. In 1813, the Americans, with about 1,700 men under the command of General Dearborn, sailed up Lake Ontario in Commodore Isaac Chauncey's ships: the *Madison* under Lieutenant-Commander Elliott, the *Oneida* under Lieutenant (Lt.) Woolsey, the *Hamilton* under Lt. McPherson, the *Scourge* under Mr. Osgood, the *Tompkins* under Lt. Brown, the *Conquest* under Lt. Pettigrew, the *Growler* under Mr. Mix, the *Julia* under Mr. Trant, the *Asp* under Lt. Smith, the *Pert* under Lt. Smith, the *America* under Lt. Chauncey, the *Ontario* under Mr. Stevens, the *Lady of the Lake* under Mr. Hinn, and *Raven*. The fleet[1] arrived about four miles west of York (now Toronto) at around 8 am on April 27, 1813. Dearborn's second-in-command, Brig. Gen. Zebulon Pike, attacked and overwhelmed Fort York and its 600 defenders under Major-General Roger Sheafe. 50 Americans were killed or wounded, and 90 British regulars and 50 Canadians and Indians were killed or wounded during the battle. Immediately after the Americans took the Fort, a powder magazine exploded, killing or wounding 232 Americans including General Pike, and 40 British regulars.

The victorious Americans burned an almost constructed 24 gun ship after taking its guns, took the 10 gun brig *Gloucester*, looted and burned public buildings in the nearby town of York including the **Provincial Parliament buildings**, and destroyed provincial records. After being detained in York a week by bad weather, the Americans crossed Lake Ontario to help attack Canadian forts on the west side of the Niagara River.

The Americans conducted a second invasion of York on July 31, 1813, when 300 American soldiers came ashore uncontested. They seized supplies and food, and burned military installations on Gilbraltar (now Hanlan's) Point on the **Toronto Islands**. The American burnings left a revengeful Canadian and British folk that led to their burning the White House in Washington on August 15, 1814, and the birth of the Stars and Stripes US anthem.

 More American soldiers per 100,000 of US population died in the War of 1812 then in the Vietnam War!

---

[1] See page 125 of "The Naval War of 1812", written by Theodore Roosevelt in 1882 and re-published in 1999 by Modern Library Paperback Edition, for information on ship type, tonnage, crew, broadside metal, and armament.

After the War of 1812

Most of the immigration to Canada prior to the War was from the US. After the War, American immigration was discouraged and British immigration encouraged. In addition to the fact that the Americans had tried to takeover Canada twice hereto (1775, 1812), Canadians were concerned with the US's Manifest Destiny concept whereby many Americans felt it was their destiny to control all of North America's land. It was a valid concern given the US had acquired the Louisiana Purchase (central US) from France in 1803, much of today's North Dakota from the British in 1818, Florida from Spain in 1819, present day Texas/New Mexico from Mexico in 1845, present day Washington and Oregon from Britain in 1846, present day Utah/Arizona/California/Nevada from Mexico in 1848, and Alaska from Russia in 1868!

The Rebellion of 1837

The town of York, often called Muddy York because of the mud streets, was incorporated as the City of Toronto in 1834 with a population of 10,000 to 12,000. Discontent developed over the governing elite's land-granting policies, and the general favoritism shown to the Church of England and its supporters. William Lyon Mackenzie, Toronto's first Mayor, led a rebellion of dissenting "radicals" against the higher government authorities in 1837. About 750 rebels congregated at Montgomery's Inn (today's Postal Station K at 2384 Yonge Street, just north of Eglinton Ave). They came largely from north of Toronto and were mostly farmers, landowners, and laborers. On December 5, 1837, they marched south along Yonge St until they met Sheriff Jarvis and approximately 20 men hiding in the vegetable garden of a Mrs. Sharpe (today's Maple Leaf Gardens on Carlton Street). A brief skirmish ensued before both sides fled. On December 7, 1837, the Governor's troops and reinforcements marched north to Montgomery's Inn to defeat the rebels.

Mackenzie escaped to Buffalo, USA where he garnered support from Americans to continue fighting on. Mackenzie's rebels attacked Navy Island in the Niagara River on December 14, 1837, but were driven back shortly thereafter by Canadian troops. Canadians also burned the US rebel supply ship, the Caroline.

Two of Mackenzie's supporters, Peter Matthews and Samuel Lount, were hanged in the Toronto jail at present day 1 Toronto St at King St East on April 12, 1838. William Lyon Mackenzie was imprisoned for 18 months in Rochester, New York by the US government. He was later pardoned by the Upper Canada Governor in 1850, returned to Toronto, and lived at 82 Bond St (today **Mackenzie House**) until his death. Interestingly, William Lyon

Mackenzie's daughter Isabel married John King and their son William Lyon Mackenzie King became Canada's 11th prime minister!

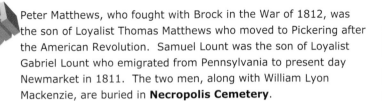

Peter Matthews, who fought with Brock in the War of 1812, was the son of Loyalist Thomas Matthews who moved to Pickering after the American Revolution. Samuel Lount was the son of Loyalist Gabriel Lount who emigrated from Pennsylvania to present day Newmarket in 1811. The two men, along with William Lyon Mackenzie, are buried in **Necropolis Cemetery**.

The first person killed in the Rebellion, rebel Colonel Moodie, is buried 10 yards inside the main entrance to Holy Trinity Cemetery in Thornhill.

<u>1867 and the Birth of Canada</u>

Canada was born after the Fathers of Confederation met in P.E.I. A significant impetus to Confederation was fear of take-over by the Americans based on events including the American induced Trent Affair of 1861, the US Annexation Bill passed in the House of Representatives in 1866, and the Fenian (Irish American) attacks in 1866. The Bill indicated the provinces and territories of Canada be "...constituted and admitted as States and Territories of the USA" by being bought from Great Britain for $85,750,000 and other considerations, and by being bought from the Hudson's Bay Company for $10,000,000.

Just as the US national anthem has a Canadian connection, the Canadian national anthem has an American connection. Calixa Lavallee, born in 1842 in Quebec, wrote the music for O' Canada in 1880. He lived in the US in 1865-72 (he served as Lieutenant during the Civil War) and in 1880-91 (he died in Boston in 1891). His remains were moved to Montreal in 1933. The French version of O' Canada has been unaltered since 1880, but the English version was only finalized in 1968 and declared Canada's national anthem only on July 1, 1980!

The Weekend: What's Best to Do?

This Section is for those of you who might ask, "What should I do if I only have a weekend in Toronto?" I've taken a few family situations and have assumed the family arrived by car near dinnertime Friday. Departure is after dinner on Sunday. Each itinerary only scratches the surface of great things to do, but will give you a good overview of Toronto's wonders.

Family #1: adult(s) with kid(s) who want the common tourist spots.

Friday
1. Check-in at your hotel and have dinner at Mr. Greenjeans.
2. Visit the Eaton Centre and abutting **Trinity Church** and **Maze**, and **Chinatown (West).**

Saturday
1. Have breakfast at your hotel, The Senator Restaurant, or Jenzer's Deli in the **Sheraton Centre**'s underground food court.
2. Stroll down Yonge St to the **Hockey Hall of Fame** on Front St. Turn right or west until you reach Bay St, then turn left or south past the **Air Canada Centre** until you reach Queen's Quay. Head through Harbour Square Park toward the Toronto Island Ferry dock and you'll see a boardwalk off to the right. Follow this boardwalk along the lakefront and you'll come to **Harbourfront** and Queen's Quay Terminal (see Tour 6). Have lunch at one of the hot dog cart vendors, Café Deli, Il Fornello's, or the Boathouse Bar & Grill.
3. Have dinner at The Old Sphagetti Factory, Joe Badali's, or Gretzky's.
4. Go to the **CN Tower** and neighbouring **Skydome**.
5. Stroll Bloor-Yorkville and have coffees/hot chocolates at Lox Stock & Barrel in Hazelton Lanes.

Sunday
1. Have breakfast at your hotel or grab a commuter's breakfest in **Union Station** on the train departure/arrival level (see Tour 2).
2. Visit the **Ontario Science Centre**, a great spot for families.
3. Have dinner at Marche's or Panorama.

Family #2: adult(s) with kid(s) who want common tourist spots, plus.

Friday
1. Check-in at your hotel and have dinner at Mr. Greenjeans or Gretzky's.
2. Go to the movies at the **Paramount Theatre**.
3. Cap the evening with a short stroll one block north on John to Queen St West. Grab a cup of coffee from Second Cup on the southwest corner. Walk along Queen St West to Spadina Ave and back. Spend a buck to have your say on video at the **Speaker's Corner.** There is an excellent nighttime view of the color-lit **CN Tower** and **Skydome** from here.

Saturday
1. Breakfast in your hotel, Fran's, or the Golden Griddle. Or, a lite breakfast of coffee/tea and muffins/sweets can be had at the many "Second Cup", "Starbucks" and other cafes.

2. Go early to the **St. Lawrence Market**.
3. Catch the **Toronto Police Museum, Cloud Forest, Eaton Centre, Old City Hall**, and Financial District on your way to the ferry docks.
4. Ride the **Toronto Islands** ferry to Centre Island for a fabulous view of Toronto's magnificent skyline. If your kids are under 13, spend a couple of hours at the very park-like **Centreville** amusement park, try the maze, and walk the southern pier over Lake Ontario. (If your kids are teenagers or young adults, instead of Centreville, head to **The Docks** entertainment complex after having lunch at **Marche's**).
5. Return via ferry and have a late lunch at **Marche's** at BCE Place. A great open market-like restaurant where you stroll among the food stations and have your meal prepared on the spot. Kids will love it, but get there early to avoid long line-ups.
6. Stroll **Old York** Town area. See Tour 11.
7. Have dinner at **The Old Spaghetti Factory** or **The Brownstone** and catch a live show at the **Royal Alex Theatre, Elgin and Winter Gardens Theatres, Lorraine Timsa Young People's Theatre, Canon Theatre, Roy Thomson Hall, Air Canada Centre,** or **Skydome.**

Sunday

1. Have brunch at **The Hothouse**. Voted the best brunch in the city, a seat on the south end of the restaurant facing busy Front St gives you the added pleasure of people watching.
2. Head to The Beaches. See Tour 12.
3. Have dinner at **Lick's**, the colorful and novel premium burger/ice cream shop the kids will love, or at Whitlock's outdoor patio across the street.
4. Take Queen St East west to the Yonge and Queen Streets start point.

Family #3: loves sports; mostly grown children.

Friday

1. Check-in at your hotel and have dinner at **Gretzky's**.
2. Walk through the Entertainment District down to the **CN Tower** to watch a Toronto Argonaut Canadian football game at the neighbouring **Skydome** or play a round or hit a few balls at the **City Core Golf** just west of the Skydome on the west side of Spadina Ave. Another choice if there's no game on at the Skydome would be to visit the **Hockey Hall of Fame.** Or grab your rollerblades or bikes and do the **Martin Goodman Trail** to Kew Beach and back.

Saturday

1. Start at Yonge and Queen Streets. Take a pre-breakfest morning 4 mile roundtrip jog/run west along Queen St West past the **Eaton Centre, Old City Hall, Nathan Phillips Square**, and **Osgoode Hall**. Turn north on

University Ave until you reach Queen's Park Circle. Follow it on the right until you reach Bloor St West or Queen's Park if you want the shorter route. Turn right until you reach Bellair St on the north side of Bloor. Turn left on Bellair until you reach Yorkville Ave and then turn left until you reach Avenue Rd. Turn left for 150 yards and turn right on Bloor St West for about 100 yards until you reach the entrance of Philosopher's Walk on the south side of Bloor. Turn left along the Walk until you reach Hoskins Ave. Turn west for about 30 yards and then south on Tower Rd in **University of Toronto** grounds. Pass under Soldiers' Tower and you'll come to King's College Circle. Follow it left and you'll come to King's Rd. Turn left until you reach College St. Follow College St for 200 yards to University Ave, and turn right back to Queen St. Or you can workout or swim at your hotel or at the **YMCA**. In winter, consider a brisk skate at **Nathan Phillips Square**, **Harbourfront**, or at **Ryerson.**

2. Have breakfast in your hotel or at the **Golden Griddle** and then head to the **Hockey Hall of Fame**. Have lunch at **Marche's** or **Movenpick**.

3. Depending on your sport, you can go windsurfing or sailing in Toronto's Outer Harbour, mountain-biking or hiking in the Don or Rouge Valleys, rock-climbing at **Joe Rockhead's**, go-karting at Centennial Park, giant swing riding at **The Docks**, swimming/high diving at the **Summerville Pool**, skating at **Nathan Phillips Square**, skiing at Earl Bales Park or **Uplands Ski and Golf Centre**, golfing at the **Don Valley Golf Course**, drive ranging at **The Docks** or at **City Core Golf**, frisbee-golfing on the **Toronto Islands**, beach volleyball at **Woodbine Beach Park** & Ashbridge's Bay, basketball at the **YMCA**, skateboarding at **Cummer Skateboarding Park**, or horseback riding at **Sunnybrook Stables.** See the *monument* at Birch and Gange Avenues honouring Lionel Conacher as the Canadian male athlete of the first 50 years of the 20th century, and the *plaque* at the CN Tower honouring "Bobbie" Rosenfeld for being the Canadian female athlete of the first 50 years of the 20th century.

4. Have dinner at **The Keg Mansion** steakhouse.

5. Catch a game at the **Air Canada Centre** (NBA basketball, NHL hockey, and lacrosse), the **Skydome** (MLB baseball and CFL football), Maple Leaf Gardens (junior hockey), or Centennial Stadium (pro soccer).

Sunday

1. Have breakfast at **The Senator** or in the **PATH system**. Take your bike on the subway or ride it north almost 4 miles on Yonge St through several beautiful neighbourhoods and commercial street landscapes until you reach the Lawrence subway station. Travel one block south to St. Edmunds Dr, head into the Alexander Muir Park, and follow the path (see "Toronto Adventure Trail") if you're up for another 10 miles through **Sunnybrook Park**, Serena Gundy Park, Seton Park, and the Don Valley. If you make it, you'll be one of the few people who have done so

(including me, of course). Bring lots of water. The Don Valley trail will end at Lakeshore Blvd and join with the Martin Goodman Trail near Cherry St.

2. Follow Cherry St south along the **Martin Goodman Trail** until you reach Polson St and fantastic entertainment complex, **The Docks**.
3. Follow the Martin Goodman Trail west back to Yonge St, turn right or north, and you'll reach Queen St in less than 10 minutes.

Family #4: loves high society, arts, shopping, and architecture.

Friday

1. Check-in at your hotel, put your fine clothes on, and have dinner at Canoe, North 44°, or The 360 Restaurant. Attend a live show at the **Elgin and Winter Garden, Canon Theatre, Roy Thomson Hall, Royal Alexandra Theatre**, the **Ford Centre of Performing Arts**, the **Hummingbird Centre**, or The St. Lawrence Centre.
2. Top the evening off with a drink at the **Roof Lounge** of the Park Hyatt Hotel, or the Avenue Lounge in the **Four Seasons Hotel**, or the Panorama atop the 55 story Manulife Centre.

Saturday

1. Have breakfast at Movenpick in Yorkville.
2. Visit the **Thomson Gallery**.
3. Visit the **Royal Ontario Museum**, the **Gardiner Museum of Ceramic Art**, the **Bata Shoe Museum**, and/or the **Art Gallery of Ontario**. Shop Bloor-Yorkville.
4. Have dinner at Sassafraz, Bistro 990, Bellini's, or Sotto Sotto's.

Sunday

1. Have breakfast at Kalendar's in Little Italy (see Tour 5).
2. Stroll through University of Toronto grounds (see Tour 10) or **Cabbagetown** (see Tour 14).
3. Shop at Queen's Quay Terminal, and checkout the many upscale antique and home décor shops in Mount Pleasant.
4. Have dinner at Centro or North 44°.
5. Stroll along Bloor St West and Yorkville (see Tour 9).

Family #5: the couple or family who wants to experience different cultures.

Friday

1. Check-in at your hotel, and head to Little Greece's Astoria for dinner.
2. Go to the Second Cup in **The Village** (couples).
3. Stroll down Yonge St from Bloor St back to your hotel.

Saturday
1. Have breakfast at **Maggie's**. Walk west on Queen St West from Yonge St and see **Old City Hall**, **City Hall**, **Nathan Phillips Square**, **Osgoode Hall**, **Campbell House**, and Queen St West.
2. Visit **Chinatown (West)**, Kensington Market, and Little Italy (see Tours 3 and 5).
3. Have lunch at **Saigon** in Chinatown or at **Sensation Café** on Baldwin St. Visit Roncesvalles Village and Bloor West Village (see Tour 8).
4. Visit Hillcrest Village, Corso Italia, Bloorcourt Village, Bloordale Village, Little Korea, Markham Village, and Bloor St in the Annex (see Tour 18). Have dinner at **JJ Muggs** on Bloor St in the Annex.

Sunday
1. Have brunch at **The Hothouse Café** or **Il Fornello's** (Greektown).
2. Visit Little India, Queen Broadview Village, and Leslieville.
3. Visit The Beach and have lunch at **Lick's**, **Whitlock's**, or Lion on the Beach (see Tour 12).
4. Have dinner in Yorkville at **Yamato's** (watch your food being prepared in front of you) or at the **Sultan's Tent** (be entertained by a belly-dancer).

FOR KIDS!

Let's face it: it pays to keep kids gainfully occupied on trips or else the "relaxing holiday" is not. Here is a partial list of things to do for kids.

1. **Toronto Islands** ferry, maze, and **Centreville Amusement Park**.
2. Play at **Ontario Place**.
3. Play at the **Canadian National Exhibition**.
4. **CN Tower** and its Skydeck glass floor and/or Edge Arcade.
5. Shop at Eaton Centre.
6. Eat at Marche's in BCE Place.
7. Test your skills at the **Hockey Hall of Fame**.
8. Catch the latest movies at the **Paramount** or **Uptown Theatres**.
9. **St. Lawrence Market** (downstairs, and especially Domino's).
10. Walk Yonge St from Dundas to Bloor (especially the Arcade video game parlour, fast food joints, music video stores, jeans stores, and 1,000,000 Comics and its thousands of comic books). FREE.
11. Eat at The Old Spaghetti Factory.
12. Beach it up at Ashbridge's Bay or Rouge Beach Park. FREE.
13. Walk, bike, or rollerblade the **Martin Goodman Trail**. FREE.
14. Have lunch or ice creams at Lick's in **The Beaches**.
15. Ice skate at **Nathan Phillips Square** or **Harbourfront**. FREE.
16. Go kart at **Centennial Park** or **401 Indy Go Karting**.

17. Watch the Raptors, Maple Leafs, or Rock at the **Air Canada Centre**.
18. Catch a Blue Jays or Argonauts game at the **Skydome**.
19. Play at **The Docks**. This place has it all!
20. Visit and try life in Toronto's first development, **Fort York**.
21. Have fun pretending to be a 1800's school kid in a re-enactment at **Enoch Turner School**.
22. Take a tour of **ChumCity TV** at 299 Queen St West and maybe get chosen to be a dancer on the Electric Circus show. FREE.
23. Speak your mind for $1 via taped video at **Speaker's Corner.**
24. Learn about the sugar industry at the **Redpath Sugar Museum**. FREE.
25. Visit the **Royal Ontario Museum**, especially the dinosaur exhibit.
26. Visit the **Bata Shoe Museum**.
27. Take a pottery class at the **Gardiner Museum of Art**.
28. Make pottery at The Clay Room (see Tour 16).
29. Check out the Toy Terminal in the **Queen's Quay Terminal**.
30. Play video and virtual reality games at **Playdium Mississauga**.
31. Downhill ski at Uplands, Centennial Park, or Earl Bales Park.
32. Catch a live show at the **Lorraine Timsa Young People's Theatre** or "The Mousetrap" at the **Toronto Truck Theatre**.
33. Take a walk-in dance lesson at **The National Dance of Canada** for only $11, tax included (see the "SPORTS and ACTIVITIES" section, p. 176).
34. Partake in any of the _many_ festivals and events throughout Toronto such as the **Milk International Children's Festival**, and the **Beaches Jazzfest** (see "Attractions, Festivals").
35. The **Children's Own Museum** (best for kids 8 and under).
36. Learn about the Toronto harbour and ships at The **Pier Museum**.
37. Try canoeing or kayaking (for older kids) at **Harbourfront Canoe and Kayak School**.
38. Check out Toronto's first Post Office, its model of 1837 Toronto, and write a letter with quill pens, at 260 Adelaide St East. FREE.
39. Catch a live Broadway style show at the **Princess Alexandra Theatre**, **Princess of Wales**, **Elgin and Winter Garden Theatres**, **Toronto Centre for the Performing Arts**, or **Roy Thomson Hall**.
40. Go for an outdoor swim at **Sunnyside Pool**, the Riverdale Park East pool, or **Summerville Pool** in **Woodbine Beach Park**. FREE.
41. Visit the **Riverdale Farm**. FREE.
42. Visit the **Metro Toronto Zoo**.
43. Visit George's Trains at 510 Mount Pleasant Ave.
44. Visit the serenity and beauty of **Allan Gardens** and greenhouse. FREE.
45. Visit Toronto's castle, **Casa Loma,** and nearby **Spadina House**.
46. Try Queen's Quay Loblaw's cooking classes for children.
47. Be part of the audience at live tapings of the Royal Canadian Air Farce Show and The Red Green Show (see "HOLLYWOOD NORTH"). FREE.
48. Visit the **CBC Museum**. FREE.

49. Learn about Canadian inventors at the **Ontario Innovations Museum**.
50. Bike the Don Valley and/or Rouge Valley trails. FREE.
51. Tobaggan the superb hill at Riverdale Park (West and East). FREE.
52. Learn about how stocks and the stock exchange work at the **Toronto Stock Exchange Museum**. FREE.
53. Take a 25 minute one-way GO train ride to Port Credit (see Tour 2).
54. Have ice cream at the outdoor patio of the hilltop Dairy Queen on Broadview Ave and Pottery Rd. Superlative view of the valley.
55. Visit the **Don Valley Brickworks**. FREE.
56. Try the old-fashioned jail cell at the **Toronto Police Museum**. FREE.
57. Hit some balls at the **CityView Golf** range.
58. Re-live the pioneer days at the **Todmorden Museum and Discovery Centre** or at **Black Creek Pioneer Village**.
59. Visit the zoo at **High Park**. FREE.
60. Walk the free maze, or Labyrinth in Trinity Square Park. FREE.
61. Eat peanuts and toss the shells onto the floor at **McSorley's Saloon**.
62. Check out the stars on the free Canadian **Walk of Fame**. FREE
63. Play **LaserQuest** (laser tag) at 1980 Eglinton Ave East. Kids > 7 yrs.
64. Skateboard or rollerblade at the **Cummer Skateboard Park**. FREE.
65. Play in the fabulous sand of Rouge Beach Park. FREE.
66. Go bowling at the 24 hour **Newtonbrook Bowlerama**.
67. Take a movie location tour (see "HOLLYWOOD NORTH"). FREE.
68. Have some quiet time in **Lillian H. Smith Library** at 239 College St, east of Spadina Ave. A children's library and outdoor garden on the 1st floor, computers with Internet access on the 3rd floor, and the Osborne Collection of Early Children's Books on the 4th floor. FREE.
69. Play at Children's Village at **Ontario Place**.
70. Play at the two adventure playgrounds at Bathurst Pier. FREE.

TOURS

All 19 tours were designed for walking and are in or near downtown Toronto. Streetcars/buses, cars or taxis can be used to get to the starting point and back home, or by those want to skip over parts of the tour. The starting point assumes Yonge and Queen Streets, the centre point of most downtown hotels.

Tour 1. The Financial and Entertainment Districts.

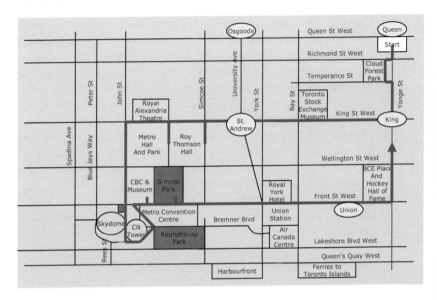

Approx. 2.5 Miles or 4.0 Km return

Key Sights: Cloud Forest Park, Stock Market Place, TD Centre, **St. Andrew's Church, Roy Thomson Hall,** Canadian **Walk of Fame, The Royal Alexandria Theatre, Metro Hall, Princess of Wales Theatre, Skydome, CN Tower, Metro Convention Centre, CBC Building and Museum,** Simcoe Park**, Royal York Hotel, Union Station,** Royal Bank Tower, **and Hockey Hall of Fame.**

Start at Yonge and Queen Streets. Walk down Yonge one block and turn right on Richmond St for about 75 yards until you reach **Cloud Forest Park**. This incredibe and FREE attraction won the Canadian Governor General's Award for Architecture in 1994. There is the enclosed Cloud Forest of trees, shrubs, and plants; a 40 foot high waterfall; the Margaret Priest designed *Monument to Construction Workers* constructed with the assistance of 13 different trade unions; an Urban Woodland of oak, sugar maple, ash and hemlock; and landscaping that won the Canadian Society of Landscape Architects' Regional Merit Award in 1995. Exit the south end of the park - you'll see a concrete stub 5 stories high that was the last (cancelled) attempt to build a Toronto skyscraper - and walk the few yards east on Temperance St to Yonge St and turn right until you reach King St.

Turn right along King St West and step into the *CIBC Bank building* at 25. This building was built in 1927-30 and has an ornate gold and stone domed hall a few yards from the entrance that's worth a FREE look. At King and Bay St, you'll be on Canada's equivalent of Wall Street. The black towers you see are part of the TD Centre, Toronto's first modern skyscrapers built in 1967. Each tower's main floor houses Canadian contemporary art for viewing and there is the FREE **Toronto Dominion Gallery of Inuit Art**.

Continue westbound on the south side of King St West until you reach the *"Megaptera" sculpture* of two whales by George Schmerholz. Directly north of you is the First Canadian Place tower complex. Enter through the doors to the left of the park and waterfalls, and turn left twice and you'll come to the FREE **Stock Market Place** (TSE). The TSE started in 1863 at 24 King St East, then moved to 234 Bay St, before moving to this site. There is no trading floor, as there once was, as trading is done via computers. Adults and kids will like the "Accumulator" that compares various investments (including hockey cards!). Film crews are sometimes in presence getting that insightful stock market analysis from a company spokesperson. The **PATH** system of shops and restaurants is down one level if you're hungry.

Rejoin King St West, cross University Ave and look right for a good view of the **Queen's Park Legislature** at the top of the avenue. **St. Andrew's Church** at Simcoe and King Streets is considered a good example of Romanesque Revival architecture. Get a close look of the wall mural *"Lineal Order"* by George Boileau, and the *sculptures of man and boy* at 71 Simcoe St before crossing over to **Roy Thomson Hall** (home of the **Toronto Symphony Orchestra**). The FREE Canadian **Walk of Fame** similar to the Walk of Stars on Hollywood Ave in Los Angeles starts here. Stars include hockey great Gordie Howe, Mary Pickford, Martin Short, Kurt Browning, William Shatner, the band Rush, and David Cronenberg. Keep an eye open for Roy Thomson Hall's extraordinary Muskoka-like and below street level *reflecting pool* as you walk the 30 yards back to King St!

Just west of the Roy Thomson Hall on King St is **Metro Hall**, a complex housing a public library and municipal government offices in several towers. Acres of landscaped open space are an oasis for some peace and quiet. The open space includes an Eternal Flame of Hope, and an unusual *sculpture, waterfall, and reflecting pool combination*.

Royal Alexandria Theatre

Immediately north is the **Royal Alexandria Theatre**. This popular stage theatre was built in 1906-7 in the Beaux-Arts style with two balconies and side boxes. The Walk of Fame continues on the sidewalk outside the Royal Alexandria. Stars include Neil Young, Michael Fox, Donald Sutherland, Joni Mitchell, Bryan Adams, John Candy, and Ivan Reitman.

Further west on King St West, you'll pass the university-campus like Peel Pub and the popular **Princess of Wales Theatre**. A block of eateries start at John St, including Hey Lucy, Fred's Not Here, The Red Tomato, Kit Kat Italian Bar & Grill, Reuben Schwartz Eatery, and **Canadian Bar & Grill**. Reuben's, a Montreal style deli, has an outdoor patio upstairs. The Kit Kat's façade has two halves of a Holstein cow hanging. The Canadian Bar & Grill is unique in serving Canadian cuisine such as New Brunswick salmon, Alberta beef, French Canadian pea soup, and Newfoundland clam chowder.

A little further west, the Fashion District's eastern boundary is Peter St/Blue Jays Way. Walk south on Blue Jays Way past the **Second City Comedy** club and **Gretzky's** (with lots of hockey memorabilia for fans of the Great One).

Continue on Blue Jays Way south of Front St until you reach the **Skydome**, a stadium with the world's first fully retractable roof. At the southeast end is Bobbie Rosenfeld Park that serves as the south entrance to the CN Tower. A lovely waterfall and pool with metal salmon, a wall sculpting of grasses by Susan Schelle, benches, and a drinking fountain makes for a nice place to have a rest. There are several hot dog cart vendors to choose from here.

Skyline from
Roundhouse Park

Immediately south is the lovely Roundhouse Park with nice benches and landscaping to take a break or have a tour or beer at **Steam Whistle Brewery**. There are drinking fountains at the south and west ends of the park, and the *coal & sanding towers, John St rail roundhouse, turntable, and water tower* (all built 1929-51) in the west end of the park.

A life-size fiberglass moose in a RCMP uniform guards the entrance to the **CN Tower**, the world's tallest building at 1,815 feet (see picture). General access begins at 9 am, but elevators to the observation decks start at 11 am and end at 7 pm. A food and shopping area, and the Edge Arcade, can be accessed without paying to go up the Tower. The Edge Arcade has video games, motion simulators, and amusements that will reward your kids for having walked with you so far. You can experience the lookout, glass floor, and Skypod for $22.49 plus taxes per person. The

360° view on a clear day from 1150 feet (about the same height as the World Towers were) is one of a kind. The 360° view from the 1465 foot high Skydeck makes the street below that much smaller. The elevator ride, with its see-through doors, is an experience in itself. The **360 Restaurant** and its full circle rotation floor offer unsurpassed views.

The escalators to the left in the CN Tower entrance area are your way to continue north out of the CN Tower and over the rail tracks to the Planet Hollywood. Small Isabella Valancy Crawford Park on Front St offers a place to rest or eat a hot dog you can buy from the many hot dog cart vendors here.

The **Canadian Broadcasting Corporation** (CBC) building on the northeast corner of Front and John Streets houses the **Glenn Gould Studio**, a museum, Radio Canada, a few shops, and TV studios. Two of Canada's most popular comedies are taped here in front of audiences. A park bench with a life size bronze sitting man provides a good photo spot near the main entrance. At the FREE museum, you can see how radio evolved, the skates worn by Kurt Browning when he landed the first quad jump in competition at the 1988 World Championship in Budapest, Hungary, a photo collection, and an interactive trivia computer screen. Exit through its south and main entrance.

 American "Rocket" Ismail scored the winning TD in the Toronto Argonauts' 1991 Grey Cup victory.

Follow Front St east for a few yards to Simcoe Park. You can view the *100 Workers* monument of plaques commemorating some of the workers who died on the job. The plaque outlines their names and the date and cause of death. There is a metal relief *Plan of York Harbour* showing Lt. Governor John Graves Simcoe's plan for the new town of York, and a *steel map of Upper Canada* originally done by Elizabeth Simcoe on birchbark in 1794. Further east on

Front St are The Lone Star Café, Loose Moose Tap & Grill, The Armadillo, **Joe Badali's**, East Side Mario's, and The Fish House, all good middle of the road eateries. The northwest corner of University and Front once housed the *1818 built home of Bishop Strachan* of St. James Church (later Cathedral). It was here that the Loyalist troops amassed before marching to Montgomery's Tavern to defeat the Rebels in 1837 (see "In The Beginning").

On the northeast corner is the **Royal York Hotel**, once Toronto's tallest building. Take a quick peek at the ornate grand foyer inside the main entrance. The Game Trek store with its Star Trek chess sets and the Julius Vesz Pipesmith store with its smoking pipes and Civil War chess sets may appeal to some. South of the Royal York is **Union Station**, the site of many movies and TV productions. It was built in 1915-20 in the Beau-Arts style. A *Monument to Multiculturalism* donated by the Italian Canadian community adorns the front of the building. The station isn't really worth walking through, so go from the Royal York Hotel to its easterly neighbour the Royal Bank Tower. Its exterior looks like gold because it partially is. It has thousands of ounces of gold in its windows!

Royal Bank Tower

Turn north on Bay St for 50 yards and you'll see the Spanish designed Atrium of *BCE Place*, BOMA International Building of the Year, at 181 Bay. Walk through here to the east end and you'll come to fun-filled **Marche's**.

The Masquerade is near **Marche's** and is a funky place to eat, but not as kid conducive. The **Hockey Hall of Fame** is one level down. An interesting bronze statue is outside on Front St for FREE viewing. A monument commemorates Canada's hockey victory over the Russians in 1972.

Walk north on Yonge St two blocks back to the starting point on Queen St.

Tour 2. PATH System (for rainy days).

Key Sights: About 400 stores, restaurants, and services, **Union Station, Hockey Hall of Fame, Stock Market Place,** The Bay, **Thomson Gallery, Nathan Phillips Square,** Eaton Centre, Trinity Square Park and Maze, **Church of the Holy Trinity**.

There are sometimes those rainy or freezing days when people don't like to be walking outside: the 10 kilometer or 6.2 mile PATH system might help. **PATH** is basically an underground city that starts at Union Station and goes as far north as the Atrium on Dundas St West. The Royal York Hotel, Toronto Hilton, and Sheraton Centre are directly linked to PATH. PATH consists mostly of the various office complexes' malls or "centres" that cater to the daytime business crowd. Each Centre has 50-75 stores, services, restaurants, and inexpensive fast food in "Food Courts". About 400 in total. Many of the office complexes have waterfalls, art, and sculptures, especially on their main street levels.

Union Station, the PATH's southern end, is both a subway station and a train station with several spots to grab a coffee and bun, or other fast food: Second Cup, The Bagel Stop, Cinnabon, mmmuffins, McDonald's, Country Style, The Croissant Tree, Michel's Baguette, and Jugo Juice. Amuse-o-Matic Centre offers video games and pinballs. Maybe a comfortable, double-decker GO Train for a quick 25 minute each way ride to Port Credit is your style? – $7.20 return, tax included/adult and $3.60/child 5-11 or seniors 65+; www.gotransit.com/fare/fndfare.asp#frcity.

Hockey Hall of Fame

Heading north along the PATH, you can visit the **Royal York Hotel** (see Tour 1) or the **Hockey Hall of Fame** in BCE Place. You'll have your pick of stores and eateries as you continue north through the Royal Bank Plaza, TD Centre, Canadian Pacific Tower, First Canadian Place, The Exchange Tower (try the FREE **Stock Market Place**), Oxford Tower, and Shops of the Sheraton. Fast food places include Cultures, Druxy's, and The Bagel Stop. I find First

Canadian Place Centre's "Marketplace" to be the nicest of a nice lot. Inexpensive lunches can be had at Greenleaf's salads, Grainfield's Bakery, The Chocolate Factory, Bacchanalia where you can get 4 oz meat sandwiches for $3.99, or check out Soup it Up! and its 8 soups for $2.79/12 oz to $6.79/32 oz. The downside? No immediate area seating!

Once you reach the **Sheraton Centre**, you can either continue north to City Hall (see Tour 3) or turn east into The Bay. The food court below the Sheraton has two of the few non-hotel spots downtown where one can get a bacon and egg breakfast: Mr. Souvlaki and **Jenzer's Deli**.

The Bay, officially the Hudson's Bay Company (HBC), founded in 1670 to trade fur, is an unbelievable store with 10 huge floors of virtually everything. Head to the 8th floor if you are hungry. The **City View** cafeteria is inexpensive and offers beautiful views through floor to ceiling glass windows of Old City Hall, City Hall, **Nathan Phillips Square**, Osgoode Hall, the Eaton Centre, and *Trinity Church*. The Arcadian Court, in a huge bright grand ballroom, offers mid-price meals under chandeliers and 40 foot ceilings. Note the *black and white photos* in the lobby from the HBC Corporate Collection, including the "Cigarette Department": three young women in the 1950's with smoke lounge type cigarette trays slung from their shoulder to sell cigarettes.

 The wonderful **Thomson Gallery** of Canadian art, mostly from the famous Group of Seven. The stairs to the gallery start outside the Arcadian Court.

From The Bay, the PATH enters the Eaton Centre. 300 stores of shopping that is a favourite of teenagers. There's a food court, including a **Marche's**, and several middle of the road restaurants like **Mr. Greenjeans.** You can pop out for a few seconds into the rain and catch a glimpse of the **Church of the Holy Trinity** and Trinity Square Park and Maze (see Tour 3).

To see whether the weather will improve enough for you to resurface, have a look at the weather beacon on top of the Canada Life Assurance building (see picture) at 330 University Ave just west of Nathan Phillips Square. Green lights running up the beacon mean clear and warmer for the balance of the day. Flashing red lights running down means rain and cooler.

Tour 3. Queen St West, Kensington Market and Chinatown.

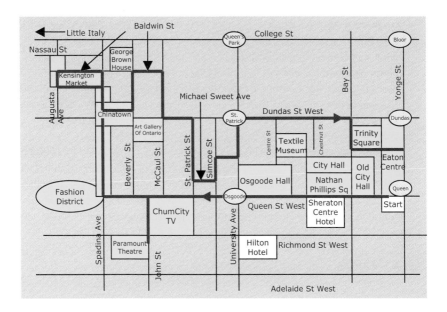

Approx. 3 Miles or 4.9 Km return

Key Sights: Old City Hall and **Clock Tower**, **Nathan Phillips Square**, **City Hall**, **Osgoode Hall**, **Gibson House**, **ChumCity TV**, **Queen Street West ("Little Bohemia")**, **Paramount Theatre**, Spadina Ave, Kensington Market, **Chinatown (West)**, **Art Gallery of Ontario**, *Grange House* **and** Grange Park, Trinity Square Park and Maze, **Church of the Holy Trinity**, Eaton Centre.

Start at Yonge and Queen Streets. You could start in the Eaton Centre, but the shoppers in the family may spend most of the day there. So... walk west along Queen St *past* the Eaton Centre to the **Old City Hall**. Built in 1889-1899 of Credit River Valley sandstone, it was designed in the Romanesque Revival architectural style. Outside the front entrance and steps is a World War I Memorial and an incredible view south along busy Bay St. Just inside the entrance doors are several *historical plaques*, the most noteworthy being the one naming the first Canadian casualties of enemy action in World War II: R.T. Knox, L.E. Sword, and J.F. Bailey. You'll have to clear security to enter the huge foyer of **Old City Hall FREE**, but it's worth the few minutes to have a look at *1899 wall murals* by George A. Reed, the mosaic tile floor, painted glass, and marble on the walls.

The 300 foot high **Old City Hall Clock Tower** is hard to miss seeing or hearing. The clock and bells, the largest being "Big Ben" at 11,648 lbs, were installed in 1900 and can be heard ringing for quite a distance. Across Bay St is **Nathan Phillips Square** (named after Toronto's first Jewish mayor) and **City Hall** (designed by Finn Viljo Revell). The Square's **Peace Garden** shows what can be accomplished with such a small space. Then Prime Minister Pierre Trudeau turned the sod in 1984 and Pope John Paul II kindled an eternal flame with an ember from Peace Memorial Park in Hiroshima. Towards the entrance to the **City Hall** is Henry Moore's 1966 sculpture *"Three-Way Piece No. 2 or The Archer"*. If you go into City Hall and look left, you'll note a very large and detailed 3D working architects model of Toronto by building! To the right are the washrooms, drinking fountain, a snack shop, and a Public Library. Go back out the way you came in – you'll be looking south, towards Queen St and the reflecting pool complete with fountains and an overhead moose on a diving board. This spot is a very popular FREE skating arena in winter, especially at night with 100,000 Christmas lights sparkling like candy.

Head west, past a *statue of Winston Churchill* and you'll see the wrought iron fence of **Osgoode Hall,** on a site originally named Lawyers' Hill. The fence was built to keep cows out (true when it was first built in 1829-32). The lawn is an oasis of mature trees and meticulously maintained flowers and shrubs.

 Cross University Ave to the historical **Gibson House** (and US Consulate a block north if you need it).

You are now yards away from the part of Queen St I personally like to call "Little Bohemia" for its eclectic mix of people, stores, art, buildings, pubs, and restaurants. A few interesting ones include the Queen Mother Café, the Condom Shack, Lush Fresh Handmade Cosmetics, M.A.C., the Black Bull Pub with its great outdoor patio, Cannabis Culture Shop at 241, Friendship House at 280 (where the TV series "Street Legal" was filmed), Roots clothing at 358, Silver Snail at 367 (don't miss toy store), Active Surplus at 347 who claim to "buy and sell anything", the Chicago Diner and Bird's Nest with its live blues and funk entertainment, 3rd Quadrant Comics and Malibar Theatrical Costumes on McCaul a few yards north of Queen, and….

 ChumCity TV. The number of musical stars that have played here is incredible and exciting for any young person. Mini-concerts by stars like Shaggy, Destiny's Child, Jessica Simpson, Sloan, and many others are often held here, sometimes with the garage door windows opened and people spilled out over Queen St. Don't miss the City TV van crashing through the east wall of the building or **Speaker's Corner** on the corner of John and

Queen Streets. For one loonie, you can speak your mind on any topic on video. Interesting videos are aired on TV every Sunday!

Walk south on John St to Richmond St and the **Paramount Theatre.** A great place to catch a movie, the building itself is entertaining with its huge escalators and rooftop colored cube. A three level Chapters bookstore with Starbucks on the second level can be fun to flick through books, magazines, and music DVDs. Try Al Frisco's and **Montana's** across from the Paramount if you're hungry. Hooter's, Palamino's, and Milestone's are only yards away. This block up to Queen St sometimes hosts street parties with concerts, trick ski jumping, and more.

Chinatown (West)

Make your way back to and then west along the south side of Queen St until you reach the west side of Spadina Ave. To the west and south is the Fashion District where you can get almost any clothes, cloths, fabrics, and sewing supplies. Turn right on Spadina and walk past Chinese, Vietnamese, Laotian, and Thai outdoor fruit/vegetable stands, fish stands, stores, restaurants, and a Chinese film theatre. Knowledge of Chinese or Vietnamese will be useful, although not required. At Dundas St West, you'll see what looks like Hong Kong to your right – **Chinatown West!**

From the corner of Dundas St West and Spadina St, continue west on Dundas St. A short block later you'll see Kensington St running north off of Dundas. (A couple of blocks west and north at Augusta and Wales Avenues is Denison Square, a beautiful little park with children's wading pool – the park is named after Colonel Denison, whose family was one of the very first settlers in York and who once owned all the land in this area). This is the southern part of the Kensington Market, a colorful, unique, and somewhat zany street market. *Very* colorful stores offer seafood, coffees, fruits/vegetables, clothing, Persian rugs, furniture, bulk foods, linens, spices, health foods, and more.

Take Kensington St to Baldwin St, then left to Augusta St, then right to Nassau St, and then right to Spadina. Look left to see the spire of the (once) *Presbyterian Theological School* built in 1874 in the Gothic Revival style. Retrace your path a little by following Spadina south on the east side back to Queen St. Follow Queen St east to Beverley St and turn left to 186 Beverly.

Kensington Market

 The **George Brown House**, built in 1874-77, was the home of George Brown who founded the Globe newspaper (today's Globe and Mail), co-founded the Anti-Slavery Coalition of Upper Canada, and co-founded Canada. He died here after being shot at work by an irate employee. He emigrated from Scotland to New York, where he lived for 6 years before he came to Toronto in 1843.

The house's foyer is a sight to behold with its 13 foot ceilings, wood paneling, grand staircase, and foyer fireplace! The rest of the house is also spectacular and full of interesting things like the library and vault.

Follow Baldwin St east to arrive at a quaint streetscape of mostly restaurants. The fancier French restaurant **La Bodega**, the one-of-a-kind Café La Gaffe, **Sensation Café**, the Chinese food restaurants Eating Garden and Baldwin Palace (vegetarian), and Smoke Shop, Tobacco, and Cigars make this area a rewarding place to spend an hour or so.

 Many Americans dodging the Vietnam War made the Baldwin St area home, according to American born John Hagan, author of a book on the subject, called "Northern Passage".

Head south on McCaul St from Baldwin until you reach Dundas St. There is the **St. Patrick's Catholic Church** and German Parish. The church is very

European in look inside. The **Art Gallery of Ontario** (AGO) is on the corner, fronted by Henry Moore's *Large Two Forms sculpture*, and is worth a visit if you're an art lover. Behind the AGO is the late Gregorian *Grange House* built in 1817 and Grange Park, and the Ontario College of Art founded by George A. Reed (who painted the murals in the **Old City Hall**). If you hungry, the Village by the Grange fast food market on the southeast corner offers Greek, Thai, Chinese, Japanese, West Indian, pizzas, subs, fish and chips, and coffee.

Walk east along Dundas St West one block to St. Patrick St and then south one block to **Michael Sweet Ave**. This avenue was dedicated to the Toronto police officer killed on duty while responding to an armed robbery on March 14, 1980. Walk east to Simcoe St and then north to a walkway off to the right between the office towers. Walk 30 yards to University Ave and the **Royal Canadian Military Institute** at 426 University Ave. The building was built in 1912 and *two "9 pounder guns"*, the type used at the Battle of Waterloo and the 1853-56 Crimean War, guard its entrance.

Continuing north to Dundas St West, there are two *war monuments* in the traffic island along University Ave. One monument identifies 7 Canadians from Ontario who were awarded the prestigious Victoria Cross in World War I and II. The other, Oscar Nemon's Modernist style "Per Ardua Ad Astra", was dedicated by Queen Elizabeth II to honor Canadian airmen of World Wars I and II. A block east on Dundas St West is Centre St and the **Museum of Textiles** if you have an interest. Otherwise continue on east to Bay St and turn right or south to the crosswalk. Behind you is the...

Larry Sefton Park built and donated by the United Steelworkers of America to commemorate the birth of the Canadian section of the union.

Cross Bay St to the south side of the Marriot Hotel and Trinity Square Park. The park houses a creek, waterfalls, park benches, small clock tower, maze, and the **Church of the Holy Trinity** (once on the outskirts of Toronto if you can believe it). It was built in 1847 of bricks from the Don Valley in the Gothic architecture style. There is a list of names outside the front door of homeless people who "died as a direct result of homelessness". The maze, or more accurately the Labyrinth, was based on the 11-circuit labyrinth in Charles Cathedral in France that was built in the 13th century.

Enter the popular **Eaton Centre** and enjoy perusing the three levels of shops, restaurants and services, as well as the atrium and "flying" Canadian geese. It's a short block south back to the starting point at Yonge and Queen Streets.

Tour 4. Fashion and Queen St West Gallery Districts.

Approx. 1.8 Miles or 2.9 Km (plus 1.8 miles or 2.9 km to start point) return

Key Sights: 100s of stores, restaurants, cafes, services in a vibrant, eclectic street scene.

Take the westbound TTC streetcar 501 to Spadina Ave. (If you're driving, park at the $1/hour municipal parking lot at Augusta Ave, three blocks west of Spadina on Queen). Walk south along the east side of Spadina Ave to King St West and return north along the west side to Queen St West. This area is laden with fur stores and buildings of early 1900s vintage. Cosmopolitan Fur at 174, Yukon Furs at 197 Spadina, Charisma Fur at 196, Canadiana Fur at 198, Paul Samaras Furs at 188A, Paul Magder Furs at 202, and Elite Furs at 204. Other fashion stores include Bridal Fashions and World of Bras at 161, and T.O Leather Fashion at 116A. Eateries include a McDonald's at Spadina and Adelaide, the Great Canadian Bagel and Second Cup at 147, and Fusaro's (Italian) at 147.

Turn west along Queen St West. This section is even more eclectic than the Queen St West of Tour 3. There are over 100 stores along this strip. It is where most of the Fashion District's sewing and sewing supplies stores are.

Some of the interesting stores include Sugar Mountain candy at 571, Art Deco home accents at 536, Short Man by Brown's fine men's clothing at 545, Rotate This vinyl and CDs at 620, Royal Antique (Indian) at 624, Miss Behav'N lingerie at 650, Morba's home accents at 665, Cabaret Nostalgia costumes at

672, McBurne & Cutler's stuffed full bookstore at 698, Lynn Robinson Gallery home accents at 709, Antiques on Queen at 717, Extraordinaire hair salon at 722, Doc's Leathers at 726, Dexterity home accents at 773, The Australian Boot Company boots and clothes at 791, and World Art & Décor African goods and magazines at 803.

Some of the interesting services and eating establishments include Central Billiards at 470, Fressen's herbivorous cuisine at 476, Epicure Café at 512, Java House at 537, Vienna Home Bakery at 626, Prague Deli's delicatessen at 638, Second Cup at 652, Irie Food Joint (Caribbean food) at 745, and Dufflet's Pastries at 787 (supplier of many cafes and restaurants, and considered to have among the city's best cakes).

Other points of interest include *Edward Leadley House* at 25 Augusta Ave, built in 1876 (a magnificent century home with elaborate covered porches and gingerbread trim); the Underground at 508 has a roof over the entrance covered in exposed spikes; 540's roof is plastered with bikes and bike parts; and the building at 500-504 has very unique gables and metalwork near the roofline. The southeast corner of Trinity Bellwoods Park has a metal relief map where Garrison Creek (in which people fished for salmon) once ran. The Creek is now buried in a Victorian brick pipeline. The park has a community centre, a baseball diamond and skating rink, a playground, lots of open space, tennis courts, and the 1903 gateway to Trinity College. The Trinity College building was demolished in 1956 as the College earlier became part of the University of Toronto on Hoskins Ave in 1925. The "new" Trinity College's entrance houses the plate from the original cornerstone laid by Trinity College founder John Strachan in 1851 at its original site in Trinity Bellwoods Park).

 A plaque commemorates Major-General Aeneas Shaw, a Loyalist and member of the Queen's Rangers during the American Revolution, who settled near the park in 1793.

The City administration officially recognized Queen St West between Bathurst St and Roncesvalles Ave as the **Queen West Gallery District**. The district has 28 galleries! **Art at 80** has eleven art galleries in one historic building at 80 Spadina Ave, south of Queen St West.

Take the eastbound TTC streetcar 501 back to Yonge and Queen Streets.

Tour 5. Little Italy.

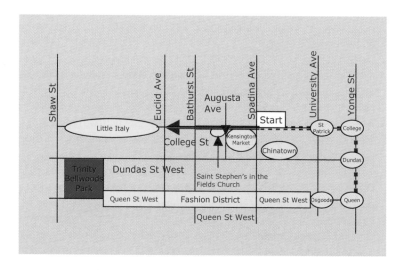

<u>Approx. 1.8 Miles or 2.9 Km (plus 3.1 miles or 5 km to start point) return</u>

Key Sights: *post and chair artwork,* **Saint Stephen's-in-the-Fields Church**, *1878 Kensington Fire Hall, 1913 Bank of Nova Scotia building, Latvian House, Johnny Lombardi Way,* and 300 fantastic shops, restaurants, and nightclubs in Little Italy alone (57 restaurants/cafes/bars!).

Take the westbound TTC streetcar 506 from the College Subway station on Yonge St. Get off at Augusta Ave, which is the top end of Kensington Market. Walk west along College: the stretch west of Augusta Ave is interesting, but Little Italy only starts at Euclid Ave. "Little Italy" is known for culture, eating, nightclubs, and shopping. "Little Italy" was so-named because of the high concentration of Italian immigrants that made this area home in the 1950s. Hollywood stars like to partake in this area's many fine restaurants and bars.

Points of interest include the *post and chair artwork* on the southwest corner of College and Augusta Avenues; **Saint Stephen's-in-the-Fields Church** built in 1858; the *Kensington Fire Hall (no. 8 station)* built in 1878 and located next to Saint Stephen's-in-the-Fields; the *Bank of Nova Scotia building* built in 1913 at 440, the *Latvian House* with its greek pillars and hallway homeland painting at 491, and *Johnny Lombardi Way* and Johnny's CHIN Radio/TV International at 622. CHIN Radio, 100.7 FM, offers radio/television in 30 languages and hosts the famous annual picnic and beauty/talent contest.

A small sample of the 300 shops, restaurants, and services include Amato Pizza (gourmet pizza) at 380, El Eden Equatorian variety at 396, Eli's Factory Outlet (clothing) at 398 and identified by Toronto Life magazine as a place "Where to Get Good Things Cheap", Bistro 422 which offers the "Reindeer Lapland" at 422, **KOS Bar & Grill** (50s Diner) at 434 with its $4 bacon and egg breakfest, Starbucks at 544, the beautiful Kalendar at 546 (also the site of a Ford car commercial), Magnolia Fine Foods at 548, Riveria Bakery at 576, Bar Italia at 582, Udeal Hotel and Restaurant Supplies at 599, Balfour Books at 601, MVP Italian music and videos at 604, Cupps Café at 622, and the Silician Ice Cream Company at 712.

At Little Italy's western end, Shaw St, take an eastbound TTC streetcar 506 back to College Subway station at Yonge St.

Tour 6. Harbourfront and Toronto Islands.

Approx 2.0 Miles or 3.3 Km (plus 1.6 miles or 2.5 km to start point) return

Key Sights: Harbourfront, Pier 6, Queen's Quay Terminal, **Music Garden Park**, **Toronto Islands (Centreville Amusement Park**, **Clothing Optional Beach**, *Maze,* Haunted *Gilbraltar Point Lighthouse*, place of *Babe Ruth's first home run*).

Start at the foot of Yonge on Queen's Quay. Walk 150 yards west and 50 yards south to the Toronto Island ferry docks. A lakefront promenade is off to the right. Follow the promenade for 10 minutes past condos, **Pier 6** and its Second Cup coffee shop, and through landscaped areas until the **Queen's Quay Terminal**. This converted warehouse with its 8-story atrium is quite popular with gift shoppers. Save the t-shirts for your relatives - this is a great place to get gifts for YOU to remind you of your trip to Toronto. Unique gifts from YNK Notables; dolls, including Anne of Green Gables from Dollina; fine Inuit art from Harris Gallery or Artic Canada; The Canadian Naturalist; Mr. Music Box; FirstHand Canadian Crafts; and

 The **Toy Terminal**! This may be one of the few places where the adults and the kids will both need to be dragged out of the place. Puzzle masters, models, train sets, chess sets, paint by numbers, dolls, war games, yahtzee, slot gaming machines, board games (including a Civil War game) are just part of this store's offerings.

Il Fornello's and the **Boathouse Bar &Grill** are great spots to stop, eat, and enjoy a view of the harbour. There are a few fast food places on the second floor at the southeast end that have some seating with great views as well.

 The **Café Deli** is a pleasant spot to get good food inexpensively. It offers deli sandwiches, pizza slices, salads, and bagels all under $6. It also offers Breyer's ice cream during the summer and Reunion Island coffees via two separate parts of the store.

The lakefront promenade continues along the east and south sides of Queen's Quay Terminal until you reach **Harbourfront**. This area, built on landfill, is... fantastic! Arts, crafts, live theatre at the **duMaurier Theatre/Power Plant**, a wading pool with radio-controlled boats (the FREE Natrel skating rink in winter), an amphitheater, and more.

 The **Milk International Children's Festival** is just one of many events during the year that are fantastic for families. Blow glass, make jewelry, watch Chinese acrobats, make crafts, learn magic, be entertained by buskers, and see live concerts and theater.

Continue on the promenade or head back to Queen's Quay (the road) if you've lost the promenade. Continue west and you'll pass the Radisson Plaza Hotel and the extraordinarily landscaped **Music Garden Park** just past Spadina Ave. Retrace your steps or take the streetcar back to Bay St. Head south to the entrance to the **Toronto Islands** ferry docks. Grab a picnic basket and take the 15 minute ferry ride to the very popular Centre Island. You will enjoy views of sailboats in the harbour, small planes landing at the Island airport, and of course downtown Toronto. The Toronto Islands only became islands in 1858 after a large storm broke through a narrow part of a peninsula.

 Sports fans might like to know the Toronto Islands were the site of a baseball diamond/park where Babe Ruth hit his first professional home run!

There is an island map where you get off the ferry. Stay left for about 200 yards and you'll reach **Centreville Amusement Park**. FREE if you just want to wander the grounds, see the animals, or eat (rides cost extra). A super time for families, especially those with kids 13 and younger.

 The *hand carved wooden carousel* at Centreville is one of only 30 left in existence today. It was built circa 1908 by G.A. Dentzel Steam & Horsepower Company of Pennsylvania, U.S.

Return to the entrance and ticket booths. Turn left over the bridge and you'll come to a large water fountain and gardens. The FREE maze is off to the left. With the maze entrance also serving as the only exit, you can sit on the park bench by the entrance and the kids can safely have fun for a long time.

Continuing south from the maze, you'll be able to see the Pier extending out into Lake Ontario. There is a beach, although few swim there, a snack shop, bicycle rentals, and many paved paths. If you follow the path to the right or west, you'll eventually come to the haunted *Gilbraltor Point Lighthouse*, the "**Clothing Optional" beach,** and Gilbraltor Point near present day Hanlon's Point (yes, where the Americans burned buildings in 1813). If you don't want to walk all the way back, follow the path to the Hanlon Point ferry dock.

If you want to see cottages in the city, visit Wards Island on the east part of the islands and you'll see a neighbourhood of very cottage-like homes in use.

On your way back to the starting point, follow Bay St north until you reach the **Air Canada Centre (ACC)**. This facility now hosts the Toronto Raptors and Maple Leafs, as well as concerts. It still incorporates parts of the *Toronto Postal Delivery building* that once stood at the site. Go through the Bay St doors and there are several plaques identifying the architectural and historical aspects of the building (many of which remain part of the ACC). Tours are available that will show you the Maple Leafs' dressing room and the Raptors' practice facility, among other things. A few yards outside the west doors, just past the ticket booths, you'll see the *Search Light, Star Light, Spot Light statues*, by John McEwen and each weighing 11 tons.

Follow Bay St north to Front St East, east to Yonge St and north to Queen.

Tour 7. Ontario Place and Canadian National Exhibition.

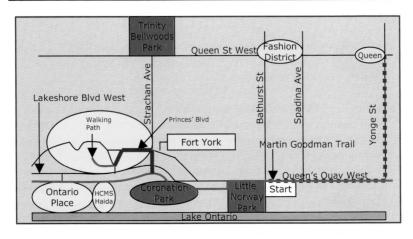

Approx 2.7 Miles or 4.3 Km (plus 3.8 miles or 6.1 km to start point) return

Key Sights: HMCS York, *Queen's Wharf Lighthouse,* Coronation Park, *World War II monuments,* **Canadian National Exhibition** (incl. *Princes' Gates,* **Marine Museum,** *Princess Margaret Fountain, Sculptures for the Gardens of the Gods,* **"Sir Douglas Fir",** *historic CNE buildings, The Carlsberg Carillion, Shrine Peace Memorial,* **Fort Rouillè** (1750-51), **Scadding Cabin** (1794)), and **Ontario Place** (incl. the **HMCS Haida** warship).

Start at Bathurst St. and Queens Quay (TTC streetcar 509 from Union or TTC streetcar 511 southbound along Bathurst after transferring from westbound TTC streetcar 501 on Queen St). There is a lovely park called Little Norway Park near the foot of Bathurst St, named for the World War II Norwegian air force training base that once stood here. A Norwegian flag still flies. A little west on Lakeshore Blvd, you'll come to Coronation Park and the HMCS York "stone frigate" used by the Navy reserves for training and other activities. The friendly folks here may let you have a peek. Look north to the red *Queen's Wharf Lighthouse* built in 1861 standing by its lonesome in a fork in the road. It was originally at the foot of Bathurst St and was used to mark the only navigable entrance to Toronto Harbour at the time.

Further west in Coronation Park, you'll see a small boat harbour and *a World War II Monument* near the large flagpole and flag about 50 yards south of the trail. A most intriguing metal relief map of the Atlantic shows where individually identified Canadian ships and German U-boats were sunk! There is another relief map indicating 1,081,865 of Canada's 11,300,000 enlisted participated in World War II. 700,000 were under 21 years old!

Walk north of the lake for 75 yards to a very noticeable trail. The trees here were planted in 1937 to commemorate the veterans of the Canadian Expeditionary Force in 1914-18, the Fenian Raids in 1866, the Northwest Rebellion of 1885, and the Boer War 1898-1902.

 Coronation Park is also the site where the Americans invaded Toronto for a second time on July 31, 1813.

Yards later you will reach the traffic lights at Strachan Ave and Lakeshore Blvd. Cross Lakeshore and walk through the *Princes' Gates* just ahead of you, so-called as they were opened by Princes Edward and George in 1929. The nine pillars on either side represented the nine Canadian provinces at the time (Newfoundland was not part of Confederation until 1949).

You are now in the **Canadian National Exhibition (CNE)** grounds (FREE when the CNE is not on). Walk west one block (you're on Princes' Blvd) and look southeast or left. You'll be able to see the limestone **Marine Museum** built in 1841 (now closed). It was originally called New Fort and renamed to Stanley Barracks in 1897. It was also one of the first recruiting centres for assembling and training red-coated RCMP constables. Outside the building for FREE viewing on the surrounding grounds is a ship propeller, the Ned Hanlon Steam Tug built in 1932 and undergoing a restoration, an anchor, "marine triple expansion steam engine" for ships, *monument to Ned Hanlon,* and a historic railway engine. Hanlon won 300 rowing victories in a row plus the U.S. championship in 1878, the England championship in 1879, and the World Championship in 1880. The parking lot to the west was once the Exhibition Stadium site (1976-1999) where the Blue Jays and Toronto Argonauts played, and concerts were staged.

Go back to Princes' Blvd and continue west past the "Better Living Centre" building. You'll see *the Princess Margaret Fountain*, a replica of a water fountain in St. Peter's Square in Rome, Italy. It was presented to the CNE in 1929 by George Gooderham of Gooderham & Worts. (and rebuilt in 1958). Look directly north and you'll see the *"Press" Building* built in 1904. A plaque indicates this building, along with the *Music Building, Horticulture Building, Arts & Crafts & Hobbies Building, and the Fire Hall/Police Station*, all built in 1907-1912, are the "largest and finest group of early 20th century exhibition buildings in Canada." "…[T]hey reflect the influence of the 1893 World's Columbian Exposition of Chicago in their creative classical decoration and ordered integration to a site plan." Turn around and walk back toward the Princess Margaret Fountain and you'll note the stone *Sculptures for the Garden of Greek Gods* on your right. Straight ahead you'll see *The Carlsberg Carillon* (bells tower).

You also can't miss the 184 foot tall "**Sir Douglas Fir**" flagpole. It was cut from a 350 year-old Vancouver Island fir with a tip diameter of 15 inches and a base diameter of 33 inches. It weighs about 35,000 lbs and was donated by Travel South USA in "...appreciation to the many Canadians who visit our States and for the friendships that have evolved over the years."

A few yards southbound toward the lake is the 20 feet or so high *Shrine Peace Memorial*. Gifted in 1930 to commemorate "the peaceful relationships existing for over a half century between Canada and the U.S.". It is surrounded by a lovely rose garden overlooking Lake Ontario and Ontario Place, 100 yards away.

Follow the most southerly walking path west and you'll come to **Fort Rouillè** historic site. Also commonly known as Fort Toronto, Fort Rouillè was built in 1750-51 by order of Marquis de la Jonquière to strengthen French control of the Great Lakes. While it was destroyed in 1759, there is a concrete wall base in the ground that shows the Fort's exterior walls. A plaque also shows the Fort's interior building locations. While not historically of the same time, there are three *cannons* (two from 1843 and one from 1856) guarding the site.

Scadding Cabin, Toronto's oldest existing building, is nearby. John Scadding, manager of John Graves Simcoe's estate in England, came to Toronto in 1793 with Simcoe, was granted 250 acres directly east of the Don River, and built this cabin there in 1794. Take the southerly walking path back east to Ontario Dr, cross over, and walk a few yards to the west bridge to **Ontario Place**. Tucked away left of this bridge is a plaque honoring the Queen's Rangers, the first British regiment raised in Britain specifically for service to Ontario.

Cross the bridge to **Ontario Place**. You'll get a lovely view of **Ontario Place**, Lake Ontario, **Canadian National Exhibition** grounds, and the city skyline. **Ontario Place** has a great children's village, water park, a 5 story tall IMAX film theatre with stupendous films, the **HMCS Haida** warship (separate cost), the Molson Amphitheatre for concerts, the west island for restaurants/pubs, and more. There is a FREE shuttle bus from/to Union Station outside the main entrance to **Ontario Place**. Or head back to Princes' Gates and catch TTC streetcar 511 back to Queen St, remember to get a "transfer", get off at Queen St, and take TTC streetcar 501 east back to Yonge St.

If you have a car, time and energy, go to **Fort York** at 100 Garrison Rd, east of Strachan Ave and north of Fleet St. Built in 1793, Fort York was attacked on April 27, 1813 by the US. American explorer Zebulon Pike was killed here. Today, Fort York has Canada's largest collection of original War of 1812 buildings. A few blocks northeast of Fort York is Toronto's first burying ground at Niagara and Portland Streets (northeast of Bathurst and Front Streets). A Captain Neal McNeale, killed in the Battle of York on April 27, 1813, and other soldiers of War of 1812, are buried here.

Tour 8. Sunnyside Beaches and Bloor West Village.

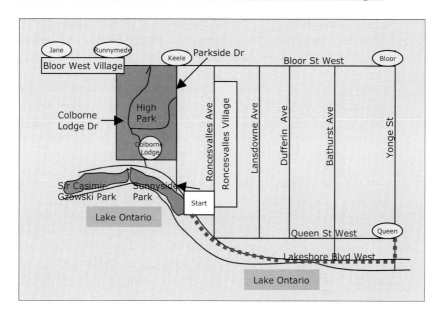

Approx. 3.6 Miles or 5.8 Km (plus 3.6 miles or 5.8 km to start point) return

Key Sights: Budapest Park, **Sunnyside Pool, Pavilion and Courtyard,** Sunnyside Park, Sir Casimir Gzowski Park, *Sir Casimir Gzowski Monument, Trans Canada Trail pavilion, Lion's Monument, Palace Pier* (historic site of big band concerts/dances), *Sheldon Lookout*, **High Park**, Bloor West Village, Roncesvalles Village, and the *Katyn Monument*.

Take westbound TTC streetcar 508 along King St West to Parkside Dr. Walk south about 200 yards under the Gardiner Expressway – you'll get a sense of why Torontonians say the lakefront is cut off from the city. If you drive, take Lakeshore Blvd West west until you reach Ellis Ave and then make a U-turn and come back to the second of two municipal parking lots along this stretch (near Colborne Lodge Dr and Parkside Dr).

A few minutes to your east is a crème colored building at 1601 Lakeshore Blvd that really doesn't look like much. Built in 1922, it was once a *dance hall* where Tommy & Jimmy Dorsey and Count Basie played. Continuing westward, there is Budapest Park with a children's playground, wading pool, and lots of shady space for a BBQ. The **Sunnyside Pool, Pavilion and Courtyard** complex in **Sunnyside Park** is a great spot to go for a swim while overlooking the beach and pedestrian traffic. There is a boardwalk along the beach and a path for biking and rollerblading.

Further westward is the Sir Casimir Gzowski Park and *Sir Casimir Gzowski monument*. Born in 1813 in St. Petersburg, Russia, Gzowski emigrated to the US in 1834 before emigrating to Canada in 1841.

Gzowski was a railway builder, soldier, and entrepreneur, and was credited with building the International Peace Bridge between Fort Erie and and Buffalo in 1870-73. He also helped organize the Toronto Stock Exchange and Toronto Philharmonic Society. He is buried in **St. James Cemetery.**

You'll come to another, larger children's playground and wading pool, the Sunnyside Café food concession near the foot of Ellis Ave, and then the *Trans Canada Trail pavilion*. The pavilion identifies local people and groups that contributed to developing part of the Trans Canada trail. The 10,700 mile long trial will be the longest recreational trail in the world. Nearby is the *Lion Monument* that marks the eastern end of the Queen Elizabeth Way (QEW), Canada's first superhighway, opened by King George VI in 1939. The QEW remains the main highway between Toronto and New York State to this day.

Continuing west, you'll reach a suspension bridge over the Humber River. The Humber River was the western boundary, and Lake Ontario the southern boundary, of 1100 acres of land granted to Sir John Graves Simcoe on Jan 13, 1796. The Humber River was also the western boundary of England's first purchase of land in the Toronto area from the Mississauga Indians. Past the bridge is the *Sheldon Lookout*, for a spectacular view of Toronto's skyline and lakefront. A few more yards and you'll see a concrete footing monument. This is all that remains of the *Palace Pier*. Built in 1941, it went out over the lake 300 feet and served as a big band dance hall.

If you drove, check out **Bloor West Village** and **Roncesvalles Village**:

Return to your car and drive up Colborne Lodge Dr into **High Park** to **Colborne House** and the John and Jemima Howard *tomb*. Return to Lakeshore Blvd West and go east (left) until you reach Parkside Dr. Turn north until you reach Howard Park Ave and turn left into the park. You will quickly come to a magnificent ½ acre children's play village, a duck pond, a grove of Japanese Cherry trees, a fast food pavilion, and a 100 yards further along, a FREE outdoor zoo.

When you're done with **High Park**, walk
or drive west to Bloor St West at the
northern end of **High Park** and turn west
one block into charming Bloor West
Village (www.bloorwestvillage.com).
Street parking is at a municipal parking
lot at 265 Willard Ave near the west end of Bloor West Village and north
of Bloor St West. There are about 200 stores, restaurants, and services
shoulder-to-shoulder along this 1-mile stretch that ends at Jane St, with 14
bakeries and delicatessens, and 29 restaurants and cafés!

The delightfully tempting bakeries and delicatessens include Anna's Bakery
& Deli at 2396, Kingsway Meat & Deli at 2342, Max's Market at 2299 (a real
gem!), Durie Deli at 2302, Bread & Roses Bakery/Café at 2232, Sunglow
Bakery & Delicatessen at 2226 (you can get the Deutsche Press paper
here), Meat Market Delicatessen at 2216, and Sweet Gallery at 2312.
Caviar can be had at Snappers Fish Market at 250 Durie St, 20 steps north
of Bloor St, or flowers at several outdoor flower stands.

On the way back on Bloor St West, turn south or right on Dundas St West
and go to Roncesvalles Ave and Roncesvalles Village. The "village" is a
commercial strip of more than 100 stores, restaurants, cafés, deli's, and the
like along a little over ½ mile strip lined with gas lampposts. Definitely
worth a stroll and maybe a stop at one of the cafés or Polish restaurants.

Interesting stores include Village Meat & Deli at 415, the Sunflower Café
(with perogies for $7, and Polish beet soup), Second Cup at 385, Butler's
Pantry (Café) at 371, Pascal's Baguette and Bagels at 363, The Old Country
Shop (German foods and gifts) at 355, Alternative Grounds (café) at 333,
Renaissant home accessories at 331, Polskie Smakolyki Warmia Deli at 323
(the poppy seed strudels have 1 ½ of poppy seed!), Dresser's gifts and
home accessories at 307, C'est Cheese specialty cheeses and foods at 305,
Chicago Butcher Shop (with deli and bakery) at 289, *St. Vincent de Paul
Church* (built in 1915), and Roncesvalles Bakery at 173. At the foot of
Roncesvalles Ave, on The Queensway and in Beaty Boulevard Park, is the
Katyn Monument to 15,000 Polish soldiers that vanished in Russian POW
camps at Kozelsk, Ostashkov, and Starobelsk. 4,000 were found in mass
graves at Katyn, near Smolensk.

If you took the TTC: Double back to Colborne Lodge Dr and head into **High
Park**. When you finished exploring **High Park**, head to the north end of **High
Park**, Bloor St West, and head into Bloor West Village (about 0.7 miles one

way from **High Park**). If you want to skip **High Park**, TTC bus 80 comes along Lakeshore between Ellis Ave and Parkside Dr and goes to the Keele St Subway Station on the Bloor subway line. If you run out of energy in **High Park**, take TTC bus 506 on Howard Park Ave near Parkside Dr east to Yonge St.

Tour 9. Bloor-Yorkville.

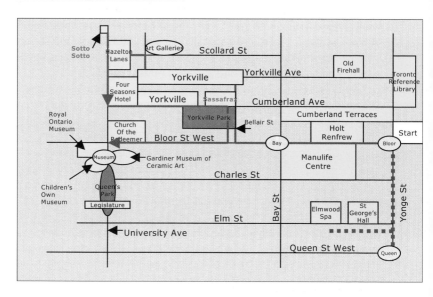

Approx. 2.4 miles or 3.8 km (plus 2.7 miles or 4.3 km to start point) return

Key Sights: *Young Women's Christian Association building, St. George's Hall, "Oddfellows Hall", Masonic Hall, Postal Station F, Potter's Field cemetery site,* **Toronto Reference Library**, Manulife Centre, Hazelton Lanes, Village of Yorkville Park, **Sassafraz**, **Four Seasons Hotel**, Sotto Sotto, **Royal Ontario Museum**, **Children's Museum**, *the Building of Household Science,* **Gardiner Museum of Ceramic Art**, **Isabel Bader Theatre**, *Victoria University, St. Michael's College,* **Bistro 990**, **Sutton Place Hotel**.

Start at Yonge and Queen Streets. Walk up to Bloor St and experience the stroll along Yonge St - millions of people have – teenagers in particular will like the stores along this walk, such as: The Arcade and Sunrise Records north of Dundas St, World of Posters at 355, the Toronto Sports Shop, 1,000,000 Comics at 530, Grey Region comics and models at 550, Dr. Marten's boots at 594, Central Surplus camping and hunting gear at 610, Bootmaster at 609, the venerable House of Lords hair salon at 639, Lush hand made cosmetics at 665, Gameland at 718, and the **Uptown** (movie theater) at 764.

There are several historical and architectural points of interest. The *Young Women's Christian Association building* at 18 Elm St was built in 1890 and now serves as the prestigious Elmwood Spa. *St. George's Hall building* was built in 1891 and used by the St. George Society to aid English immigrants until 1988. It was also the site of several Group of Seven (famous Canadian painters) meetings. The 100 store College Park built in 1928-30 on the southwest corner of Yonge and College was originally the *Eaton's College store*. The *"Oddfellows Hall" building* on the northwest corner of Yonge and College Streets was built in 1891. The very noticeable *Masonic Hall buildings* at Yonge and Gloucester Streets was built in 1888 and won a 1973 award for architectural restoration. *Postal Station F at 675 Yonge St* was built in 1905.

Cross Yonge St to Bloor St West, look right and you'll see the 416,000 sq.ft. **Toronto Reference Library**. The northwest corner was once *The Potter's Field cemetery* for almost 1,000 persons. This stretch of Bloor St West is fabulous at night, especially near Christmas with street decorations and lights augmenting the normally bright streetscape. At Balmuto St, attention shoppers! You can enter the 50 store Manulife Centre on your left with stores like William Ashley (fine china) and Birks Jewellry, a Cineplex Odeon theatre, and the underground shopping mall, or pop into the 25 store Holt Renfrew Centre on the north side of Bloor and shop at Holt Renfrew, Eddie Bauer, GAP, or Calderone. Connected underground to the Holt Renfrew Centre is the 70 store Cumberland Terrace.

Walk yards west past Bay St to Bellair St and turn north to Yorkville Ave and the Village of Yorkville founded in 1830. Check out Paisley's Antiques at 77 and housed in a 1867 built home. Car buffs will enjoy Prestige Art & Gift Gallery at 101. **Bellini's**, dinner host to Whoopi Goldberg, Leslie Nielson, Brooke Shields, Danny Devito, Bono, Madonna, and other stars is also at 101. Remy's at 115 and **Marche's** (a personal favourite) are both popular eateries. Art galleries? Try Edward Day Gallery at 33 Hazelton St and Gallery Gevik at 12 just north of Yorkville Ave, or the following galleries on Scollard St, a few yards north of Yorkville and Hazelton: Drabinski Gallery at 122, Gallery One at 121, Beckett Fine Art at 120, Gallery 7 at 118, and Revolver Contemporary Art at 112. You'll also notice the *Toronto Heliconian Club building* (built in 1876 in the Gothic style) at 35 Hazelton. It was founded in 1909 as a forum for women in the arts.

Cross Hazelton and you'll see a short laneway to the upscale Hazelton Lanes shopping complex. The Hazelton outdoor courtyard/patio is turned into a cozy skating rink in winter. Exit Hazelton Lanes on Avenue Rd and walk north a few hundred yards to **Sotto Sotto**, a Hollywood star favourite.

Return to the corner of Yorkville Ave and Avenue Rd. One of Toronto's best hotels and a Hollywood star favourite is the **Four Seasons Hotel** (catch glimpses of your favourite star during the **Toronto International Film Festival**). Walk south one block to Cumberland Ave and turn left. Yorkville and Cumberland are popular streets to cruise in one's hot car.

The Village of Yorkville Park is an amazingly beautiful park that offers a prairie wildflower garden, a fragrant herb rock garden, several native ecosystems, and 650 tonnes of Canadian Shield granite. Hollywood favourite **Sassafraz** (see picture) is across the street.

Go south on Bellair to Bloor and then turn right. The upscale shops continue to Avenue Rd. The four corners at Avenue Rd/Queen's Park house the 1879 built *Church of the Redeemer;* the Hyatt Regency Hotel; The **Royal Ontario Museum** (ROM), and *the Building of Household Science.* Head south to the **Children's Own Museum** and **Gardiner Museum of Ceramic Art**.

South of the Gardiner Museum is *Annesley House*, built in 1902 as a home for proper young women established by several elite women of the time. Cross Charles St to granite pagodas replicas dedicated to Dr. Avison, who founded the first occidental style hospital in Seoul, Korea. One building east is the modern looking **Isabel Bader Theatre** and a path leading into the beautiful Victoria University campus. This is an oasis of historic buildings of courtyards, architectural grandeur, statutes of art, and landscaping. To your right is Queen's Park with its magnificent 200 year-old oak trees.

At St. Joseph St, turn left, and notice the beautiful and superbly maintained grounds of St. Michael's College (part of University of Toronto). When you reach Bay St, turn south to **Bistro 990** and **Sutton Place Hotel**, both Hollywood favourites. Turn left on Wellesley St West for one block to Yonge St. Turn right to return to Queen St (or take the subway on Wellesley St East, yards east of Yonge St).

Victoria University

Tour 10. University of Toronto and Queen's Park.

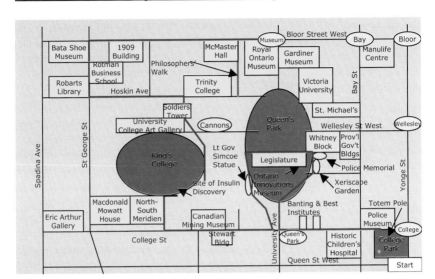

Approx. 2.3 Miles or 3.7 Km (plus 1.2 miles or 2 km to start point) return

Key Sights: College Park, **Toronto Police Museum**, **Royal Ontario Museum**, Philosopher's Walk, **Bata Shoe Museum**, University of Toronto (Varsity Arena, McMaster Hall, *315 Bloor St West*, *Soldiers' Tower*, *Geodetic Observatory*, *1758 cannons*, site of insulin discovery), **Canadian Mining Hall of Fame**, Taddle Creek, *Ontario Power Generation Building*, *George Gooderham House*, Queen's Park and **Legislature**, **Ontario Innovations Museum**, *portraits of General Isaac Brock and Lt. Gov. John Graves Simcoe*.

Part I

Start at Yonge & Queen Streets. Walk north along Yonge St past the Eaton Centre until you reach Gerrard St West. Walk about 100 yards west, and almost directly across from the main entrance to the **Delta Chelsea Hotel** is a walkway north into College Park. The reflecting pool is a lovely skating rink in winter. Head north into the back entrance of College Park and see the *Three Watchmen totem pole* carved by Haida Indians of British Columbia.

Directly north of College Park on College St are Toronto Police Headquarters and the FREE **Toronto Police Museum** (donations via a donation box are appreciated). Note the *original stone entrance of the YMCA building* preserved and embodied in the newer headquarters building. Lots of great stuff here, including the holding cell that will give your kids an idea of what it might be like to be incarcerated even for a few minutes.

Come back out onto College St and turn right or west to Elizabeth St. At 67 College is the original *Victoria Hospital for Sick Children.* The hospital was the first in Canada dedicated to pediatrics. Built in 1889, it is now used for the Canadian Blood Services. The world famous Toronto Hospital for Sick Children is now in much larger and modern facilities just south of this site.

Walk one block west past the Best Institute and Banting Institute to University Ave/Queen's Park Circle. Turn right along Queen's Park Circle until you cross Grosvenor St. On your left is Ontario's legislative building known as **Queen's Park**. On your right are the provincial government administrative buildings. Turn right into the gardens that horticulturists will much enjoy. Various trees, shrubs, and plants including the Smoke Tree and Blue Heaven Juniper are planted here and are identified with small plaques.

 There is also a **Xeriscape Demonstration Garden** of water conservation landscaping, a concept first developed by the City of Denver Water Department.

Law enforcement folks will appreciate the nearby **Ontario Police Memorial**, a wall of names commemorating fallen police officers that served Ontario. Come back to Queen's Park Circle and turn right or north. A few yards later you'll see two **cannons** that were part of the armament of the French warship "Le Prudent", captured at Louisbourg by the British in 1758. The building behind the cannons is the *Whitney Block* built in 1924 in honor of Sir James Whitney, Ontario's sixth Premier. This building was made almost exclusively of Ontario sourced materials: blue dolomite from Queenston (near Niagara Falls), marble from Bancroft, granite from Coe Hill, limestone from Shelburne, and other materials from Dundas, Toronto, Guelph, Belleville, and Mimico.

 Whitney's father was from St. Lawrence County, New York and he came to Toronto after the War of 1812. Whitney's mother was also from New York State.

Cross Queen's Park Circle (road) to **Queen's Park**. The red sandstone buildings were named after the beloved Queen Victoria and were built in the Romanesque Revival style in 1886-92. The design was by Richard Waite of Buffalo, New York.

There are exhibits of Ontario's history in the Legislative Chambers, the FREE **Ontario Innovations Museum**, oil on canvas *portraits of General Isaac*

Brock and Lt. Gov. John Graves Simcoe, and FREE guided tours from 9 am-4 pm on Mon- Fri. See *Upper Canada's "Mace"* captured by the Americans in 1813 and not returned until President Franklin D. Roosevelt did so in 1934! Return home if you're tired or have other plans, or continue with Part II.

Part II

Cross the road due west from Queen's Park to the University of Toronto (U of T) and its many treasures. U of T was Ontario's first university in 1827 and was originally called King's College. It is now Canada's largest university with 55,000 students!

See the life size stone statues of Sir Isaac Brock, Lt Governor John Graves Simcoe, General Wolf, and Champlain on the side of the Canadiana building at 14 Queen's Park Circle West. Stroll south to see a plaque honoring Maud Leonora Menton (1879-1960), the first woman in Canada to receive a medical doctorate in 1911 and who later was the co-founder of the Michaelis-Menton equation on the behavior of enzymes.

Turn right on College St and you'll come to Taddle Creek Rd, named after the Taddle Creek that ran north-south along here and down through Toronto at least as late as 1842. The building to the south is the *1892 Stewart building* designed by the same architect who designed Old City Hall (E.J. Lennox).

The Mining School and FREE **Canadian Mining Hall of Fame** are at 170. The FREE **Eric Arthur Gallery** of Architecture is at 230, just west of King's College Rd. Return to King's College Rd, turn left, and you will discover a treasure chest of items in the short block north to King's College Circle:

- A plaque to honor the first women students (9) started in 1884 only after provincial legislation allowed women to enter university classes.
- The meridian (ie. true north-south axis) of Toronto line that was accurate until 1908.
- The *Toronto time sundial* set parallel to the Earth's axis of rotation.
- The site of the Ontario School of Practical Science where more than 15,000 engineers and architects were trained from 1877-1966.
- A plaque to honor Elizabeth Gregory MacGill, the first woman to graduate from U of T engineering (1927).
- The round *Convocation Hall building*.

Follow King's College Circle right to where Canadian doctors Banting and Best discovered insulin on May 17, 1921 (Banting was the first Canadian to win a Nobel Prize). Walk a block north until you reach Hart House Circle and turn right. A monument for members of the Queen's Own Rifles killed in action at

Soldiers' Tower

Limeridge on June 2, 1866 sits on the crest of the hill. Notice the two large painted murals in the road underpass just to your right? Cut northwest across the green space toward the *two cannons* from 1758 recovered from the British victory over the French at Louisbourg. Nearby is the 1908 Geodetic Observatory building.

The tall stone **Soldiers' Tower** is clearly in view. Built in 1924, it lists the names of U of T attendees who died in service during World Wars I and II. **University College Art Gallery**, what the New York Times called "one of Toronto's hidden gems", is just yards west. Otherwise, walk through the Tower and north one block on Tower Rd up to Hoskin Ave. To your right is Wycliffe College built in 1891 and used for filming in Chevy Chase's "Dirty Work". North across the street is the immense architectural and landscaped beauty of the circa 1925 *Trinity College*. The entrance houses the plate from the original cornerstone laid by Trinity College founder John Strachan in 1851 at its original site in Trinity Bellwoods Park.

Walk west along Hoskin to St. George St and the imposing *Robarts Library*. Turn right on St. George and see incredible examples of old and new architecture and how well they work together. The **Bata Shoe Museum** is on a corner of St. George and Bloor St West, as is the *George Gooderham House* built in 1890 and now used as the exclusive York Club.

Walk east on the south side of Bloor St West. The building at *315 Bloor St West* was built in 1909 and originally used for the Meteorological Service of Canada. Next comes **McMaster Hall**, now used as the Royal Conservatory of Music, built in 1881 in the High Victorian style. Philosopher's Walk appears next. Its gate was erected in honor of Queen Alexandra and dedicated in 1901 to commemorate the Duke and Duchess of Cornwall and York's visit. The gate was relocated here from the north end of Queen's Park where it first stood as part of six rusticated stone pillars, iron fences, and ornate lamps.

To return to the start point, take the TTC subway located at the ROM and travel a few minutes southbound back to Queen St.

Tour 11. Old York (Town).

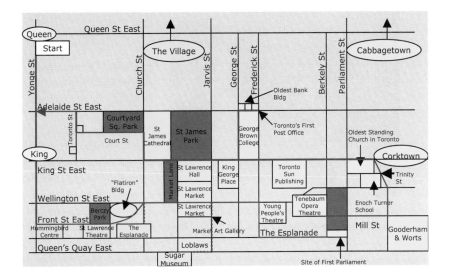

Approx. 3 Miles or 4.8 Km return

Key Sights: Hummingbird Centre, Flatiron Building, Berczy Park, St. Lawrence Theatre, **St. James Cathedral and Park, St. Lawrence Market, The Esplanade, Old York,** *Captain Yeo's plaque,* **Redpath Sugar Museum** and *Bill Wyland mural,* **Martin Goodman Trail,, Lorraine Timsa Young People's Theatre,** *Joey and Toby Tannebaum Opera Centre,* **Parliament Square Park, Gooderham & Worts, Enoch Turner School,** *King Edward Hotel.*

Flatiron Building

Start at Yonge and Queen Streets. Walk down Yonge St to Front St and **The Hummingbird Centre** for the Performing Arts on the corner (the back entrance is just north of the public parking). Walk east one block to the St. Lawrence Theatre of Performing Arts and Berczy Park. Berczy Park is famous for Daniel Besant's 1980 *Triumph D'Oleil wall mural* on the west side of the iron shaped *Flatiron Building*. The Flatiron was built in 1892 as headquarters of the rich Gooderham family of "Gooderham and Worts"

St. Lawrence Market

fame. This seems to be the site for unusual buildings as the Flatiron stands where the "Coffin" used to be.

Stores and restaurants in historical buildings on both sides of Front St are quite inviting for shopping. You can get groceries, deli, and hot meals (whole cooked chickens for $5.99!) at the bright and cheery Dominion, camping and other gear at European Bound, a pint at the Jersey Giant pub, wine and liquor at the LCBO, fast food at the Wendy's (at 75), coffees at the Second Cup and Starbucks, or pancakes and other meals at the 24 hour **Golden Griddle**.

Continue east on Front St until you reach Market and Jarvis Streets and the popular **St. Lawrence Market** (circa 1803). Open from 8 am to 6 pm on most days (closed Sunday), the heaviest traffic is on Saturday mornings when the market opens at 5 am. A must do if you love exotic foods, crafts, and other household items in European market-like conditions. Adults and kids love this place. Fresh and inexpensive meals can be had, often with one or several street musicians performing. You can also view historic paintings of Toronto in the FREE **Market Gallery** upstairs. Take the elevator in the main front entrance.

Alex Farm Products and Olympic Food & Cheese offer an astounding array of cheeses in densely packed stores. The Future Bakery has pastries to die for. Mike's Seafood and Domenic's Seafood markets will dazzle your eyes with the fresh seafood in refrigerated display cases. Mustachio's has veal and eggplant sandwiches that you'll need both hands to eat. Domino's downstairs, a deli and candy/nut store, must have the smallest aisles in North America. You can eat outside on the veranda while soaking in the sun if eating in a beehive of activity is not your style. Excellent nearby public parking can be found at the south end of Market or Church Streets.

On the northern side of Front St is the north hall of the St. Lawrence Market that is a farmers' market and is open Sundays when the South Market is not. The Harvey's & Swiss Chalet restaurant next door is a good place to get burgers and chicken in a clean and plain family setting at reasonable prices. On the northeast corner of Front and Jarvis Streets is a monument to the War of 1812 Admiral, *Sir James Yeo's and his flagship "St. Lawrence"*, erected at the original waterfront of the Town of York. A short side trip to the Queen's Quay Loblaws supermarket, the **Redpath Sugar Museum**, the harbour, and the huge *Bill Wyland mural* of whales would require you to walk south on Jarvis St to Queen's Quay (road) about 250 yards south. Loblaws has FREE parking for customers, a great Marchetta's (part of Marche's restaurant chain) and upstairs eating area with a view over the harbour and Bill Wyland's mural, and live musicians on weekends. See ocean going ships unload yards away.

From Jarvis and Front Streets, continue on east until you reach the **Lorraine Timsa Young People's Theatre (YPT)** at the corner of Front and Frederick Streets. This is a wonderful theatre for kids – every seat in the theater is a great seat. The actors often run through the two aisle-ways, creating a whoosh of air, and giving the audience the sense of being in the scene.

A house once stood on the northwest corner of Front and Frederick Streets that was home to William Warren Baldwin from 1804-1807, William Lyon Mackenzie from 1824-1826, and Joseph Cawthra from 1837-1842. William Warren Baldwin also built the now demolished *William Warren Baldwin House* in 1835 on the northeast corner of Front and Bay Streets (now BCE Place). East of the YPT is the Toronto Sun Publishing Company, publishers of the Toronto Sun. Take Frederick St south to The Esplanade (Street) and turn left or east. This whole area is an excellent example of how well public and co-operative housing can be planned and developed. Walk until you reach Berkeley St a few blocks down. You'll pass right by the front door of both a public pool and public elementary school and will likely not even notice! Toronto's third jail, built at Front and Berkeley Streets and used from 1840-1860, was just east of the current day *Joey and Toby Tanenbaum Opera Theatre*. Cross over Berkeley St and you'll see **Parliament Square Park**.

 This is the area where Ontario's first **Provincial Parliament Buildings** built in 1798 were before the Americans burned them to the ground in 1813 as part of the War of 1812!

Continue 75 yards through the park and you will reach Parliament St. Mill St starts across the street and just to your left. Follow Mill St one block to the **Gooderham & Worts (G&W) buildings**. Once part of the British Empire's largest booze empire, the buildings were built circa 1859. They now are used in films and TV productions (see Hollywood North). Note that this area is in the midst of being transformed from industrial to residential. Two nearby high-rise condo apartments have incorporated parts of G&W into their buildings. At the northeast corner of Mill and Trinity Streets is the six story "Rackhouse" that G&W used to age 3,000 31.5 gallon oak whiskey barrels.

Follow Trinity St north a block until you reach the fabulously restored **Enoch Turner School**, at 106, Ontario's oldest standing school building from 1843. Great fun for both kids and parents is partaking in the 1800's classroom re-enactment. The kids and you will howl with laughter on what the teacher expected of our kids of that time! Abutting the Enoch Turner School is the **Little Trinity Church**, built in 1842 and located at 425 King St East, and the oldest standing church in Toronto. It's considered an example of early Gothic Revival architecture. It was a common place of worship for the generally poor Irish folks of **Corktown** (King and Sackville Streets area).

Walk west on King St until you reach the main entrance of the Toronto Sun newspaper building at 333. A life size *metal sculpture* of two adults on a bench and a child on the ground all reading newspapers is FREE for viewing. It is called "Unity" and was sculpted by Czech born Lea Vivot. Continue west on King St and you'll pass Trianon at 247, with its upscale home furnishings, and D&E Lake Ltd at 239, jam-packed with antique and fine books, maps and manuscripts, prints and paintings. There's a Starbucks at 185 in the *King George Place building* built in 1836. Arts on King at 169 offers glassware, pottery, carvings, jewelry, ironworks, wax creations, prints, and more to decorate your home. The *Sovereign House* at 172 was built in 1907.

At George St, the western boundary of the original ten-block town of York, turn right or north until you reach Adelaide St East. At 252 is the *Bank of*

Street in Old Corktown part of Toronto

Upper Canada building built in 1827 in the Georgian style, with its superb Roman Doric portico. Next door is the *De La Salle Institute* building built in 1871. The most interesting building is at 260, built in 1833-35: Toronto's (not York's) first and still working **Post Office**. Don't miss the fascinating model of Toronto in 1837. It provides a feel for what the buildings looked like, where they were, their history, and how the original town grew into today's metropolis. It also shows that the no-longer existing Taddle Creek[2] ran along present day Queen St and just east of Sherbourne St to a swampy area where the Don River emptied into Lake Ontario. This swamp just east of the original town is one of the reasons the town primarily grew westward. Kids can also try their hand at writing letters with quill pens.

Return to King St and head west to Jarvis St. The northwest corner houses the *Canadian Bank of Commerce building* at 144, where the Township of York Council held its meetings from 1907-50. The southwest corner houses the **St. Lawrence Hall**, built in 1850, and which for many of its early years was Toronto's chief social and cultural centre. Its Corinthian façade and graceful copula are architectural beauties that can be seen from the street. Inside is the Great Hall where two Fathers of Canadian confederation, Sir John A. MacDonald and George Brown, spoke to crowds up to 1,000 people. The Anti-Slavery Society met here as well (Ontario abolished getting new slaves in 1793 and abolished slavery fully in 1833). One can envision the throngs of people being swayed to one political objective or another under the ornate ceilings, gigantic hanging chandelier, and upper deck/balcony.

Immediately west of the St. Lawrence Hall building is **Market Lane Park** and an innocuous looking *granite slab face sculpture* with an old water pump in the middle. It is hard to believe this was once the commerce centre for Toronto and that public punishment of criminals took place here. Stocks once stood here were last used in 1834.

Cross King St to get to **St. James Park and Gardens** on the north side. The garden is considered to be in the 19th century Victorian style with a wrought iron fence, ornamental water fountain, and a bandshell. The most unique sight is the

Drinking Fountain

working wrought iron drinking fountain just off the sidewalk! The small one on the back is for humans, the big one on the front is for dogs and the like. Continuing westward, you'll come to **St. James Cathedral** on the corner of King and Church Streets. Built in 1803-7, it was

---

[2] About the only other remnants of Taddle Creek are Taddle Creek Rd (see Tour 10) and Taddle Creek Park in The Annex neighbourhood at Lowther Ave and Bedford Rd.

Toronto's first church. Prior to that, its congregation met in the original Parliament buildings, later destroyed by the Americans in the War of 1812. The mother church for Anglicans in the Diocese of Toronto, it was rebuilt in 1853 after a fire. The St. James Parish House north of the church was built in 1909. The church interior is reminiscent of European churches. Of interest is the fragment from the St. James Church in Piccadilly, London, England in the wall of the entrance vestibule (also where a scene of the movie "Dogmatic" was filmed). The fragment was part of the damage the London church endured in the World War II air raids of October 1940. St. James also hosts an annual blessing of animals by the Archbishop of Toronto, where people bring their pets for blessing. A zony (cross between a zebra and pony) was blessed in 2001! Immediately south of the church's entrance, across King St, is the tiny Toronto Sculpture Garden of sculptures, statues, and a waterfall.

Toronto's first jail built in 1797 was west across the road at the northwest corner of King and Church Streets. Walk about one block north on Church St until you reach Court St and Courthouse Square Park. This small urban park has beautiful waterworks and gardens, and leads to a covered walkway south to King St. It also backs on to the old York Courthouse at 57 Adelaide St East, built in 1853, where an original prison cell remains downstairs for people to see, and where Toronto's last public execution took place.

Walk west on Court St a few yards to Toronto St. The building at *10 Toronto* was built in 1851-53 in the Neo Classical style and used once as a post office. Turn right and you'll see the Consumers Gas buildings at 17 and 19 Toronto St, built in 1852 and 1876, respectively, and currently used for the upscale **Rosewater Supper Club**. The old *Excelsior Life building* at 36 was built in 1914. It is one of the plainest designs by famed architect E.J. Lennox.

Turn south on Toronto St about 50 yards until you reach King St East. This was the site of Toronto's second jail used from 1824-1840, and the site of several executions. Turn right for one block. Just past Victoria St is a laneway going

Historic Entrance to the
Rosewater Club

north. It leads to an incredible courtyard of glass sculptures, park benches, and 3 zany water fountains. The glass sculptures look impenetrable, but you can walk around them on your way to Adelaide St East. The *Birkbeck Building* built in 1908, is considered to have rich Edwardian Baroque architectural details. The building's John White Hall was used in filming "Nero Wolfe" and

"Queer Folk". It also has an Otis elevator made in 1908 that needs an attendant. Walk two blocks north along Yonge St back to Queen Street.

Tour 12. The Beaches and Ashbridge's Bay.

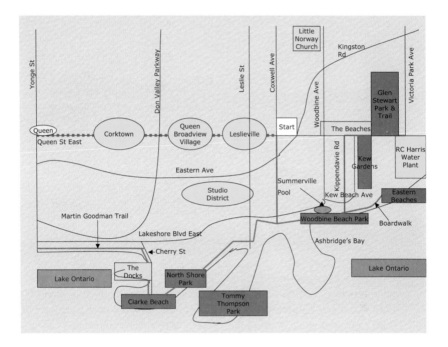

Approx. 1.8 Miles or 2.9 Km (plus 8.4 miles or 13.4 km to start point) return

Key Sights: Kew Gardens, beach volleyball, Ivan Forrest Gardens, Summerville Pool, **Martin Goodman Trail** (part), **Woodbine Beach Park/Ashbridge's Bay**, Whitlock's, Lick's.

The Beaches is a fabulous place to spend the day, or more, with something for everyone in the family. Start at Yonge and Queen Streets. Take TTC streetcar 501 east to Coxwell Ave. Walk south one block along Coxwell to Woodbine Park, once the home of Woodbine (and then Greenwood) Racetrack where Northern Dancer and Secretariat raced. The area is now an interesting new housing development and park. Continue south one block until you reach **Woodbine Beach Park** and Ashbridge's Bay right on Lake Ontario.

Ashbridge's Bay was named after the Ashbridge's family who came here from Pennsylvania in 1793.

This is a wondrous playground in summer with superb BBQ facilities, shelters, sand beach, the **Martin Goodman Trail** for biking and rollerblading, beach volleyball, a boardwalk along the beach with superb views of the lake and beach, restaurant, and a kid's playground. Follow the boardwalk east to the

Beach Volleyball at **Woodbine Beach Park**
and Ashbridge's Bay

enormous above ground Summerville Pool – you can't miss it with its high diving towers. Just north of the pool is Kew Beach Ave. Walk one block east until you reach Kippendavie Ave and turn left for two blocks to Queen St East. Turn right and you'll be right in the thick of this wondrous area.

Interesting stores include Habanos on the Beach at 1905, offering specialty tobaccos and gifts, Christmas on the Beach at 1891, and the circa 1905 *Fire Station and Clock Tower* at 1904. The kids will love Sugar Mountain candy store, Lick's gourmet burger/ice cream heaven at 1962A, Toy Circus at 2036, and Mastermind Educational at 2134. Shoppers will like Alf's Antiques at 1915/17, The Second Spin at 1947 for its thousands of used CDs, Midco at 1964 for its stationary, office, school and their excellent art supplies, The Artisans at 1974A for its masks, Seagull Classics at 1974 for furnishings and lighting, the Running Room at 1977 for its jogging stuff, and the Three Dog Bakery at 2014 for its dog goodies.

Need food? Try Bakeworks at 1946 for quick sandwiches, Lion on the Beach at 1958 for pub grub, **Whitlock's** at 1961 for fine dining, Nevada at 1963, Second Cup at 1948 or 2102 (nice outdoor patio or Starbucks at 1984 for coffee and sweets, Meat on the Beach at 1965 for delicatessen food, Juice Zone at 1966½ for fruit juices, Nutty Chocolatier at 2179 for specialty candies, and Nova Fish and Chips (traditional English fish and chips) at 2209.

Kew Gardens is my favourite of the many marvelous parks in Toronto. It extends from the hub-bub of Queen St East to the boardwalk and beach. It has a lovely multi-level library built in 1915 in mock-Tudor style, a band shell that hosts the fantastic **Beach Jazzfest** and its musicians, a playground and wading pool for little children, monuments, gardens, outdoor hockey rink, baseball field, and majestic red oaks trees.

Beaches Jazzfest

Tour 13. Garden District and The Village.

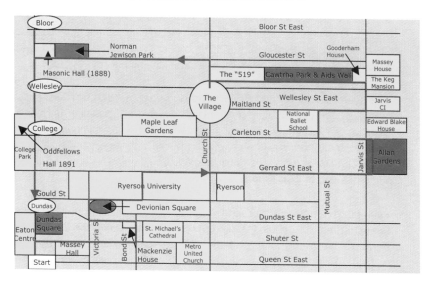

Approx. 3.6 Miles or 5.8 Km return

Key Sights: Massey Hall, Mackenzie House, Ryerson University (*St. James Square, Coat of Arms, The Toronto Normal School, Egerton Ryerson statue*), **Allan Gardens, The Village,** Second Cup (Village Central), **The National Ballet School** (plus *"Friends' Meeting House"*), **Maple Leaf Gardens, Jarvis House, The 519, AIDS Wall,** *Massey House,* Cawthra Park, *E.R. Rundle House, G.H. Gooderham House,* The Keg Mansion, *Jarvis Collegiate, Edward Blake House, home* of Sir Oliver Mowat.

Start at Yonge and Queen Sreets. The Garden District, an area bounded by Carlton St on the north, Queen St on the south, Sherbourne St on the east, and Yonge St on the west, was pronounced as such on Sept 30/2001.

Walk north on Yonge to Shuter St. Turn right and you will see **Massey Hall.** This historic music and stage hall, named after the elite Massey family of Toronto, hosted many world-class celebrities. Continue on to Bond St and turn north to **Mackenzie House** at 82. This was the last home of William Lyon Mackenzie, Toronto's first Mayor, and leader of the 1837 Rebellion.

Follow Bond St to Dundas St East, turn left for one block to Victoria St, and then turn right. You'll pass the Ryerson reflecting pool (skating rink in winter) in **Ryerson University.** Turn right on Gould St and you'll see a *statue of Egerton Ryerson,* the "founder of the school system in Ontario". Go through the entrance and you'll be in Ryerson's interior *St. James Square.* Note the very old *Toronto Normal School's façade,* dated 1847, once part of the first teachers' college. Walk through the façade and through the doors to the entrance to Ryerson's underground gym facilities. Continue on north through St. James Square to the *Coat of Arms built of Ohio sandstone dated 1896,* designed by Lt.-Governor John Graves Simcoe and Egerton Ryerson.

Exit Ryerson onto Gerrard St East and turn right to **Allan Gardens** just past Jarvis St. These FREE gardens in glass houses are spectacular in their abundance of plants, colors, and fragrances. There is a monument to Scottish poet Robbie Burns, author of "Auld Lang Syne", at the east side of the park. Exit **Allan Gardens** on the north side and you'll be on Carleton St. This is the south end of **The Village,** as Toronto's gay district is known.

Follow Carleton west or left until you reach Mutual St. Turn right or north on Mutual St until you reach Maitland St. On your left is **The National Ballet School**. Part of the complex is the *Friends' Meeting House,* built by Quakers in 1911. Turn right or east on Maitland for a block to reach Jarvis St, named by Samuel Peters Jarvis in 1845. The Jarvises were among the first land grantees of York town when Samuel's father William received land in 1796.

Samuel killed an adversary in a duel and served in the War of 1812. Lovers of architecture and history will love Jarvis Street, as it continues to have some of the grandest century homes built in Toronto.

Oakham House at 322 was built in 1848. The house at 372 was built in 1856 and was the home of Sir Oliver Mowat, a Father of Confederation and Premier of Ontario for 24 years. The *Edward Blake House* at 467 was built in 1891 and was also the home of a Premier of Ontario. 469 and 471 are extraordinary yellow brick century homes. *Jarvis Collegiate* at 495 was established in 1807 on this site, but the current building is dated to 1924. It is one of the oldest public secondary schools in Ontario. 15 stunning murals by George Reid, who also did the murals in Old City Hall. A little further north of Wellesley St on the east side is **The Keg Mansion** steakhouse in the palatial historic building known as *Euclid Hall* at 515. Abutting the restaurant at 519 is *Massey House*, built in 1885-93, and once the home of the famous Massey family. Raymond became a famous Hollywood actor, and Vincent became Canada's first Canadian born Governor General in 1952. Hart House (named after Hart Massey) in the University of Toronto and Massey Hall are also named after this family. Across the road at 504 is the *Gooderham House*, built in 1891 in the Romanesque Revival style, and now home to Angelini. The century homes at 506, 510, 512, and 512 make for a nice row to give one a sense of what this street was like in the 1800s. 514 Jarvis St is the *E.R. Rundle House* built and designed by E.J. Lennox in 1889. Covered porches, sandstone, gables, wrought iron fence, spire, and lion column holding up the upper porch are some of the touches you don't see on today's houses.

A short street one block north of Wellesley, Cawthra Square, leads to Cawthra Park. A few yards in and you'll come to the **AIDS Wall** monument to those who died of the affliction. The building in the park is known as **The 519** – a community centre well used by the gay/lesbian and other community groups. A popular spot for the community is the Second Cup café at 545 Church St, where people get coffee and congregate outside on "the steps". This area's **Pride Toronto** parade (and Halloween parties) provides sights you'll rarely see! You will see the Rainbow flag frequently here.

Cross Church St after leaving Cawthra Park, head north to Gloucester St, and then turn left or west. One block later, after passing **Bumpkin's** and Norman Jewison Park, you'll be at Yonge St. The **Brownstone** is on this corner in the *1888 Masonic Hall building*. Turn right on Yonge St and walk to Bloor St. Walking Yonge St from Queen to Bloor Streets is a favourite activity among visitors and young people in particular. There are restaurants, dollar stores, fitness gyms, coffee shops, music stores, fashion and shoe stores, and many more stores packed shoulder to shoulder on both sides of the street the whole way. You will also see people of all kinds. Retrace your steps south along Yonge St. If you wish to see *Maple Leaf Gardens*, turn left at Carleton St and it's a few buildings east. Now that the Toronto Maple Leafs no longer play here, this once venerable hockey shrine is really not much to see. Continue south to **Dundas Square** and **Eaton Centre** at Dundas St. Dundas Square, opening in the summer of 2002, is a black and green granite lined City Square with large video screens, water fountains, and underground parking. Jazz festivals, street performers, movie nights, and dancing events will be held here. The **Eaton Centre** is a very popular indoor shopping mall with almost 300 shops, restaurants, and services.

Tour 14. Cabbagetown.

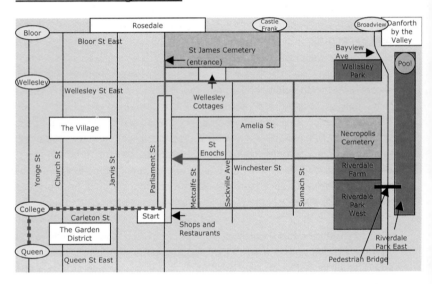

Approx. 2.2 Miles or 3.6 Km (plus 2.7 miles or 4.3 km to start point) return

Key Sights: *Darling Terrace*, **St. James Cemetery**, *St. James the Less Chapel*, *Wellesley Cottages*, Wellesley Park, *384 Sumach St*, **Necropolis Cemetery**, **Riverdale Farm,** Riverdale Park, *St. Enoch's Presbyterian Church*, *Winchester Hotel*. This tour will appeal most to people interested in architecture, history, and urban planning.

Cabbagetown is a great mix of residential, historic homes, stores, restaurants, parks, and the arts. It came to be known as Cabbagetown from the cabbages grown in the front yards of the generally poor citizens at the time. Today, Cabbagetown is an excellent example of a once run-down area that has been wonderfully resurrected. Compare this neighbourhood to St. Jamestown just northwest – it is comprised of several 30 story high apartments in several blocks of sterile environs that once were full of houses like in Cabbagetown.

Take TTC streetcar 506 from College subway station east to Parliament and Carleton Streets. The African Art Store at 250 Carleton, Micasa at 242, and Antiques at 248 offer exotic and unique home decorations. Daniel et Daniel at 248 has exquisite baked goods. Around the corner, heading north on Parliament, is Johnny G's, a popular restaurant with fantastic prices ($3.75-$9.95). Across the street at 495 is Letteri's Expresso Bar & Café, a great spot for coffee, panini, salads, squeezed juices, and pizzas – nice view of the Carleton/Parliament intersection too. Peartree is at 505/507 and Jet Fuel Coffee Shop is at 519. The **Danny Grossman Dance Theatre** and Canadian Children's Dance Theatre are at 509. Green's Antiques is at 529 and Nettleship's Hardware Store at 576 is a pre-Home Depot neighbourhood hardware store and has been serving the area since 1920.

Darling Terrace, several Victorian homes next to each other, was built in 1877 and is at 562-66. A few yards north of Wellesley is **St. James Cemetery,** the mid 1840s successor to the St. James Cathedral burying grounds. If you love history, this national historic site is an enthralling place. One is "greeted" at the main entrance by the *St. James the Less Chapel*. Built in 1860, it is considered <u>one of the finest examples of Gothic Revival church architecture in Canada</u>. You can also obtain a map of famous people gravesites at the office, just inside the main entrance. The names include several of Toronto's early Who's Who like Enoch Turner, William Jarvis (Loyalist from Connecticut), John Scadding, Egerton Ryerson, EJ Lennox, John White (Upper Canada's 1st Attorney General, killed in a duel by John Small in 1800), John Ridout (killed in a duel by Samuel Jarvis in Canada's last duel), William (father) and Robert (son) Baldwin, James Worts, George Gooderham, William Allan, Sir Casimir Gzowski, Mary Ridout, Laura Mary Ryerson (heroine of "Lusitania") James Cockburn (a Father of Confederation), Peter Russell (Lt. Governor John Graves Simcoe's right hand man), and

 Sir William Pearce Howland (a Father of Confederation). He was born in New York State.

At Wellesley St, turn right/east until you reach Wellesley Cottages Lane and the *Wellesley Cottages* built in 1886-87 for laborers. Further along is the pleasant Wellesley Park that once was the site of Cabbagetown's only major factory. Notice the concrete dish that is one of the many city wading pools for children in summer. Follow the path to the right and you'll see several homes whose front lawn is the park! Their garages are behind the houses along a

laneway. You'll come to Amelia St, the Necropolis Cemetery's north boundary.

Turn left on Sumach St and walk one block to 384 to view a superb Victorian home with gingerbread trim and porch. Back to Winchester St and turn right to the **Necropolis Cemetery** entrance (see picture). The buildings were built in 1872 and have beautiful architectural details: slate shinges, gingerbread trim, and a copper roof peak. The small chapel interior is a miniature version of a large cathedral. Many prominent people are buried here (see "Attractions").

Immediately south of the Necropolis Cemetery is the FREE **Riverdale Farm** and Riverdale Park. This is a superb place for families with small children.

Follow Sumach south to Carleton St, turn right to Metcalfe St, a particularly attractive street lined with beautiful historic homes. *St. Enochs Presbyterian Church,* built in 1891 in the Romanesque style, is located at Metcalfe and Winchester Streetsand is now used as the Toronto Dance Theatre. Follow Winchester St west to Parliament St and the *Winchester Hotel* built in 1881-88. Further south on Parliament at 502-508 are large Victorian houses built in 1879 and considered premier examples of Second Empire style. Take TTC streetcar 506 along Carleton back to College Subway Station.

Horse grazing near Francey Barn at Riverdale Farm.

Tour 15. East End.

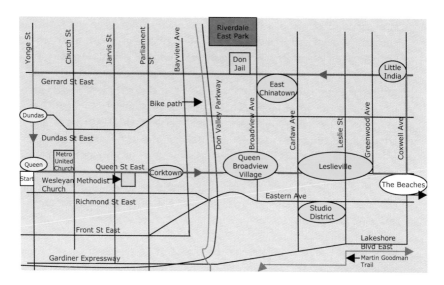

Approx. 7.5 Miles or 12 Km return

Key Sights: St. Paul's Basilica, Corktown, Queen Broadview Village,
*sidewalk inscription in metal, Ralph Thornton Town Hall and Cultural Centre
(1913), 1885 Poulton Block,* **Leslieville,** *Ashbridge's Home,* **Studio District,
Gerrard India Bazaar, Chinatown (East), Don Jail,** Toronto Jail.

Take eastbound TTC streetcar 501 from Queen and Yonge Streets. You'll pass
the site on Berti St, yards south of Queen and west of Yonge, where Sir
Sanford Fleming developed and "sold" the concept of international standard
time in 1879. You will also pass **Metropolitan United Church,** Moss Park
Armoury, Nouveau Stained Glass and related supplies at 207, the sexy clothes
of He and She Clothing at 263, Ontario Decorative Hardware at 271, *Berkeley
St Wesleyan Methodist Church* (built in 1811), **St. Paul's Basilica** at 83
Power St (where 863 Irish were buried after succumbing to typhus contracted
on the ship over to Canada), and **Corktown** before reaching the gateway to
Queen Broadview Village. The gateway is the Queen St Bridge, with its
"The River I Step In is Not the River I Stand In" overhead metal sign. This
area is a work-in-progress with its wider mix of urban styles and buildings
more likely to show their age. Nevertheless, there are several interesting
buildings, stores, and restaurants/cafes.

The *neo classical sandstone building* at 765 was designed by E.J. Lennox and
built in 1913. It was originally used as a Post Office and now serves as a

Town Hall. The *Poulton Block* at 798 is dated 1885. The *Canadian Bank of Commerce* (forerunner of today's CIBC) building was built in 1905, but today is unused and tarnished. A *sidewalk inscription in metal* on the northwest corner of Queen and Broadview says "Time is Money, Money is Time" – this should have been at Bay and King Streets, Canada's "Wall Street"!

Interesting stores include Mary Macleod's Shortbread at 639 and Bistro 67 at 641. Ignore the ugly strip mall across the road! Clutter's Antiques is at 692, Sunnybrook Meats at 738, Elbers Antiques at 777, the Gallery Wall at 783 has prints and paintings for sale, Biroche Bakery Café at 812, Juice Queen at 898 for vegetarians, and The Joy of Java café at 884. Two places worth a quick look are Newell's Café at 784, a *real* 1950's diner, and Beyond the Pale pottery store at 922 – its door sign says "open by chance or appointment"! The Real Jerk at Queen and Broadview has fed several Hollywood stars including Wesley Snipes, Omar Epps, and Mario Van Peebles.

Leslieville, circa 1884, continues on Queen St East, east of Queen Broadview Village from Carlaw to Greenwood Avenues. Leslieville is similar to Queen Broadview Village but further along in its refurbishment. Part of what's driven the investment is the growing **Studio District** a block south, with about 50 film-related companies in the area including the 9 acre Toronto Film Studios complex that bills itself as Canada's Largest Film Studio Complex. Located on 629 Eastern Ave at the foot of Pape Ave, it looks like it was airlifted out of Los Angeles. It is home to the TV show "Earth: Final Conflict", movie company Aliiance Atlantis, and the cable networks of Life, Showcase, HGTV, and Food.

The Queen St *East Presbyterian Church* at 947 is not noteworthy but check its northwest cornerstones – 1878, 1909, and 1929! At 1444 and 1473 are the site of the Ashbridge's family's first home after arriving from Pennsylvania in 1793 and the house of Jesse Ashbridge, a descendant, respectively.

Hello Toast at 993 has a very pleasant setting for lunch, as is Ten Twenty Five at 1025. You can find novel gifts such as Indian furniture at Chada Import Gallery at 1015, home accents at Saltbox at 1028, Hardware at 1022, Finders Gallery at 1093, and Poof at 1112, and antiques at Jaws Antiques at 1118. Continue east until you reach Greenwood Ave. Take northbound TTC bus 22 on Coxwell Ave to Gerrard St East (or walk the 0.4 mile), and walk east to Gerrard India Bazaar.

Gerrard India Bazaar is very unique in North America and consists almost exclusively of Indian shops. Roasted sweet corn stalls replace downtown's hot dog stands. Incense and the aroma of sweet fruits waft through the air. Try south Indian vegetarian cuisine at Udupi at 1455 Gerrard. The Dollar Joint at

1499 offers its (non-Indian) goods for $1 and under, including clothes and clay figurines. Satyam at 1445 has Indian musical instruments and religious books. Indian Record Shop at 1428 and Taj Mahal at 1408 have records, and movie and music videos for sale. Maharani Emporium at 1417 has many gifts, books, puja items, and souvenirs. Islamic Books and Souvenirs at 1395 may be a good place for those who want to learn more about Islam. Surati Sweet Mart offers gujrati, thali-paw, bhaji and other sweet goods. Toronto Cash & Carry's fruit/vegetables include the exotic desi-karela and very sweet bore/dungs. See www.indo.com for more local Indian culture.

Take westbound TTC streetcar 506 to **Chinatown (East)** at Gerrard St East and Broadview Ave. Several fruit and vegetable marts on the sidewalk make for a colorful and busy marketplace. Shops sell gifts, traditional medicine and herbs, books, and videos. Most tourists will only need a few minutes here.

Just west of Broadview and north of Gerrard St East is the **Don Jail** and Toronto Jail. The Don Jail was built in 1863/64 in the Italian Renaissance style and is still standing today. There were 70 hangings here since the first one in 1872, including the last one to be held in Canada in 1962. People are allowed to tour inside the jail during the **Doors Open Festival** FREE.

Take westbound TTC streetcar 506 back to Yonge St.

Tour 16. Greektown.

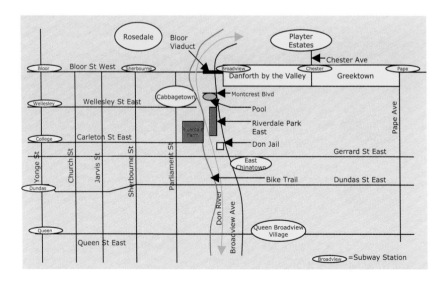

Approx. 1.2 Miles or 1.9 Km (plus 5.7 miles or 9.1 km to start point) return

Key Sights: Danforth by the Valley, Riverdale Park East, Broadview Pool, *Bloor Viaduct*, **Greektown**, *Alexander the Great statue*, Broadview Pool, **Taste of the Danforth Festival**, *Church of the Holy Name* built in 1915.

Take the subway from Yonge and Queen to Bloor, transfer to the eastbound Yonge-Bloor line, and head east. You will pass Castle Frank Subway Station, named after Lt. Governor John Graves Simcoe's summer home of the same name, and travel under the *Bloor Viaduct* and get a nice view of the Don Valley before getting off at Broadview Subway Station. Walk a few yards south to Bloor St East where Danforth by the Valley starts.

The subway ride wore you out and you need a fast food fix? McDonald's is right on the corner at 98 Danforth. Or if you're overheated, walk south two blocks on Broadview Ave to Riverdale Park East and the FREE pool. A great pool: a slide, heated, padded bottom in the shallows, waterfalls, "river" course, and a great view of the Toronto skyline.

Danforth by the Valley along Bloor is stock full of stores, bars, restaurants, cafés, services, and churches. Home accents and items can be obtained at Harvest Spa at 239, Lily Lee at 363, Lucid at 315, Alchemy at 325, and Grass Roots at 372 that offers environmental products, such as EarthGame, a cooperative game to save Earth. For kids, try Sucker's Candy Store at 448 or The Clay Room at 279. For $3-$36 per item, you can pick and paint a ceramic piece, and all necessary items are provided.

You can have coffee and delectable pastries at the lovely Schillings Exclusive café at 135, The Joy of Java Café/Bistro at 307, Timothy's at 320, or at the Second Cup at 353 with its lovely sidewalk patio. There are a few taverns and bars along this strip, such as Allens at 143 and The Black Swan Tavern at 154.

 The Playter Estates area directly northeast of Danforth Ave and Bloor St East was named after Captain George Playter, an early Loyalist settler.

 The main street is known as Danforth Ave. It was named after Asa Danforth, an American, hired in 1799 to build a road from Toronto to the east end of Lake Ontario.

Danforth by the Valley seamlessly joins to **Greektown**, considered to be North America's largest Greek community. Greektown runs along Danforth Ave from Chester Ave to Pape Ave (although there are many more stores and restaurants east of Pape Ave). The famous and popular Greek restaurant Astoria at 390 starts it off, followed by several others such as Megas at 400,

Myth at 417, Papa's Grill at 440, Greek City at 452, La Carreta (Cuban cuisine) at 469, Ampelli's at 526, The Friendly Greek at 555, Mr. Greek at 568, and **Il Fornello's** at 576 (a personal favourite). These restaurants offer Greek and other cuisine entrees for $8-$19 generally. Cafés include Cup of Mocha at 489, PAM's at 541, and Starbucks at 604. Try Athen's Pastries for sumptious Greek pastries such as baklava.

Interesting shops include Louis Meat Market at 449, The Cook's Place at 486, Textile Bazaar at 501 (all Simplicity patterns for only $2 each), Romancing the Home home accents at 511, Treasure Island Toys at 581, Traverso imported Greek clothing at 592, and Strictly Bulk Food Emporium at 638. Gamblers may want to try Champions Off Track Betting at 437.

The only points of historical or architectural interest are *Alexander the Great's statue* on the northeast corner of Danforth and Logan Avenues, and the *Church of the Holy Name* near Pape Ave built in 1915 with Greek pillars.

Tour 17. South Bayview and Ontario Science Centre.

Approx. 2.9 Miles or 4.6 Km (plus 11.6 miles or 18.6 km to start) return

Key Sights: stores and restaurants, **Ontario Science Centre**, antique alley.

South Bayview is part of the Leaside area named after John Lea, an American who came in 1819 from Pennsylvania.

To get here by TTC, take the Yonge Subway to Davisville Station and take Bus 11 along Davisville Ave to Bayview Ave. Get off at Bayview and walk north. Interesting shopping along this six-block strip includes home furnishings and knick-knacks, eateries, cafes, flowers, antiques, and novelty stores. Malmar at 1707 has the most interesting clear salad bowls with dried flowers within the bowl walls. The Sentry at 1633 will amuse the youngsters and military buffs with toys, models, toy soldiers, and "Men At Arms" war books. Smoke a cigar at The Smoking Cigar shop at 1693. View art at the State of the Art Gallery at 1541A. Check out some books at the quaint Sleuth of Baker Street at 1602. Have a creamy ice cream at Baskin & Robbins at 31 Millwood Rd on the corner of Bayview, or knock yourself out at Chocolate Messenger at 1645. For the cerebral set, try Strategy Games & Accessories at 1685 for games like Risk, chess, Axis and Allies, and Stratego.

Need some body fuel? Try Duff's famous chicken wings at 1604, McSorley's Saloon restaurant/pub at 1546, Diner '55 at 1614, a 50's style diner, Tea Emporium at 1592 (its Taiwanese gunpowder green tea is the lowest cost item at $8.30/100 gms), and popular neighbourhood Second Cup at 1593. It has a sidewalk seating area for European style people watching, an interior full of couches and sofa chairs, hard-to-get seats in a front window cranny, and good coffee. Rahier Patissiere at 1717 has sumptuous baked goods and coffees/teas in a European café setting.

Walk north one block past Soudan Ave to Eglinton Ave East. There is a McDonald's on the corner if you need a fast food fix. For hikers/bikers, the trail down to Harbourfront in downtown Toronto starts ½ mile north of Eglinton Ave East on Bayview. For antique hunters, turn left 0.6 miles to **Mount Pleasant** and antique alley. Catch eastbound Eglinton Ave East TTC bus 34 to Don Mills Rd, and either transfer to the southbound Don Mills TTC bus 25 or walk the 0.3 mile south to the **Ontario Science Centre**.

 The **Ontario Science Centre** is chock full of the most entertaining stuff for the whole family. Open everyday except Christmas, from 10 am - 6 pm from July 1 – Sep 4 and from 10 am - 5 pm the rest of the year. $12/adult, $7/child from 13-17, $6/child from 5-12, $7/senior 65 and over, and FREE for kids under 5. On-site parking is $7. The OMNIMAX Theatre admission is extra, but buying a combined admission is less expensive than separate admissions. 770 Don Mills Rd. (416) 696-1000, www.ontariosciencecentre.ca.

To return home, take TTC northbound Don Mills bus 25 to the westbound Eglinton Ave East bus 34 all the way to the Yonge St Subway Station (terminus). Take a southbound train back downtown.

Tour 18. Hillcrest Village, Corso Italia, Bloordale and Bloorcourt Villages, Bloor St in the Annex.

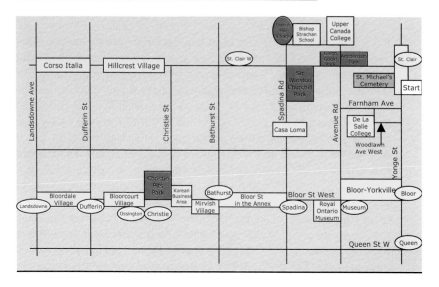

Approx. 8.4 Miles or 13.4 Km (plus 5.1 miles or 8.2 km to start point) return

Key Sights: Amsterdam Park, Glenn Gould Park, **Timothy Eaton Memorial Church**, **Casa Loma** and **Spadina House**, **Canadian-Hungarian Cultural Centre**, Korean Business Area, **Mirvish Village**, over hundreds of stores, restaurants, and the like through several ethnic communities.

Start at Yonge and Queen Streets. This tour will appeal to the person(s) who loves shopping streets with over 500 restaurants, pubs, bars, cafes, stores selling goods and services, and who wants to see more of Toronto's diversity and culture than is the case in downtown's popular tourist attractions.

Take the Yonge subway to St. Clair Ave. Transfer to westbound TTC streetcar 512 along St. Clair Ave West as you cut through the very wealthy Forest Hill community just north and south of St. Clair. You'll pass historic **Timothy Eaton Memorial Church** and, at the north corners of St. Clair Ave and Avenue Rd, Amsterdam Park and Glenn Gould Park. Amsterdam Park has a *replica of the fountain at the Peace Palace at The Hague* in the Netherlands. (If you're driving, drop in at **Casa Loma** and **Spadina House** about 0.5 mile south of St. Clair Ave West on Spadina Rd. Or spend an hour at one of the outdoor cafes in the lovely Forest Hill Village about 0.5 mile north of St Clair Ave West on Spadina Rd). Get off at Vaughan Rd just past Bathurst St about

1.7 miles from Yonge St and you're in the **Hillcrest Village** street shopping strip. The **Canadian-Hungarian Cultural Centre** at 840 is a worthwhile stopover when it is open to the public.

A 0.5 mile further west on St. Clair Ave West is the **Corso Italia** street shopping area starting at Dufferin St and ending at Lansdowne Ave. About 150 shops, restaurants, and services to choose from: everything from fine clothing, leather shoes, jewelry, fruit/vegetables stores, grocers, restaurants, cafes, sports bars, dollar stores, furniture, and gift shops. Lampposts, "Corso Italia" street signs, and potted plants add to the area's flavor. Chestnuts for sale replace the hot dog stands of downtown. McDonald's at 1168 St. Clair Ave West may be the only Americanized part of this street. The stores include Bun King Bakery at 1170, Genesis fine men's wear at 1188, Nido Restaurant at 1218, Centro Trattoria Frommaggi at 1224 has an appealing old world look and a wide range of cheeses (as well as being a site for the Cher movie "Moonstruck"), Fabian Italian leather shoes at 1224, Tuccalore Bar Café at 1240 is a quaint spot to pick up a cappuccino or ice cream. Complement it with fresh baked breads (on site) and sweets from Tre Mari Bakery at 1307, which also offers chicken, veal, or sausage dinners for $6 and a small seating area. The Connection Bar & Grill at 1368 and Eden Trattoria at 1335 both have outdoor patios that get sun most of the day. Tanya's Gifts at 1327 offers chinaware, art, pottery, and plates, and Carlo's Gifts at 1331 offers from kitchenware to mini-pool tables.

When you're done, turn left or south on Lansdowne on TTC bus 47 until you reach the 100 stores/services of Bloordale Village on Bloor St West between Lansdowne and Dufferin Streets. This area is showing some wear and tear, but is worth a quick stroll to get a peek at the enormous diversity of Toronto. In a few blocks, you'll see the Little Burma Gift and Variety at 1278, the West End MiniMart Food (specializing in African and West Indian foods) at 1280, Bombay Trading Company at 1194, Bangladesh Grocery and Video at 1176 Bloor St West, Brisa De Liz Portugese Bakery at 1174, Islamic Information Centre at 1168, and Croatian Toronto Credit Union at 1165.

Continue east along Bloor St West to Bloorcourt Village (between Ossington Ave and Christie Pits). About 150 stores, restaurants, and services, and the *Bloor Eastdale library* built in 1912. This area, like Bloordale Village, is quite diverse. Ethiopian restaurants include Queen Sheba at 1051, Tinkisk Restaurant at 842, and Ethiopia at 810. Nearby Sawa Restaurant and Sports Bar offers Eritrean cuisine. *St. Anthony's Catholic Church* built in 1921 is at 1037, Beirut Palace offering Lebanese food is at 1006, Calabrese Fruit Market & Grocery is at 922, and Top Taste Jamaican food is at 758 Dovercourt a few yards north of Bloor St.

The stretch of Bloor St West from Christie to Euclid Streets could be called "Little Korea" but is officially known as the Korean Business Area. There are about 125 stores, restaurants, and services before you reach Mirvish Village, including Latin Video Tours at 616 that offers Latin videos and music.

One block further east is **Mirvish Village** on Markham St, and the 54-year old Honest Ed's. It is best to do this part of the tour after sunset as Honest Ed's and Bloor St West are particularly attractive at night. The 75 yard long block that comprises Mirvish Village contains David Mirvish Books (of Art), Victory Café in a Victorian era house, Galor Gallery, Butlers Pantry Café, and the Purple Whale Bar & Grill (with its 15' whale hanging over the entrance). Honest Ed's holds a birthday bash or thank you to the customer bash pretty well every year in the third week of July. Drinks, food, souvenirs, prizes, kid rides, and entertainment are FREE. There's a McDonald's across Bloor St for those who must.

 Bloor St in the Annex offers over 100 shops, sidewalk cafes and rooftop bars along Bloor St West between Mirvish Village and Yorkville. This is one of the liveliest parts in Toronto, especially at night and on the weekends.

Examples of the great places along this stretch include Paupers and its Rooftop Patio at 539 (entrees $4-$10), **Bloor Cinema** at 506, Second Cup at 539, the very colorful **Lee's Palace** for live rock'n'roll at 529, **JJ Muggs** at 500, Dooney's Café (items $3.95-$7.95) at 511, Sushi on Bloor (items $2.50-$15.50) at 515, Future Bakery and its outdoor patio at 483, **Brunswick House** (a Toronto institution) for drinking and gambling at 481, The Cheese Diary at 454, **Country Style** and its huge Hungarian food portions and plain surroundings at 450, Mel's Montreal Deli at 440, Elizabeth's Meat & Delicatessen at 410, Outer Layer body lotions and message oils at 406, Tutti Fruitti candy store at 402, Sweet Fantasies seasonal ice cream parlor at 398, **Nataraj Indian Cuisine** at 394, voted best Indian restaurant in 2001 by Eye and Now Magazine readers, and The Rajputs Indian restaurant at 388 (entrees from $7.95-$9.95).

Tour 19. North Toronto (Yonge St).

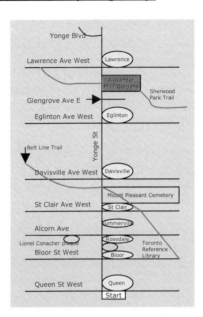

Approx. 7.2 Miles or 11.5 Km (plus 2.7 miles or 4.3 km to start point) return

Key Sights: the spine of Toronto and the world's longest street, Yonge St, **Toronto Reference Library**, **The Belt Line Trail**, **Lionel Conacher plaque**, and Postal Station K (site where the rebels in the 1837 Rebellion aggregated before marching to Toronto), Yonge-Lawrence Village.

Part I (Yonge St between Bloor and St. Clair Streets)

Start at Yonge and Queen Streets. I've walked Yonge St from Lake Ontario to past Steeles Ave, Toronto's northern municipal boundary – a marvellous way to get a close-up view of many Toronto attractions and neighbourhoods. Most people, though, will likely want to take the subway up to Yonge-Bloor Subway Station. Exit the subway and start walking north on Yonge St past **Toronto Reference Library**, The Cookbook Store at 850, and the eastern boundary of Yorkville. A block north is the Masonic Temple and now CTV venue, Canadian Tire's original main store in Canada (ca. 1937 – the original and first store was at Yonge and Gould Streets in 1923), and Ridpath's Fine Furniture at 906. As you continue north, you'll see Ramsden Park on your left and the western boundary of one of Canada's wealthiest neighbourhoods, Rosedale, on your right. This stretch is not as densely packed with stores, but there are still some notable ones to try like **Thai Magic** at 1118 and Matthew Berger Antiques at 1162.

A block north you'll see high the *CP Railway Station* tower (built in 1881) in upscale Summerhill Village. Summerhill has a higher density of antique and home décor shops, similar to Mount Pleasant. The lovely stores of Patachou Bakery & Café, Olliffe Butchers, Harvest Wagon, and All The Best home décor are all located at 1103. At Birch Ave, turn left one block to Gange Ave to see the **Lionel Conacher plaque/monument**. Other interesting stores include D&E Art & Books at 1199, RG Perkins Antiques Ltd at 1198, Orchids Imports at 1202, Horsefeathers Design home décor at 1212, Decorum home décor at 1210, Latalier Antiques at 1224, Ellen Reeves Antiques at 1230, Absolutely home décor at 1236, Pallete Fine Art Gallery at 1260, Braem and Minette Antiques at 1262, and Treasures Antiques at 1282.

Another block and you will come to Yonge-St. Clair and its many jewels. Yonge-St. Clair's neighbor to the east is the upscale Moore Park residential neighbourhood, and its neighbor to the west is historic Upper Canada College. Yonge-St Clair has some good value spots for lunch or dinner, or just coffee and cake. One block south of St. Clair is **Il Passione Italiana**, the original Swiss Chalet at 1411 (popular chain of roasted chicken restaurants), Mega Wraps at 1391A for the health conscious who want a quick inexpensive meal, the delightful **Boccone's** at 1378 and Starbucks.

North of St. Clair one block is **Il Fornello's** and its tasty brunch, Bregman's with its mouth-watering baked goods, and Second Cup café. The shops stop at Heath St, two blocks north of St. Clair St, and give way to the gothic looking *Yorkminster Park Baptist Church* built in 1927, the historic **Mount Pleasant Cemetery**, and **The Belt Line Trail** for biking/walking. The shops pick up again about 0.3 mile north at Yonge-Davisville. To return home, take the subway south from the St. Clair Station at Yonge and St. Clair.

Part II (Yonge St between Davisville Ave and Blythwood Rd.)

Either continue on from Part I or start at Yonge and Queen St and take the subway up to Davisville Subway Station.

North Toronto was founded in 1890. Its villages of Davisville and Eglinton were annexed by Toronto in 1912. Right at Yonge and Davisville, things kick off with Starbucks at 1911. Other interesting places include Windpromotions Boardsports at 2010, Mysteriously Yours Dinner Theatre at 2026, **St. Louis Bar & Grill** at 2050, Sugar Mountain at 2299, Yonge Eglinton Centre at

2300, **Grazie** at 2373, Postal Station K (site where the 1837 Rebellion rebels aggregated before marching to Toronto), The Anne Johnston Heath Station at 2398 (built in 1932 – the original North Toronto town hall was built on this site in 1891), The Source for Snowboards at 2454, **Centro** at 2472, Redwood Grille at 2495, Ultimate Truffle at 2487 ½, **North 44°**at 2537, The Butchers at 2632, Roots at 2670, and the hugely popular Sporting Life at 2665.

If you want to return to your hotel, take the subway south from the Eglinton Station at Yonge and Eglinton. The 24 hour bus 97 also runs along Yonge St.

Part III (Yonge-Lawrence Village: Yonge St from Lawrence Ave to Yonge Blvd)

Either continue on from Part II or start at Yonge and Queen Streets and take the subway up to Lawrence Subway Station.

This part of Yonge is integral to the surrounding residential neighbourhoods, much like North Toronto's. Noteworthy stores among the 250 include Dick Young's flowers at 3180, Capital Tea at 3196 (including teas from China, Japan, China, and Africa), Rainbow Candies at 3198, Crime Scene at 3212, Paradise Games at 3278, Mastermind Educational at 3350, Maryann's Fabrics at 3213, Starbucks at 3252, Artisically Yours (make your own clay pottery) at 3377, Richardson's Tartan at 3435, Wildfire at 3436, Trappers at 3479, Loblaws (including a Marchetta's) at 3501, and Play It Again Sports at 3456.

Yonge Blvd is the original northern city limit of Toronto. A tollgate once stood here in 1830-1850, and the Yonge St streetcar stopped here in the 1920s. North of here, suburban planning and growth dominate the urban landscape.

Typical Building Architecture and Density in the
Yonge-Lawrence Village

ATTRACTIONS

General

Air Canada Centre (ACC). This entertainment complex is home to the
Toronto Maple Leafs and Toronto Raptors. Entrance to the Galleria area is
FREE. "Behind the Scenes" tours are offered Mon-Sat 10 am-3 pm, and
Sunday 11 am -3 pm. $9.50/adult, $7.50/students and seniors, and $6.50 for
children 12 and under. Admission to sport games, theater, and concerts are
charged separately. Your chances of getting Leaf tickets without going to a
"ticket scalper" are slim, but you can try at www.ticketmaster.ca. You may
have more luck in getting Raptor tickets. (416) 366-3865, www.raptors.com.
40 Bay Street, south of Front Street. (416) 815-5500,
www.theaircanadacentre.com.

Allan Gardens. The Gardens were established
in 1858. The beautiful glass Palm House built in
1910 contains an unbelievable array of plants
and flowers. A popular spot for wedding photos.
Open year round 9 am-4 pm Mon-Fri and
10 am-5 pm weekends and holidays. 19
Horticultural St, 4 blocks east of Yonge on
Gerrard St East. (416) 392-7288,
www.collections.ic.gc.ca/gardens/opening.html. FREE.

Bata Shoe Museum. This museum has over 10,000 historic and celebrity
shoes. The architecture of the building alone is worth a peek. Open Tues/Wed
and Fri/Sat 10 am-5 pm, Thur 10 am-8 pm, Sun noon -5 pm. First Tuesday of
every month is FREE. $6.00/adult, $2/child, $10/family (two adults/two kids),
$4/senior or student. www.batashoemuseum.ca, (416) 979-7799. 327 Bloor
St West, just west of the Royal Ontario Museum.

Black Creek Pioneer Village. This 19th century village of over 40 buildings
on 40 acres is an excellent way to immerse your family in the life of the times.
Some shopping and dining, and special events such as the Pennsylvania
German/Mennonite Annual Pioneer Festival, round out the experience. Open
May 1- Dec 31, except Dec 25. Hours vary, but are 10 am-5 pm daily during
July-Sep. $9/adult, $7 for seniors and students (with ID and 15 years old and
over), $5/child 5-14, and free for accompanied children under 5. 1000 Murray
Ross Parkway on the southeast corner of Jane St and Steeles Ave. Take TTC
bus 60 (Steeles Ave West) from Finch Subway Station until you reach Murray
Ross Blvd, one block east of Jane St. (416) 736-1733, www.trca.on.ca.

Campbell House. This circa 1822 house of Georgian architecture was located on Adelaide St East before it was moved to its present location. It is the oldest remaining building from the Town of York. It was the home of Sir William Campbell (1758-1834), a United Empire Loyalist, who fought with the British during the American Revolution and was taken prisoner at Yorktown in 1781. He was eventually released and later moved to Toronto in 1811. Open Mon-Fri from 9:30 am – 4:30 pm and from noon – 4:30 pm on weekends and holidays from late May to early October. 160 Queen St West, at University Ave. $4.50/adult, $2/child, $10/family, $2.50/senior. (416) 597-0227, www.advsoc.on.ca/campbell/index.html.

Canadian Broadcasting Corporation (CBC) Centre. Behind the scene tours of this television and radio facility cost $7/adult or $20/family. You can visit the **Glenn Gould Studio**, production sets, the CBC Museum, the radio studio, the Graham Spry Theatre, or see live tapings of two of Canada's most popular TV shows, The Royal Canadian Air Farce and The Red Green Show (see "HOLLYWOOD NORTH" re free tickets). 250 Front St West.
(416) 205-8605, www.cbc.ca. FREE.

Canadian-Hungarian Cultural Centre. This large Hungarian community centre, considered by some to be the largest outside of Hungary, houses a Hungarian military museum, the Dr. Halaz Janos library of more than 24,000 books, a 500 seat auditorium, and Hungarians paintings. 840 St. Clair Ave West. (416) 654-0536.

Canadian Mining Hall of Fame. Several wall plaques honoring the people considered to have made the greatest contributions to the Canadian mining industry. Included is Noah Timmins – the town of Timmins was built on his company's property and the town was named after him. Famous country singer Shania Twain hails from Timmins. Also included are the four men who started the Klondike gold rush. Through the front doors of the University of Toronto's 1905 Mining Building and in the first hallway on your left. 170 College St. FREE.

Canadian National Exhibition (CNE). First established in 1879, this 3 week extravaganza on CNE grounds is a great family outing. An amusement park, live music, farm exhibit, garden show, lumberjack and dive shows, talent shows, the Inferno show, the exceedingly popular Air Show, demonstrations of dance, Heritage Festivals, and much more. Open August 16 – Sept 2, 10 am to midnight. General admission $9.00/adult, $6.00/child under 6 ("babes in arms" are free), $6.00 seniors over 55, $23 for an All Day Amusement Park pass (otherwise you pay per ride). www.theex.com.

Casa Loma. This 98-room castle was built by Sir Henry Pellatt in 1911-14 to a E.J. Lennox design and has been used in films like The X-Men. Attractions include the extraordinary architecture, the stately interior, a long underground tunnel to the Spanish castle looking stables designed by E.J. Lennox in 1906, landscaped gardens, a Café, Gift Shop, and periodic events. Open daily 9 am – 5 pm. 1 Austin Terrace, 2 blocks north of the Dupont subway stop on Spadina Rd. $10/adult, $6.50 for seniors over 60 and children 14-17, $6.00 for kids 4-13. (416) 923-1171, www.casaloma.org.

Centreville. This amusement park is in a very attractive park-like setting on the Toronto Islands (Centre Island). Attractions include a variety of rides, mostly suitable for kids up to 13, a train ride, a small farm, water rides, miniature golf, a wading pool, a great "sky ride", an arcade, an antique carousel, and a small town setting of food concessions. Entry to the grounds is FREE, but an All Day Family ride pass for 4 costs $15.20+tax per person. Individual ride passes are $18.65+tax, and children 4 feet tall and under are $13.05 each. Open daily from 10:30 am, generally to dusk. (416) 203-0405, www.centreville.ca.

Children's Own Museum. An interactive discovery play centre for kids under 8. Open daily 10 am-5 pm. $4.75/person, and kids under 1 are FREE. 90 Queen's Park, south of Bloor St. (416) 542-1492, www.childrensownmuseum.org.

Chinatown (East). A small slice of downtown Hong Kong, you'll find both Chinese and Vietnamese shops selling Far East medicine and herbs, markets selling produce, and restaurants. Located on Gerrard St East between Broadview and Jones Avenues. You can either drive east along Gerrard St East from Yonge St, or you can take the Yonge subway line to the Bloor subway station, transfer to the Bloor subway line until you reach Broadview, and then transfer to the Broadview streetcar for the short trip south to Gerrard St East. You can also take the Queen St East streetcar and walk up 5 blocks to Gerrard St East. FREE to window-shop.

Chinatown (West). A strip of almost exclusively Chinese stores mostly on Dundas St West between McCaul St and Spadina Ave. Looks a lot like Hong Kong. Even more stores, this time mixed with Vietnamese and Thai stores, are around the corner on Spadina Ave. FREE to window-shop.

ChumCityTV. Ground breaking TV and music station with periodic free mini street concerts (e.g. Shaggy, Destiny's Child), a truck hanging out the side of its east wall, **Speaker's Corner** where you can have your say on video and maybe television for $1, and home to TV shows like Much Music, Electric Circus, Ed the Sock, and Fashion Television. (416) 591-7400, ext 2770 to book a free tour, www.citytv.com. FREE.

Cloud Forest Park. This incredibly unique attraction won the Canadian Governor General's Award for Architecture in 1994. There is the enclosed Cloud Forest of trees and shrubs; a 50 foot high waterfall; a steel based Monument to Construction Workers designed by Margaret Priest and constructed with the assistance of 13 different trade unions; an Urban Woodland of oak, sugar maple, ash, and hemlock; and landscaping that won a 1995 Canadian Society of Landscape Architects' Regional Merit Award. FREE.

CN Tower. This 1,815 foot high structure is the world's tallest free-standing structure. Elevators to the top start at 11 am and go until 7 pm, or until 10:30 pm if you're dining at the top. General access to the shopping area starts at 9 am. Cost for the lookout, glass floor, and Skypod is $22.49 plus taxes per adult, $17.49 plus taxes per child 4-13, $20.49 plus taxes for seniors, and FREE for kids 3 and under. Cost for the lookout and glass floor only is $15.99, $13.99, $10.99, and $0.00 respectively. You can book your tickets via the Internet. Located at 301 Front St, 3 blocks west of Yonge St (and 2 blocks west of Union Station subway). Walk past the Planet Hollywood restaurant and the entrance is to your left. (416) 868-6937, www.cntower.ca.

Colborne Lodge. The 1837 home of John George Howard and his wife Jemima, the people who donated High Park to Toronto in 1873. The Howards tomb is on site, as is a cannon from 1834. Open from Mar 10 – Oct 31, daily from 10 am – 4 pm. 3.50/adult, $2.75 for seniors/students and $2.00 for children (12 and under). South end of **High Park** on Colborne Lodge Dr, north of The Queensway or south of Bloor St West. (416) 392-6916, www.city.toronto.on.ca/culture/colborne.htm.

Corktown. Named after the 1800s settlement of mostly poor Irish folks from Cork, Ireland. There are several buildings still from the late 1800s in the area, as well as some of the shortest streets in Toronto (Bright, Wilkin). Buildings include **Enoch Turner School House**, *Little Trinity Church*, *St. Paul's Church*, *Dominion Square (1873)*, *Dominion Hotel (1875)*, and *Davies Terrace (1877)* (the last four are on Queen St East between Power and Sumach Streets).

Don Valley Brickworks. This 40 acre site was once used to manufacture bricks. Today it is open to the public to explore the buildings, wetlands, and parks. Some exposed walls demonstrate the clay deposits that made this site useful to make bricks from 1882 - 1989. Don Valley bricks were used in Casa Loma and U of T. A "Discovery Walk" trail runs west of the Brickworks and can be accessed from the Brickworks. A great view of Toronto's downtown skyline can be had from the top of the hills (see picture). Open all year. FREE.

Dundas Square. Opening in the summer of 2002, this black and green granite lined city square will have large video screens, water fountains, and underground parking. Jazz festivals, street performers, movie nights, and dancing events will be held here. Dundas St East at Yonge St. FREE.

Eaton Centre (see "Shopping").

Elevated Wetlands. A working experiment of several 20 feet or so high containers of shredded tires and plastics as "earth" supporting wetland plants. Located along the Don Valley Parkway near Don Mills Rd and the Don Valley bike path. FREE.

Enoch Turner School House. The oldest standing school building in Toronto, built in 1848. Open 9:30 am – 4 pm Mon to Fri. Admissions (inexpensive) vary depending on the day and time of year, so call (416) 863-0010 or see www.toronto.com/E/V/TORON/0011/68/19/.

Eric Arthur Gallery. This architecture gallery is the first in Toronto. 230 College St at the University of Toronto's School of Architecture, Landscape and Design. Open Mon-Fri 9 am - 5 pm and Sat noon - 5 pm. FREE.

Gardiner Museum of Ceramic Art. Historic and contemporary pieces. A "Clay Pit" where you can make your own classes will keep the kids amused. On-site restaurant. Open from 10 am Mon-Sat. Closes at 6 pm Mon/Wed/Fri, at 8 pm on Tues/Thurs, and at 5 pm on Sat/Sun. 111 Queen's Park Circle, south of Bloor St West. $10/adult, $6/senior and student. FREE on the first Tuesday of each month. (416) 586-8080, www.gardinermuseum.on.ca.

George Brown House. Built in 1874-77, this fabulously restored house was the home of George Brown who founded the Globe newspaper (today's Globe and Mail), was a co-founder of the Anti-Slavery Coalition of Upper Canada with Sir Oliver Mowat, and then later was a co-founder of Canada. Brown was shot in 1880 at his Globe office on King St, just east of Yonge St, and died shortly after at home. He is buried in **Necropolis Cemetery**. 186 Beverley St at Baldwin St, just north of Chinatown West.

Gerrard India Bazaar is unique in North America and is comprised almost exclusively of Indian shops. Roasted sweet corn stalls replace downtown's hot dog stands. Incense and the aroma of sweet fruits waft through the area. Restaurants, clothing stores, Indian movie videos, and more. Gerrard St East (Coxwell to Woodfield Avenue).

Gibson House. This 1851 dated house is the second home of David Gibson and family. Their first home near Yonge St and Finch Ave was burned down by the government in retribution for Gibson's involvement in the 1837 Rebellion. A good spot to get a feel for Toronto's rural past. $2.75/adult, $2.25/seniors and youth (age 13-18), $1.75/child (age 2-12). 5172 Yonge St, yards north of the Mel Lastman Square complex at Yonge St and Park Home Ave. Take the Yonge subway line to the North York Subway Station and walk north a block on Yonge St. Open Tue - Sun but days and times vary depending on the season. (416) 395-7432.

Glenn Gould Studio. Named after the famous pianist, this 340 seat venue is used for live concerts of chamber music, studio jazz, classics, piano, and more. In the **Canadian Broadcasting Corporation (CBC) Centre** at 250 Front St West. (416) 215-5555, www.glenngouldstudio.cbc/ca.

Gooderham & Worts Historical Buildings. Several buildings built in the 1800s for use in the G&W booze empire. Currently used for movie sets, although new development is under consideration. You cannot enter the site, but the buildings are right at the road and can be well seen. FREE viewing.

Greektown. Danforth Ave, between Chester Ave and Dewhurst Blvd. The largest Greek community in North America, with 400 shops, restaurants, and services. Host to the enormously popular Taste of the Danforth Festival. See Tour 16. www.greektowntoronto.com.

Hanlan's (Clothing Optional) Beach. Take the Toronto Islands' ferry to Hanlan's Point. Walk left or south past the softball fields and the beach is off to the right behind a narrow band of forest and sand dune. FREE.

Harbourfront. What a fantastic place! Music, dance, performing arts, festivals, readings, crafts, artists' gardens, and more. Hosts several festivals and events including the **Milk International Children's Festival** of the Arts (the glass-blowing workshop is a unique thrill), and the World Leaders Festival of Creative Genius. Also the home of the duMaurier Theatre Centre, Queens Quay Terminal, Premiere Dance Theatre, Natrel skating rink, Power Plant Contemporary Art Gallery, Norigen Stage, and more. 231 Queen's Quay West. www.harbourfront.on.ca. FREE mostly – special events and activities charged for separately.

High Park. An extraordinary oasis of 399 acres containing Grenadier Pond, a small zoo, historic **Colborne House**, landscaped gardens, forest areas, pool, 2 playgrounds, greenhouse, tennis courts, nature trails, fishing, toboggan hills, outdoor skating rink, mature woods, open and covered picnic areas, the Sculpture Symposium of 7 sculptures, restaurant, washrooms, the "Dream Site" outdoor amphitheatre, and leash-free dog run zones. The small zoo, or "animal paddocks", contains buffalo, American Bison, Yaks, Llama, Barbary Sheep, and Scottish West Highland cattle. Bird-watchers have seen about 235 bird species in the park. Bloor St West (north end) or The Queensway (south end), between Parkside Dr (east end) and Ellis Ave (west end). FREE.

Hockey Hall of Fame. Housed in the circa 1885-86 Beaux-Arts Classicism style Bank of Montreal building. Hockey memorabilia, interactive games, and a special section highlighting "Wayne Gretzky – The Legend". Open every day except Christmas, New Year's Day, and Induction Day (Nov 12). Mon-Sat 9:30 am – 5:00 pm during June 25-September 3. Yonge and Front Streets – entrance via BCE Place. $12 for adults, $8 for kids 4-8 and seniors, FREE for kids 3 and under. (416) 360-7765, www.hhof.com.

Japanese Canadian Cultural Centre. The Centre has classes in various cultural activities, art shows and lectures, a library of Japanese books, and a gift shop selling Japanese goods like origami supplies. 6 Garamond Court, near Don Mills Rd and Eglinton Ave East. (416) 441-2345.

Jewish Discovery Place Children's Museum. $2.50 per person. Albert J Latner Jewish Public Library with over 40,000 items of Judaica, is next door. 4588 Bathurst St. (416) 636-1880, ext. 456

Joey and Toby Tanenbaum Opera Centre. Houses the Imperial Oil Opera Theatre. 227 Front St East. (416) 363-6671, www.coc.ca.

Kensington Market. A very colorful open street marketplace offering fruits and vegetables, nuts, clothing, cafes, delicatessens, dried food goods, health foods, and much more.   Along Kensington, Baldwin, and Nassau Streets a few blocks northwest of Spadina Ave and Dundas St West.

Lionel Conacher Plaque/Monument. Lionel Conacher was an excellent athlete in hockey, football, baseball, and lacrosse. He was chosen the Male Athlete of the First Half Century (20th). Birch and Ganges Streets, just west of Yonge St and south of Summerhill Ave. FREE.

Mackenzie House. The last home of William Lyon Mackenzie, Toronto's first Mayor and leader of the 1837 Rebellion against government authorities. Late-Georgian architecture. Houses a working newspaper press. Open Tuesday, Wednesday, Thursday, Friday, Weekends: noon–5 pm. $3.50/adult, $2.75 for seniors & students, and $2.50 for children 12 and under. 82 Bond St, two blocks east of Yonge St, south of Dundas St East. (416) 392-6915, www.torontohistory.on.ca.

Maple Leaf Gardens. Once the home to Toronto Maple Leafs and their rabidly faithful fans. Built in 1931, it was the last of the original six NHL hockey stadiums to succumb to retirement. The Maple Leafs now play out of the Air Canada Centre. The College St Subway Station has large pictures of the Maple Leaf greats and some of their key statistics. 60 Carleton St.

Marine Museum. This limestone building was built in 1840 to replace the aging Fort York. It was originally called New Fort and renamed to Stanley Barracks in 1897. It was also one of the first recruiting centres for assembling and training RCMP constables. Outside the building on the surrounding grounds is a "marine triple expansion steam engine" for ships, an anchor, a ship propeller, the Ned Hanlon Steam Tug built in 1932 and undergoing a restoration, a historic railway engine, and a monument to Ned Hanlon. Hanlon won 300 rowing victories in a row, including winning the U.S. championship in 1878, the England championship in 1879, and the World Championship in 1880. Currently closed, but you can still access the items outside for FREE.

Martin Goodman Trail. This 17 mile (28 km) long paved trail is ideal for biking and rollerblading. It runs along the lakefront past many top tourist attractions like Sunnyside Pool, Harbourfront, Ontario Place, the Canadian National Exhibition, **Clarke Beach**, Ashbridge's Bay, and **Kew Beach**. www.ryerson.ca/vtoronto/wwwsite/themes/cultrec/html/goodman.htm. FREE.

Massey Hall. Built in 1893 by Hart Massey. This venue has a very storied history of concerts, conventions, and speeches by royalty and celebrities. Examples include: Robert Peary spoke here, Tom Longboat was married here, Luciano Pavarotti sang here, heavyweight boxing champ Jack Dempsey sparred here, and Bob Dylan held a concert here. www.masseyhall.com.

Metro Convention Centre. 460,000 square feet of space used for large shows, exhibitions, and special events such as the Auto Show. 255 Front St West. (416) 585-8000, www.mtccc.com.

Mount Pleasant Cemetery. The final resting place for Prime Minister Willam Lyon Mackenzie King, the men who co-discovered insulin (Sir Frederick Banting and Dr. Best), 22 victims of the Empress of Ireland ship sinking, famed pianist Glenn Gould, Arthur Peuchen (a survivor of the Titanic), 119 people from the S.S. Noronic disaster, and many other prominent people. The cemetery was founded in 1876 and is located from Yonge St to Bayview Ave, to Merton and Moore Streets. The main office and entrance is on Mt. Pleasant Rd, just south of Davisville Ave.

Museum of Textiles. 10,000 textile articles, and a hands-on room for kids. 55 Centre Ave, just northwest of City Hall. $5/adult, kids under 12 FREE. (416) 599-5321.

Music Garden Park. Music or art lover, or not, this park is extraordinarily innovative and unique. The City of Toronto states the Park was designed "...to interpret in nature Bach's First Suite for Unaccompanied Cello with each dance movement within the suite corresponding to a different section in the garden." Based on an idea of American cellist Yo-Yo-Ma. Open year round. 475 Queen's Quay West, west of Spadina. Take the Harbourfront LRT (TTC streetcar 509 or 510) from Union Station. www.city.toronto.on.ca/parks/music_index.htm. FREE.

Nathan Phillips Square. A large public square fronting City Hall that hosts concerts, exhibitions, demonstrations, and several festivals. A large reflecting pool in summer becomes a very popular skating rink in winter. Also contains the Peace Garden. Then Prime Minister Pierre Trudeau turned the sod in 1984 and Pope John Paul II kindled an eternal flame with an ember from Peace Memorial Park in Hiroshima. Towards the entrance to the **Toronto City Hall** is Henry Moore's 1966 sculpture *"Three-Way Piece No. 2 or The Archer"*. 100 Queen St West, west of Yonge St. FREE.

National Ballet School. A world leader in ballet, offering ballet, academic training, and residence at the same location. Alumni include Karen Kain and Veronica Tennant. Site also houses the *Friends' Meeting House* of Quaker origin and built in 1911. 105 Maitland St. www.nationalballetschool.org.

Necropolis Cemetery. The buildings here are 1870s vintage and are beautiful architectural examples. The small gothic style chapel interior seems like a shrunken version of a large cathedral. Three leaders of the 1837 Rebellion are buried here: William Lyon Mackenzie (and three of his children), Samuel Lount, and Peter Mathews (see "In the Beginning"). Also buried here are George Brown, a Father of Confederation, Ned Hanlan, Joseph Bloor (Bloor St namesake), two soldiers killed in the Fenian attacks, Thornton Blackburn (a former slave who escaped to Canada via the Underground Railway), and William Peyton Hubbard, the first black person elected to Toronto City Council in 1894. Mackenzie's children were moved from the Presbyterian Burying Grounds at Richmond and Sherbourne Streets in 1911/12. 984 other people's graves were also moved from "The Potter's Field" cemetery at the modern day northwest corner of Yonge and Bloor Streets. 200 Winchester St. FREE.

Old Firehall. The original playhouse for The Second City comedy troupe, the renowned breeding ground of world-class comedians such as Gilda Radner, Eugene Levy, Martin Short, and John Candy. Now primarily used for "Gilda's Club", a free, non-residential, emotional and social support community for men, women and children and their family and friends living with cancer, in memory of Gilda "Roseana-danna" Radner. 110 Lombard St, two blocks east of Yonge St and two blocks south of Queen St. (416) 214-9898, www.gildasclubtoronto.org.

Old York. See Tour 11. The original 10 block plan of Old York, now Toronto, was surveyed by Alexander Aitken in the 1790s for Lt. Governor John Graves Simcoe. A metal relief version of the plan resides in Simcoe Park on the north side of Front St West, between Simcoe and John Streets. The land set aside for a church and market in this survey has been used for a church (St. James Cathedral) and market (St. Lawrence Market) to this day! The survey established the use of north-south and east-west roads, rural concessions 100 "chains" (6,600 feet) apart, and a 1 chain (66 feet) road allowance between each concession every 12 miles that are noticeably apparent today. The 66 feet road allowance remains a standard in 21st century municipal planning! Old York today is a superb example of how the City of Toronto and local residents have maintained and improved this gem of a neighbourhood. FREE.

Ontario Innovations Museum. A one-room museum where you can view various Canadian inventions including ginger ale (Canada Dry) in 1907, the zipper, biodegradable plastics, Macintosh apples, the synthesizer, telephone, and basketball. Queen's Park (Ontario Legislative Building). FREE.

Ontario Place. A great children's village, waterpark, a 5 story tall IMAX film theatre with stupendous films, the **HMCS Haida** warship (extra admission), the Molson Amphitheatre for concerts and the like, the west island for pubs, restaurants, and more. Most of the park is only open during late spring, summer, and early fall. $9/adult, $5/child (5-15 yrs old), $6/senior 55 and over, and FREE for kids under 5. Prices include taxes. An extra $13/person 4 years old and up for the Play All Day Pass entitles you to the rides, IMAX films, HMCS Haida, and Children's Village. A season's pass is $39/person 4 years old and up and offers admission to Ontario Place, the benefits of the Play All Day Pass, and admission to the CNE. There is a FREE shuttle bus from/to Union Station outside the main entrance to Ontario Place. Or head back to the Princes' Gates and catch TTC streetcar 511 back to Queen St. Get a transfer from the driver upon embarking, get off at Queen St, and take TTC streetcar 501 east back to Yonge St. (416) 696-3147, www.ontarioplace.com.

Ontario Science Centre is chock full of the most entertaining stuff for the whole family. Often have special treats like "Circus", where you can walk the high wire. Open everyday except Christmas, from 10 am - 6 pm from July 1 – Sep 4 and from 10 am - 5 pm the rest of the year. $12/adult, $7/child from 13-17, $6/child from 5-12, $7/senior 65 and over, and FREE for kids under 5. On-site parking is $7. The on-site OMNIMAX Theatre costs extra, but you can get a package admission that is less expensive than buying separate admissions. 770 Don Mills Rd. (416) 696-1000, www.ontariosciencecentre.ca.

Osgoode Hall. This complex was built over a number of years between 1829 –32 on a site previously known as "Lawyers' Hill". Today it is used for courts and is surrounded by lovely landscaping and a large wrought iron fence once used to keep cows off the property. Also once the site of Osgoode Hall Law School, now part of York University. It was here that Clara Brett Martin became the first female lawyer in Canada and the British Empire! 130 Queen St West, just west of Nathan Phillips Hall. Public tours during July and August, Monday to Friday at 1:15 pm. See www.lsuc.on.ca for interesting photos and information on the various historic elements of the buildings. FREE.

PATH. 6 miles (10 kms) of about 400 underground shops, restaurants, food courts, and services linking downtown core office buildings, malls, and hotels. The south end is Union Station and the north end is The Atrium on Dundas St West. Most of the stores and services are there for the office tower workers and close after business hours (although the PATH remains open). FREE.

Parliament Square Park. This is the area where Ontario's first **Provincial Parliament Buildings** built in 1798 were before the Americans burned them to the ground in 1813 as part of the War of 1812! Esplanade and Berkeley St.

Post Office (Toronto's First). History lovers should not miss this building built in 1833-35 and still operating as a Post Office. A model of Toronto in 1837 provides a feel for what the buildings looked like, where they were, their history, and how the original town grew into today's metropolis. It also shows that the no longer existing Taddle Creek ran along present day Queen St and just east of Sherbourne St to the swampy area where the Don River emptied into Lake Ontario. This swampy area just east of the original town is one of the reasons the town primarily grew westward. Kids can also try their hand at writing letters with quill pens. 260 Adelaide St East. (416) 865-1833, www.townofyork.com, www.web-sights.com/tfpo. FREE.

Provincial Parliament Buildings. The seat of the Ontario Government (now located in **Queen's Park)** was first located at the present day Budget car rental business site at Berkeley and Front Streets. It was burned down by the Americans in the War of 1812, rebuilt, and then again destroyed by fire due to an overheated chimney in 1824. An archaeological dig under the parking lot at this site in 2001 uncovered several artifacts from the original buildings, including a layer of charred ashes!

Pier Museum. Exhibits about the Toronto Harbour. Open May 1-Oct 31, 10 am – 6 pm. $5/adult, $4/child or senior. 245 Queen's Quay West.

Pier 6. The oldest building on Toronto's waterfront, built in 1907. Today, it is used primarily by Second Cup. Queen's Quay West and York St.

Playdium Mississauga. The 126 John St location in the Entertainment District closed down late last year. A *horrible* shame, as this was THE place to take your kids. Now, you have to drive to Playdium Mississauga to partake in the over 200 games and attractions of high energy and excitement for the whole family. Superb video and virtual reality games that put you in the action. There's Target Zone and Contact Zone for those who like shooting and martial arts games, including one game where the on screen character partially mimics your kicks and punches against his opponent. The hang-glider virtual game and the parachute landing game are two thoroughly unique and exciting games. There's an outdoor go kart track, mini-golf, basketball, and beach volleyball. There is no admission, but it does cost to play. 4 credits per $1, minimum $5. You receive free bonus credits as you buy more credits. $20 buys you 80 credits plus 40 bonus credits for a total 120 credits. 99 Rathburn Rd West, Mississauga. Take the Gardiner to Hwy 427 north, to Hwy 401 west, to Hwy 403 south, to Hurontario St south, to Rathburn Rd west. S-Club-7 played and performed here. Open 7 days/week from 10 am to as late as 2:30 am. (416) 260-1400, www.playdium.com.

Queen's Park (Ontario Legislative Building). The red sandstone buildings, known as Queen's Park, were named after beloved Queen Victoria and were built in the Romanesque Revival style in 1886-92. The design was by Richard Waite of Buffalo, New York. There are exhibits of Ontario's history just past the front doors including samples of high grade nickel ore and silver ore, a galleon model ship built from nickel, the **Ontario Innovations Museum**, an exhibit on the history of Canada's national flag, Upper Canada's "Mace" (taken by the Americans in 1813 and not returned until President Franklin Roosevelt did so in 1934!), and oil on canvas portraits of General Isaac Brock and Lt. Governor John Graves Simcoe. Guided tours from 9 am-4 pm Mon- Fri. FREE.

R.C. Harris Water Filtration Plant. This municipal water source was built in the Art Deco style and has been a site in several Hollywood films. It produces 45% of the drinking water for Toronto, Vaughan, Markham, and Richmond Hill. Tours Saturday at 10 am, 11:30am, and 1 pm. 2701 Queen St West, at the foot of Victoria Park Ave. (416) 392-3566. FREE.

Redpath Sugar Museum. The only museum in Canada exclusively for sugar. Provides interesting information on the history of the sugar industry and Redpath Corporation, and how sugar is processed. Outside, you can see the Bill Wyland mural of whales on the side of one of the buildings facing Queen's Quay. If you're lucky, you may see an ocean freighter unloading sugar. 95 Queen's Quay East. Open Mon-Fri, 10 am-noon and 1:00 pm – 3:30 pm. Call (416) 366-3561 in advance to ensure the museum is open, as the museum is part of a manufacturing facility. FREE.

Redpath Sugar Building and
Bill Wyland Mural

Riverdale Farm. This gem, once the Toronto Zoo from 1894-1974, is open 365 days a year. Historic buildings, with live farm animals in barns and pens. Buy fresh eggs, pat a horse, see ducks and geese, and demonstrations of how to milk a cow and much more. A trail leads to and around wetlands at the bottom of the hill. Open 9 am – 6 pm in spring/summer and 9 am – 4 pm in the fall/winter. 201 Winchester Ave one block north of Carlton St and four blocks east of Parliament St. Stupendous tobogganing in Riverdale Park West immediately south of Riverdale Farm. 416) 392-6794, www.city.toronto.on.ca/parks/riverdalefarm.htm. FREE.

Rouge Park. Near the Toronto Zoo, this is North America's largest urban park at over 11,600 acres. New York City's famous Central Park is 843 acres, by contrast. A trail, or technically a few trails pieced together, goes from Steeles Ave East down to within 100 yards from the shore of Lake Ontario. Camping allowed at **Glen Rouge Campground**. www.rougepark.com.

Royal Bank Tower. A noticeable office tower that glows golden yellow, as it has thousands of ounces of real gold permeated in its windows. Front St to Wellington St, west of Bay St. FREE.

Royal Ontario Museum (ROM). Houses many "galleries" of earth sciences, Egyptian mummies, dinosaurs, Chinese artifacts, artifacts from Greek, Roman, Byzantium, and Islamic civilizations, about 100 paintings by Irish born Paul Kane, and much more. Open Mon - Thur 10 am – 6 pm, Friday 10 am –8 pm, Saturday 10 am – 6 pm, and Sunday 11 am - 6pm. 100 Queen's Park at Bloor St West. $18/adult ($20 on weekends), $13/senior or student with ID, $12/child 4-12. FREE Friday nights from 4:30 - 9:30 pm, as well as one hour before closing every day! (416) 586-5549, www.rom.on.ca. You can save money by purchasing the "Toronto Museum Passport" that provides one-time admission to the ROM, Fort York, Spadina House, Colborne Lodge, Mackenzie House, Montgomery's Inn, Gibson House, Todmorden Mills Museum, and the Scarborough Museum. $25/adult, $20/senior or student with ID, $15/child. Passports are valid from May 1 to December 31, and prices include taxes. Available at City of Toronto Museums or by calling (800) 461-3333.

Ryerson University. Founded in 1948, this 15,000 full-time student school is located right downtown, northeast of Yonge and Dundas. The small campus houses some interesting sights including a *statue of Egerton Ryerson*, the "founder of the school system in Ontario", Devonian reflecting pool/rink, Ryerson's interior *St. James Square*, the *Toronto Normal School's façade*, dated 1847, that was once part of the first teachers' college, and a *Coat of Arms built of Ohio sandstone* dated 1896 and designed by Lt. Governor John Graves Simcoe and Egerton Ryerson. FREE.

Scadding Cabin. The oldest surviving building in Toronto was built in 1794 by John Scadding, manager of Lt. Governor John Graves Simcoe's estate in England. Scadding came to Toronto in 1793 with Simcoe and was granted 250 acres east of the Don River. West of Ontario St, just north of Lakeshore Blvd (you must walk the last block). FREE.

Sir Douglas Fir. The 184 foot tall flagpole was cut from a 350 year-old Vancouver Island fir with a tip diameter of 15" and a base diameter of 33". It weighs about 35,000 lbs and was donated by Travel South USA in "...appreciation to the many Canadians who visit our States and for the friendships that have evolved over the years." FREE except when the **Canadian National Exhibition** is on.

Skydome. This stadium cost ½ billion dollars. It was the first in the world to have a fully retractable roof! It is home to the Toronto Blue Jays and Toronto Argonauts. It was also home to the Toronto Raptors before the Air Canada Centre was constructed. 1 hour tours daily, offering a view of the Skyboxes, a dressing room, a film on the site's construction, Blue Jay memorabilia, and more cost $12.50/person. (416) 341-2770 for tours.

Spadina House and Gardens. Located near Casa Loma, this elegant house on six acres of Victorian and Edwardian gardens is a good visit for lovers of art and architecture. Cost is $5.00/adult, $3.50 for seniors/youths, and $3.00 for children 12 and under. 285 Spadina Rd, a short walk north of Dupont Subway Station. Open May 1 – December 31, generally Tue - Sun from noon – 5 pm. (416) 392-6910, www.city.toronto.on.ca/culture/spadina.htm.

Speaker's Corner. (See **ChumCity TV**).

Steam Whistle Brewery. Voted best microbrew in 2001 by NOW Magazine. The 30 minute basic tours of the microbrewery cost $3/person and include a taste and souvenir glass. 255 Bremner Blvd, in Roundhouse Park (circa 1929), south of the CN Tower and Skydome. (416) 362-2337, www.steamwhistle.ca.

Stock Market Place. Learn about the Toronto Stock Exchange, see market real time "tickers", play interactive games like "The Accumulator", and watch news updates on several TV screens. Open Mon - Fri 10 am – 5 pm. Exchange Tower, 130 King St West, at York St, one block west of Bay St on the north side. (416) 947-4676, www.tse.com/visitor. FREE.

St. James Cemetery, the mid 1840s successor to the St. James Cathedral burying grounds. One is "greeted" at the main entrance by the *St. James the Less Chapel*. It was built in 1860 and is considered one of the finest examples of Gothic Revival church architecture in Canada. You can also obtain a map of famous people gravesites at the office just inside the main entrance. Names include several of Toronto's early Who's Who like Enoch Turner, William Jarvis (Loyalist from Connecticut), Jarvis's son Samuel Peter Jarvis (who served at Queenston in the War of 1812, escorted a captured American General Winfield Scott during the Rebellion of 1837, and founder of Jarvis St), John Scadding, Egerton Ryerson, E.J. Lennox, John White (Upper Canada's 1st Attorney General, killed in a duel by John Small in 1800), John Ridout (killed in a duel by Samuel Jarvis in 1817), Robert Baldwin, George Gooderham, James Worts, William Allan, Sir Casimir Gzowski, James Cockburn and Sir William Pearce Howland (both Fathers of Confederation). FREE.

St. James Park and Gardens. This lovely oasis is between St. James Cathedral and Jarvis St. Mature trees, flower and rose gardens, a Victorian era garden, wrought iron fences, a band gazebo, and wrought iron drinking fountains for humans and animals. FREE.

St. Lawrence Hall. Built in 1850, it was for many of its early years Toronto's chief social and cultural centre. Its Corinthian façade and graceful copula are architectural beauties that can be seen from the street. Inside, is the Great Hall where two fathers of Canadian Confederation, Sir John A. MacDonald and George Brown, spoke to crowds up to 1,000 people. The Anti-Slavery Society met here as well (it should be noted that Ontario abolished getting new slaves in 1793, and abolished slavery entirely in 1833). One can envision the throngs of people being swayed to one political objective or another under the ornate ceilings, gigantic hanging chandelier, and upper deck/balcony. FREE.

St. Lawrence Market. Circa 1803. Open 8 am to 6 pm on most days (closed Sunday), the heaviest traffic is on Saturday mornings when the market opens at 5 am. A must do if you love exotic foods, crafts, and miscellaneous items in European market-like conditions. You can also view for FREE art from historic Toronto and other paintings in the **Market Gallery** upstairs. Take the elevator in the main front entrance. Adults and kids alike love this place. Great and inexpensive meals can be had, often with one or several street musicians performing. A north market hall is open on Sundays. FREE.

Sunnybrook Park. This approximately half-square mile park offers picnic tables and areas, walking and biking paths and trails, sports fields, restaurant, and **Sunnybrook Stables**. The stables offer horseback riding lessons to the public. Minimum age of 9 years. 50 minute lessons cost $52.50/person within a group or $85/person for private lessons. Open year round, but closed Fridays. (416) 444-4044. Park is FREE.

The Docks. Ah, a spot to keep those teenagers and young adults amused! The Docks has tons of stuff to keep people amused. Pool, sand beach, driving range, mini-putt, drive-in theater, nightclubs, pool tables, beach volleyball, rock climbing, paintball target shooting, the "Scream'n Demon" ride (you drop from over 100 feet suspended in air), a flying trapeze, and restaurants. Add a great view of the Toronto skyline and harbour, as well as being on the Martin Goodman Trail for biking, walking, and rollerblading. Pay for each activity separately or buy the Sports Day Pass for $19.95/person available on weekends and holidays. Covers the driving range, mini-putt, rock climbing, paintball, scream'n demon, gladiator jousting, beach volleyball, and billiards. 11 Polson St off Cherry St south of Lakeshore Blvd. (416) 469-5655, www.thedocks.com.

The ACT Library. Self billed as North America's largest publicly accessible library on HIV and AIDs with over 4500 books, 900 videos, 100 magazines and journals. 100 FREE handouts and pamphlets. 399 Church St, 4th floor. Open Mon-Thur 10 am-9 pm and Fri 10 am-5 pm. (416) 340-2437, www.actoronto.org.

The 519 (Church St Community Centre). Located in the heart of Toronto's gay and lesbian community. The AIDS Wall is located in **Cawthra Park**, adjoining the community centre. 519 Church St, north of Wellesley St. (416) 392-6874, www.gaytoronto.com/519. FREE.

The Village. The centre of Toronto's large gay/lesbian community. Gerrard St East to Bloor St East, and from Yonge St to Jarvis St. The centre of the Village is Church and Wellesley, especially **The 519** and the Second Cup. Favored hangouts of the gay community include Woody's at 467 Church St and Hair of the Dog at 425 Church St. Gay theatre is available at **Buddies in Bad Times Theatre** on Alexander St, near Yonge and Carleton Streets.

Todmorden Mills Heritage Museum. This 20 acre site was initially established in 1797 and houses historic millers' homes, the Brewery Gallery, the Paper Mill Gallery and Theatre, the relocated Don train station, and a wildflower preserve. Cost is $3.00/adult, $2.25 for seniors (over 60) and students, $1.50 for children 6-12, and FREE for children 5 and under. 67 Pottery Rd, east of Bavview Ave, just west of Broadview Ave. (416) 396-2819, www.city.on.ca/todmorden.

Toronto Aerospace Museum. A huge warehouse of military and commercial aircraft and artifacts. $5/adult, $3/senior or child 13-17, $2/child 3-12, and FREE for children under 3. 65 Carl Hall Rd southeast of Keele St and Sheppard Ave West. (416) 638-6078, www.torontoaerospacemuseum.com.

Toronto (Don) Jail. The site of 70 executions since the first one in 1872, the Don Jail had the last execution in Canada. This sentence was carried out in December 1962 and both men had been convicted of murder. Seven executed men were buried behind the jail in an area that became known as "Murderer's Row". These bodies were exhumed and reburied elsewhere in July 1977. 550 Gerard St East at Broadview. FREE.

Toronto Islands & Ferries. The Toronto Islands are a wonderful spot to spend time with the family. The Islands offer Centreville Amusement Park, softball parks, boat and bike rentals, a 18 frisbee golf course, a cedar maze, beaches, volleyball, tennis, open air theatre, restaurants, the Gilbraltar Light

House built in 1808, and more. A superlative view of Toronto, its harbour, and the island – alone worth taking the 15 minute each way boat ride! Boats with an open upper deck and enclosed lower deck, transporting people from the shore to the three destinations (Ward's Island, Centre Island, Hanlon's Point) on the Toronto Islands. Located 50 yards south of Queen's Quay, at the foot of Bay St. $5/adult, $3 for students under 19 and seniors over 60, $2 for children under 14, and FREE for children under 2. (416) 392-8193, www.city.toronto.on.ca/parks/to_islands. Islands are FREE.

Toronto Reference Library. Very popular library with 5 floors of books, archives, photo collections, study areas, audio-visual, PCs with Internet connections. The Arthur Conan Doyle Room has one of the world's largest collections of Sherlock Holmes memorabilia. Toronto's library system history started with a subscription library in 1810 that closed after the Americans looted it in the war of 1812. The Mechanics Institute (and library) was established in 1830 on the northeast corner of Church and Adelaide Streets, which was the forebear of the Toronto Public Library established in 1833. Open Mon-Thur 10 am - 8 pm, Fri/Sat 10 am – 5 pm, and Sun 1:30 - 5 pm. 789 Yonge St. (416) 395-5577, www.tpl.toronto.on.ca. FREE.

Toronto Police Museum and Discovery Centre. A great spot for grown-ups and kids alike. See a 1900's jail cell, confiscated weapons, infamous cases like The Dirty Tricks Gang, and a tribute to the 11 Toronto constables killed in the line of duty. 40 College St, a block west of Yonge St. Open daily 9 am – 9 pm. (416) 808-7020. FREE, although a donation box is available.

Toronto Stock Exchange (TSE) Museum. The TSE started in 1863 at 24 King St East, then moved to 234 Bay St, before moving to this site. Note there is no trading floor, as there once was, as trading is down via computers. The museum's Accumulator game that compares many different kinds of investments (including hockey cards!) would be of interest to kids. Film crews are sometimes in presence getting insightful stock market analysis from some company honcho or another. FREE.

Toronto Symphony Orchestra. Performances are held at Roy Thomson Hall on Simcoe St south of King St. (416) 593-4828, www.tso.on.ca.

Toronto Zoo. The zoo has 5,000 animals representing 459 species to see in various habitats and 7 pavilions. The Gorilla Rainforest and the polar bears are among the most popular exhibits. Camel, pony, and zoomobile rides. Open every day except Christmas Day. Summer hours from May 18 – Sep 2 are 9 am - 7:30 pm. $15/adult, $11/seniors 65+, $9/child 4-12, and FREE for kids under 4. Parking is $6 (FREE during Nov – Feb). Take the Don Valley

Parkway north to Hwy 401; take Hwy 401 east to Meadowvale Rd and north on Meadowvale about 2.5 miles. (416) 392-5900, www.torontozoo.com.

Ukrainian Museum. The museum is part of St. Vladimir's Institute, as is an art gallery, a library, and a bookstore. Different displays, such as an exhibit on "sorochka" shirts from 13 different regions of the Ukraine. Open Mon - Fri, 10 am - 4 pm. $2/person admission. 620 Spadina Ave, north of College St. (416) 923-3318.

Walk of Fame. Similar to the Hollywood Walk of Stars with its stars in the sidewalk, this Walk honors Canadians such as Neil Young, Michael Fox, Donald Sutherland, Joni Mitchell, Bryan Adams, Ivan Reitman, and John Candy. Simcoe St, north of Wellington, and King St West, west of Simcoe St. FREE.

Wave Pool. The only indoor wave pool in or near Toronto, the pool offers up to 4 foot high waves, a large hot-tub/pool, a sauna, a 160 foot waterslide, and a "beach" area for toddlers. Open most days, but it's best to call for hours. $5.50/adult (over 16), $3/senior and children 3-15, and FREE for children under 3. Family pass for 2 adults and up to 3 children is $12.75. FREE parking. www.town.richmond-hill.on.ca/townhall/pr_wave.html, (905) 508-9283. 5 Hopkins St, Richmond Hill, just southwest of Yonge and Major Mackenzie Streets.

Xeriscape Demonstration Garden of water conservation landscaping, a concept first developed by the city of Denver Water Department. Queen's Park Circle, north of Grosvenor St. FREE.

Yorkville. This one-time derelict hippy haven is now an area, a state of mind, an upscale neighbourhood. Bounded by Bay St to the east, Davenport Rd to the north, Bloor St West to the south, and Avenue Rd to the west. This is where the young, beautiful, and generally movie star types like to shop and eat. Anchored at the west end by the Four Seasons Hotel, one of the best hotels in Toronto, and in the east end by Sassafraz, one of the Hollywood stars favourite restaurants. You can view exquisite homes along Hazelton Ave, north of Yorkville Ave. The Yorkville Village Park on Cumberland St is an outstanding small urban park. FREE.

Religious Institutions

A sample of downtown Toronto religious institutions:

Beth Tzedec Synagogue. Canada's largest synagogue, also houses the Reuben and Helene Dennis Museum (pottery, coins, menorahs). 1700

Bathurst St. (416) 781-3511. www.cjc.ca/community synagogues tor.html for information on Toronto's other synagogues.

Bloor Street United Church. Built in 1887. 300 Bloor St West, east of Spadina. (416) 924-7439.

Christ the Saviour Russian Orthodox Cathedral. 102 Follis Ave, at Manning. Contains a library of over 2,000 Russian books. (416) 534-1763.

Church of the Holy Trinity. Originally on the outskirts of Toronto if you can believe it. It was built in 1847 of bricks from the Don Valley in the Gothic architecture style. There is a list of names outside the front door of the homeless people who sadly "died as a direct result of homelessness". The Labyrinth maze, based on the 11-circuit labyrinth in Charles Cathedral in France that was built in the 13th century, is near the Church's entrance. Between the Eaton Centre and the Marriott Hotel. (416) 598-4521.

Church of St. Wencelaus (Roman Catholic). Founded and attended by the Czech community. 496 Gladstone St. (416) 532-5272.

Dewi Sant Welsh Church. Services in Welsh at 7 pm of the first Sunday of each month. 33 Melrose St, yards west of Yonge St. (416) 485-7583.

 First Baptist Church. Built in 1841. Founded by a group of runaway slaves from the US. 101 Huron St, a block north of Dundas St West. (416) 977-3508.

 First Lutheran Church. The first German church in Toronto, it was built in 1898 in the neo-Gothic style. German and Hungarian language services. There is a plaque honoring a parisher and founder of the Heintzman Piano Company, Theodore Heintzman. Heintzman first emigrated to the US in 1850 and then came to Canada in 1860. 116 Bond St, just north of Dundas St East. (416) 977-4786.

 Grant African Methodist Episcopal Church. The church (not the building) was founded in 1833 by blacks escaping slavery in the US. African American. 2029 Gerrard St East near Woodbine. (416) 690-5169.

Jami Mosque. A key mosque of the Pakistani community. 50 Boustead Ave, west of Roncesvalles near High Park. (416) 769-1192.

Jarvis Street Baptist Church. Built in 1874 of sandstone in the Gothic Revival style. It was the 1st in Canada to use a U shaped galleried auditorium. Gargoyles over the entrances add to the architectural interest. 130 Gerrard St East at Church St. (416) 925-3261.

Knesseth Israel Synagogue (Junction Shul). Built in 1911-13, it is the oldest operating Synagogue in Ontario. The hall of worship faces Jerusalem. 56 Maria St, at Shipman St. (416) 961-5556, ext 16.

Knox Presbyterian Church. First Presbyterian church in Toronto. Built in 1821, and rebuilt in 1847 and 1907. 630 Spadina Ave, at Harbourd St. (416) 921-8993.

Little Trinity Church (Anglican). Built in 1843-45 in the neo-Gothic revival style. The bricks were made from Don Valley clay. 425 King St East at Parliament. (416) 367-0272, www.littletrinity.on.ca.

Lithuanian Church of Resurrection. The church has an extensive collection of Lithuanian art for viewing. 1011 College St. (416) 533-0621.

Metropolitan United Church. The cornerstone was laid by Ontario's founder of education, Egerton Ryerson, in 1870. It was built in the "High Victorian Gothic Style". Largely rebuilt in 1929 after extensive fire damage. Open for visitors during the week from 9:30 am – 4 pm. 56 Queen St East, just east of Yonge St. (416) 363-0331.

Saint Luke's United Church. Built in 1887. 353 Sherbourne St at Carleton St. (416) 924-9619.

Saint Stephen's-in-the-Fields Church. Built in 1858 in the Victorian Gothic Revival style by Robert B. Denison (grandson of Captain John Denison, one of Toronto's first settlers) at his expense. F.W. Cumberland, architect of Osgoode Hall and St. James Cathedral, was one of the church's first wardens. 365 College St West. (416) 921-6350, www.saintstephens.on.ca. A thoroughly enriching website!

Serbian Eastern Orthodox Church. Built in 1953. Northeast corner of Gerrard St East and River St. (416) 967-9885.

St. Andrew's Church (Presbyterian). Built in 1876 in the Romanesque Revival style with granite from New Brunswick and Scotland, sandstone from Georgetown, Ontario and from stone from Ohio. SW corner of King St W and Simcoe St. (416) 593-5600, www.standrewtoronto.org.

St. Anne's Church (Anglican). Built in 1907 in the rarely used for churches Byzantine style. Its interior was decorated by three famous Group of Seven artists in 1923. 270 Gladstone Ave. (416) 536-3160, www.stannes.on.ca.

St. George the Martyr (Anglican). Built in 1844 (only tower is original). 197 John St, north of Queen St W, near Grange Park. (416) 598-4366.

St. George's Lutheran Church. 410 College St. Include German language services. (416) 921-2687.

St. James Cathedral (Anglican). A magnificent interior, steeped with history, and graced with stained glass and an extraordinary organ. Canada's tallest spire (306 feet) and North America's only ring of twelve-bell chime. The bells weigh from 631 - 2,418 pounds! A few War of 1812 soldiers are buried at St. James, including John Cawthra who fought under Canadian hero Sir Isaac Brock at Detroit and Queenston Heights. Also buried here are George Taylor Denison, who led a cavalry corp against the Fenians in 1866, and Bishop Strachan, founder of U of T's predecessor. Built in 1803-7, it was Toronto's first church. Prior to that, its congregation met in the original Parliament Buildings, later destroyed by the Americans in the War of 1812. The mother church for Anglicans in the Diocese of Toronto, it was rebuilt in 1853 after a fire. The St. James Parish House north of the church was built in 1909 in the Edwardian style. The church's interior is reminiscent of European churches. Also of interest, is the fragment from the St. James Church in Piccadilly, London, England in the wall of the entrance vestibule. The fragment was part of the damage the London namesake endured in the World War II air raids of October 1940. St. James Cathedral also hosts an annual blessing of animals by the Archbishop of Toronto, where people bring their pets for blessing. A zony, a cross between a zebra and pony, was blessed in 2001! 65 Church St, at King St. (416) 364-7865, www.stjamescathedral.on.ca.

St. John's Norway Anglican Church. Built in 1893 on the site of a church built in 1855, this church was consecrated by Bishop Strachan. The Church's chimes are from Gillet & Johnson of England. The surrounding cemetery is one of the earliest in Toronto and has the graves of many United Empire Loyalists. 470 Woodbine Ave, north of Lakeshore Blvd. (416) 691-4560.

St. Mary's Roman Catholic Church. Built in 1885-89, this very European like church stands at the western end of Adelaide St West. The approximately

150 foot high church tower and spire are visible from all along Adelaide St West. Sermons mostly in Portuguese. 130 Bathurst St. (416) 703-2326.

St. Michael's Catholic Cathedral. Built in 1849 in the English Gothic style. A beautiful, European-like church with arches, stained glass, wooden pews, ornate detailing, and a 260 foot steeple. Designed by William Thomas, who also designed the St. Lawrence Hall. 65 Bond St at Shuter St. St. Michael's School built in 1900 is at 69 Bond St. St. Michael's Cathedral Rectory built in 1845 in the Victorian Gothic style and residence of bishops and archbishops is at 200 Church St, as is the St. John's Chapel (1891). St. Michael's Hospital at 30 Bond St was built in 1892 and was the site of Canada's first blood transfusion in 1917. (416) 364-0234, www.ca-catholics.net/toronto.

St. Nicholas Ukrainian Catholic Church. 4 Bellwood South at Queen St West. (416) 504-4774.

St. Patrick's Catholic Church. An European style church with both English and German parishes. 131 McCaul St at Dundas St West. (416) 598-4835.

St. Paul's Anglican Church. Built in 1913 using an E.J. Lennox High Victorian Gothic design (original part in 1861 is used as the Parish House). It is Toronto's largest church with 3,000 seats. 227 Bloor St East. (416) 961-8116, www.stpaulsbloor.org.

St. Paul's Basilica. Built in 1822 in the Italian Renaissance style. The first Roman Catholic Church in Upper Canada between Kingston and Windsor. Its architectural plan was modeled after the Major Basilica in Rome, St. Paul's Outside the Walls. The church is the first and only Minor Basilica in Toronto, receiving such status on August 26, 1999 from Pope John Paul II. There is a monument to the many Irish immigrants who died from disease. 83 Power St at Queen St East. (416) 364-7588, www.ca-catholics.net/shrines.

St. Peter's Catholic Church. Cornerstones are dated 1906 and 1925. Medieval looking exterior. Used extensively by the Hispanic community. 840 Bathurst St, just north of Bloor St West. (416) 534-4219.

Timothy Eaton Memorial Church. A large, stone church built in 1910 and dedicated to the memory of one of Canada's greatest business people. The Eaton Centre is also named after the Eaton family. 230 St. Clair Ave West. (416) 925-5977, www.islandnet.com/~temc/support.html.

Toronto Chinese Baptist Church. Built in 1866. 72 McCaul St. (416) 596-8376. www.tcbc.on.ca.

Vishnu Temple. A small park has a large statute of Mahatma Gandhi. 8640 Yonge St, just north of Hwy 407. (905) 886-1724.

Comedy Clubs

Comedy Network. FREE tickets to the taping of "After Hours With Kenny Robinson" can be obtained by calling (416) 934-4751. The Masonic Hall, 888 Yonge St at Davenport, a couple of blocks north of Bloor St and the Bloor-Yonge subway station. FREE tickets to "Open Mike with Mike Bullard", also taped at the Masonic Hall, can be obtained by calling (888) 394-6453 or (416) 934-4737. Bullard's guests have included Chyna, Vince Carter, and Pink.

CBC Comedy. See "HOLLYWOOD NORTH" about FREE tickets to The Royal Canadian Air Farce and The Red Green Show.

Second City. Comedy only or dinner/show. 56 Blue Jays Way, north of Front St. The old Second City troupe of John Candy, Martin Short, Eugene Levy, Gilda Radner, et al had performed at the **Old Firehall** (built in 1886) on 110 Lombard St. The Old Firehall is now the Gilda's Club, an organization helping those affected by cancer. (800) 263-4485, www.secondcity.com.

Theatresports Toronto. Improv comedy. (416) 491-3115, www.theatresportstoronto.com.

Yuk Yuks. Jim Carrey got his start at Yuk Yuks at age 15. 2335 Yonge St, a block north of Eglinton Ave and Eglinton Subway Station. (416) 967-6425, www.yukyuks.com.

Performing Arts Theatres

There are other 90 theatre venues in Toronto today offering one of the greatest choices of the performing arts in the world. Besides the individual phone numbers and websites of individual theatres listed below, the Toronto Theatre Alliance and its over 170 members are a theater enthusiast's friend (www.theatreintoronto.edionysus.com, (800) 541-0499). Included are web links to "T.O. TIX" where you can get half price tickets on the day of the performance (in the new Dundas Square at Yonge and Dundas Streets – call (416) 536-6468 ext 40 for shows), and "Toronto Performs" where you get show listings and information. Many people, especially visitors are not aware that you can get ½ price tickets. TO TIX is open Tue – Sat, noon - 7:30 pm. Sunday and Monday show tickets are sold on Saturday. Book your tickets earlier if you want to see the big Broadway shows like The Phantom of the Opera, Beauty and the Beast, Mamma Mia, Lion King, and Cats.

Fans of "alternative" performing arts theatre should consider the **Toronto Fringe Festival.** Fans of film theatres would appreciate the excitement and hoopla of the **Toronto International Film Festival.**

Bathurst Street Theatre. Housed in an ex-church built in 1888, this is a large theatre with 550 seats. 736 Bathurst St, south of Bloor St West. (416) 531-6100.

Buddies in Bad Times Theatre. A gay and lesbian theatre company. 12 Alexander St, north of Carleton St. (416) 975-8555.

Berkeley Street Theatre. Home to the CanStage Theatre group. 26 Berkeley St. (416) 368-3110.

Canon Theatre. A 2,200 seat theatre set among plush surroundings in a building built in 1920. Previously the Pantages Theatre. 244 Victoria St, south of Shuter St and just east of the **Eaton Centre.** (416) 364-4100.

duMaurier Theatre. A 425 seat theatre located in the popular Harbourfront complex. 231 Queen's Quay West. (416) 973-4000.

Elgin & Winter Garden Theatre Centre. The last operating double decker theatre in the world. Extraordinarily beautiful theatres housed in a building built in 1913 and refurbished with $30 million in the 1990s. Stained glass, chandeliers, ornate woodwork and painted ceilings. Tours Thursday at 5 pm and Saturday at 11 am. $7/adult and $6/students and seniors. 189 Yonge St. (416) 314-2871, (800) 461-3333, www.mirvish.com.

Factory Theatre. The theater was added in 1910 to the historic *John Mulvey House* built in 1869. 125 Bathurst St at Adelaide St West. (416) 504-9971, www.factorytheatre.ca.

Famous Players Dinner Theatre. Self billed as the world's first dinner theater dedicated to people with special needs. This theater was largely established by donations and support from founder Diane Dupuy, Phil Collins, Paul Newman, and from Canadian corporations and individuals. Open Tue-Sat. 110 Sudbury St, south of Queen St West and west of Dovercourt Rd. (416) 532-1137, www.fpp.org.

Hummingbird Centre for the Performing Arts. Previously known as the O'Keefe Centre. Hosts various forms of dance, stage, singing, and opera. 1 Front St East. (416) 393-7469, www.hummingbirdcentre.com.

Isabel Bader Theatre

Isabel Bader Theatre. A 500 seat theater newly constructed with a $7 million gift from Mr. Bader. 93 Charles St West, near the ROM. (416) 872-1111.

Medieval Times Dinner & Tournament. Knights on horseback battle each other for the King and Queen's favor in a converted hockey arena. Finger-licking food and drink included in the admission price. Good fun. $54.95/adult, $36.95/child 12 and under. Shows Fri-Sat at 7:30 pm, and Sun at 3:30 pm. 416) 260-1234, www.medievaltimes.com, (800) 563-1190.

National Ballet of Canada. All performances are held at Hummingbird Centre, the most famous being the Nutcracker in December. $26-110/person. (416) 345-9686, www.national.ballet.ca. The website offers a helpful calendar of events and map of the theater's seating sections/prices.

New Yorker Theatre. 651 Yonge St just south of Bloor St. (416) 872-111.

Poor Alex Theatre. Shows for as low as $5/person. 296 Brunswick Ave, a few steps south of the lively Bloor St West street scene. (416) 324-9863.

Premiere Dance Theatre. 207 Queen's Quay West (south end of Queen's Quay Terminal). (416) 973-4000.

Princess of Wales Theatre. 300 King St West. (416) 872-1212, www.mirvish.com.

Royal Alexandria Theatre. 260 King St West. (416) 872-1212, www.mirvish.com.

The Toronto Mendelssohn Choir. The 180 person choir performs at Roy Thomson Hall. Concerts are $20-60/person. (416) 598-0422, www.tmchoir.org.

Toronto Centre for the Performing Arts. 5040 Yonge St. (416) 733-9388, www.tocentre.com.

Toronto Truck Theatre. Agatha Christie's "The Mousetrap" has been playing here for over 22 years, the longest running show in North America. Small and church pew seating close to the stage. Perfect family entertainment. $18-20 per ticket. 94 Belmont St two blocks west of Yonge St. Take TTC bus 6 to Belmont St or walk 10 minutes south to the Bay or Bloor Subway Stations. (416) 922-0084.

Tranzac Theatre. Small, intimate setting, although the building is showing its wear and tear. Some excellent shows at ticket prices around $15/person. 292 Brunswick Ave, a few steps south of Bloor St West.

Film Theatres

Film theatres are a dime a dozen in Toronto, even after a recent industry consolidation. I've noted a few theatres of note in the downtown area.

Bloor Cinema. Voted Toronto's best repertory theatre by Now and Eye Magazines. Annual membership is $3! $4/show for members, otherwise $7. $3/seniors and children (no membership needed). Also home to the 2002 Toronto Jewish Film Festival held in late April. 506 Bloor St West at Bathurst St. (416) 516-2330, www.tjff.com, or www.bloorcinema.com.

Paramount Theatre. 13 theatres with surround sound, an IMAX theatre, stadium-style seating, huge screens, fully licensed bar, a large food concessions area with a great view over the street below, and some of the longest escalators in town. A great theater in a super location (see picture). 259 Richmond St West at John St, a few yards south of Queen St West. (416) 368-6089.

Uptown. A classic theater. 764 Yonge St, just south of Bloor St. (416) 922-6361.

Carleton Cinemas. Part of the Cineplex Odeon chain, these cinemas tend to show more unusual, none-mainstream films like the Icelandic comedy "101 Reykjavik". 20 Carlton at College Subway Station. (416) 598-2309.

For a different cultural experience, try these theatres:

Albion Theatre. Movies from "Bollywood" (Indian films). 1530 Albion Rd. East Indian and Iranian films are also screened at Woodside Theatre at 1571 Sandhurst Circle. (416) 742-1765 for both theatres. www.albioncinemas.com and/or www.indotoronto.com for further information on East Indian matters.

Long Shong Cinema. Movies from Hong Kong (Chinese films). 4350 Steeles Ave East at Kennedy Rd in the Market Village Mall. (905) 305-0122.

Art Galleries

Architecture Typical of
Yorkville: Gallery Gevik.

The city abounds with art and art galleries. The City administration officially recognized Queen St West between Bathurst St and Roncesvalles Ave as the **Queen West Gallery District**. The district has 28 galleries!

Yorkville is also home to several art galleries. Gallery Gevik at 12 and Edward Day Gallery at 33 Hazelton St, just north of Yorkville Ave, Thomas Kincaid Signature Gallery at 108 Yorkville, and the following galleries on Scollard St, a few yards north of Yorkville on Hazelton: Drabinski Gallery at 122, Gallery One at 121, Beckett Fine Art at 120, Gallery 7 at 118, and Revolver Contemporary Art at 112. Other art galleries include:

Art at 80. Eleven art galleries in one historic building in the Fashion Dstrict. 80 Spadina Ave, south of Queen St West.

Art Gallery of Ontario (AGO). A treasure-chest of great arts including old European masters, the Group of Seven, and the largest collection of Henry Moore sculptures outside of England. Includes the "Grange", one of the oldest buildings in Toronto. Some exhibits charge a separate admission. Open Tue, Thurs, and Fri 11am-6 pm, Wed 11 am-8:30 pm, and Sat/Sun 10am-5:30pm. "Pay what you can (suggested $6/person)". 317 Dundas St West, west of University Ave. (416) 979-6648, www.ago.on.ca.

Bay of Spirits Gallery. Specializing in native art from across Canada. 156 Front St West. Open Mon - Fri 10 am – 6 pm and Sat 11 am – 5 pm. (416) 971-5190, (877) 928-2858, www.artvault.com/1055/1058/11251.asp.

Chinese Art Gallery of Ontario. Small exhibit of art by Chinese artists. Open Mon - Fri, 1 pm – 5 pm. 150 Beverly St. (416) 586-9837. FREE.

Design Exchange. Hosts various exhibits, many of which are FREE. Otherwise it is $5/person and FREE for children under 12. Open Tue - Fri

10 am – 6 pm, Sat/Sun noon – 5 pm. Located in the old Toronto Stock Exchange building at 234 Bay St, south of King St West. (416) 363-6121.

John B. Aird Gallery. Various forms of paintings and prints. Located in the Government of Ontario buildings at 900 Bay St. A hunter and seal sculpture in Canadian black granite is near the building entrance. (416) 928-6772. FREE.

Justina M. Barnicke Gallery. "Social consciousness in Canadian Art". This large gallery with lovely wood floors is open Mon-Fri 11 am –7 pm, and Sat-Sun 1 pm – 4 pm. Hart House, in University of Toronto grounds near The Soldiers' Tower. FREE.

Market Gallery, The. Features changing exhibitions on Toronto's art, culture and history. Was the second site of Toronto City Council chambers (1845-1899), and its first permanent site. 95 Front St, a few blocks east of Yonge St. Take the stairs or elevator just inside the St. Lawrence Market's Front St entrance to the 2nd floor. Open when **St. Lawrence Market** is open. FREE.

Museum of Contemporary Canadian Art. Paintings, sculptures, and photographs. A Canadian artists work exhibit. Open Tue-Sun noon – 5 pm. 5040 Yonge St, about 1 mile north of Hwy 401 (at North York Centre Subway Station). (416) 395-7430. FREE.

Power Plant Contemporary Art Gallery. Open Tue-Sun 12 – 6 pm, Wed noon – 8 pm, and open holiday Mondays. $4/adult, $2/senior or student, and children FREE. Wed 5 pm – 8 pm and all day on holiday Mondays FREE. 231 Queen's Quay West (Harbourfront). (416) 973-4949, www.thepowerplant.org.

Thomson Gallery. Canadian art from the personal collection of Kenneth Thomson (one of Canada's richest people). Over 300 original works from the Group of Seven, Paul Kane, Cornelius Krieghoff (including the famous "Toll Gate"), and several others such as William Berczy's (one of Toronto's first settlers) portrait of Indian Chief Joseph Brant. 9th floor of the Hudson Bay store. Go to the Simpson Tower at 401 Bay St and take the elevators to "8th Floor – Arcadian Court" to avoid taking 8 floors of escalators in The Bay. Open Mon-Sat 11 am – 5 pm. $2.50/person. 176 Yonge St. (416) 861-4571.

The McMichael Collection (outside Toronto). In scenic Kleinburg (home to Canadian icon Pierre Burton), you can see works by the famous Group of

Seven. Works from other Canadian artists, including First Nations and Inuit, are on display as well. Take Hwy 401 to Hwy 400 north to Major Mackenzie Drive. Turn right or east to Islington Ave and turn left/north into Kleinburg. Follow the signs. $12/adult, $9/senior & students, $25/family of up to 2 adults and 3 children. 10365 Islington Ave. (905) 893-1121, (888) 213-1121, www.mcmichael.com.

Toronto Dominion Gallery of Inuit Art. Located on the ground level of the Maritime Life Tower at the Toronto-Dominion Centre. Open Mon - Fri 8 am – 6 pm, and Sat/Sun 10 am – 4 pm. Stroll around yourself or call (416) 982-8473 to book a personalized guided tour. FREE.

University Art Centre. Set amid the beautiful campus of University of Toronto's University College, this large gallery has Group of Seven paintings, Byzantine glazed and metal wares, a marble relief of St. Nicholas from circa 1400, a painting of Adam & Eve dated 1538, and more. The New York Times said this was "one of Toronto's secret gems….." Open Tues-Fri noon – 5 pm and Sat noon – 4 pm. 15 King's College Circle, Laidlaw wing, west of **Queen's Park**. (416) 978-1838. Park on Hoskin Ave and walk 100 yards south. FREE.

Annual Festivals/Events

There are more fantastic festivals and events in Toronto than one can ever hope to attend in a given year or even a span of years. The following are a *few* of the festivals and/or events that might give you a taste of extraordinary experiences Toronto can offer you. In addition, there are street buskers (performers), and FREE concerts held in Mel Lastman Square and throughout downtown Toronto in the summer. Call the City of Toronto's Special Events hotline at (416) 395-0490 for specific dates and times of events the City is hosting or Tourism Toronto at (416) 203-2600, www.tourismtoronto.com.

African Music Festival. Live bands from Africa, and African foods, crafts, and clothing. **Nathan Phillips Square** at Bay and Queen Streets. (416) 340-1717. FREE admission.

Afrofest. African music and culture, arts, crafts, games, and more. **Queen's Park**. (416) 469-5336. FREE admission.

Antiques Canada. A spring show in the 3rd week of March and a 3 day winter show in the 1st week of December. More than 100 antique, art and book dealers in 65,000 sq. ft. $7/person, FREE for children 12 and under. Metro Convention Centre. 255 Front St West. (800) 667-0619, www.antiqueshowscanada.com.

Beaches Easter Parade. A large parade to celebrate Easter. Held on Easter Sunday each year. Starts at 2 pm at the R.C. Harris Water Filtration Plant and heads west along Queen St West to Woodbine Ave. FREE.

Beaches Jazz Festival. July 18-21, 2002. 750,000 people watch 70 bands at three venues in The Beaches. A fantastic time for the whole family – families with kids will want to spend much of their time at the **Kew Gardens** venue. www.beachesjazz.com. FREE.

Bloor West Village Ukrainian Festival. Self billed as North America's largest Ukrainian street party. Held on the third weekend in September. Arts, crafts, parade, food, dances, a yarmarok (market) and cultural activities such as a Ukrainian Film Festival. Bloor St West between Jane and Runnymede (street closed). (416) 410-9965, www.ukrainianfestival.org. FREE admission.

Cabbagetown Festival. A fall festival held in the week after Labour Day in September. Dance performances, children activities, video and film shows, a street fair, arts and crafts, the Riverdale Farm, walking tours, and more. About 50,000 people attend. (416) 921-0857, www.oldcabbagetown.com.

Cavalcade of Lights. A one day festival held in late November. 100,000 lights, live music, fireworks, and a dazzling ice skating show. Nathan Phillips Square. (416) 338-0338, www.city.toronto.on.ca/special_events. FREE.

Canadian Aboriginal Festival. Canada's largest Aboriginal event, it is held in late November in the Skydome. Includes traditional teachings, art, music, food, Pow Wow dancing, a lacrosse skills competition, a 200 vendor market, and children's activity centre. $12/adult, $6/child under 12. www.canab.com.

Canadian International Air Show. Held every year since 1949. This hugely popular event at the **Canadian National Exhibition** (CNE) is a great opportunity to see some of the biggest, fastest, and most maneuverable planes and jets. Examples include the Concorde, USAF U-2, USAF B-36, the Blue Angels, the Snowbirds, F-14s, F-16s, and F-18s. Part of the CNE, but you can easily see the jets from almost any open area or beaches in downtown Toronto for FREE. Usually on the first 3 days of September. www.cias.org.

Canadian National Exhibition (CNE) Held annually since 1879, the CNE draws about 1.5 million people over 18 days. Includes the **Canadian International Air Show**, running since 1949, a huge midway, food pavilion, music shows and competitions, garden shows, horse shows, "Rising Star" competitions, and much more. Open 10 am-midnight daily during Aug 16-Sept 2, 2002 (early closing on Sept 2). (416) 263-3800, www.theex.com.

Caribana. Jul 20 – Aug 6. Two weeks of festivities, with the highlight being the vivid and exciting parade on its 1 mile route, watched by almost 1 million people. The costumes and dances of 8,000 masqueraders are spectacular. The annual Miss Black Ontario is held and there is a Kiddies Carnival parade, and there is Calyspo music and Caribbean food. The parade and the opening party at Nathan Phillips Square are FREE. www.caribana.com.

 Caravan. Over 20 pavilions each celebrating a different culture in Toronto mid June. Some include German, Russian, African, Welsh, Cuban, Tamil, and Israeli. Taste foods, see ethnic dances and cultural exhibits, and buy crafts/gifts. The Caravan Pass is the best deal, enabling one to experience many different cultures all in one day (most pavilions are close together downtown). A Pass is $20/person over 12 for the full 8 day festival ($4 off if you buy before the Festival starts). $9/person over 12 for a 1 day "passport" only. www.briankilgore.com/festival_caravan.htm.

CHIN International Picnic. Over 2,000 performers, midway rides, sporting events, live music, and a lively bikini contest. The Guinness Book of World Records lists this picnic as "the largest outdoor FREE picnic in the world." The last weekend in June, on Canadian National Exhibition grounds.

CN Tower Stair Climb for Charity. Mid-October. 1,776 steps. See www.stairclimb.org. Takes about ½ hour for the average person.

Corso Italia Toronto Fiesta. Held mid July on the weekend. Over 200 shops and FREE live entertainment at Earlscourt Park.

Creative Sewing and Needlework Festival. Exhibits, demos, fashion shows. Metro Convention Centre at 255 Front St West.

Craft Show. Accent pieces for the home, clothing, jewelry, and specialty foods. Metro Convention Centre at 255 Front St West. (888) 773-4444.

 Doors Open Festival. Held in late May, the City of Toronto hosts one of the most unique and insightful festivals I've ever seen. 100 stores, public works, museums, and many privately owned buildings are "open" for the public to view. The historic and now closed Don Jail is a favourite. (416) 338-3888, www.doorsopen.org. FREE.

Diwali Parade (Hindu Festival of Lights) down University Ave, across Queen St West to Nathan Phillips Square where a party is held. FREE.

Festival of Chariots. A parade down Yonge St in mid July celebrates the return of Hare Krishna. FREE.

Fringe Festival of Independent Dance Artists. First 3 weeks of August. Various venues throughout downtown, although the main venue is **Buddies in Bad Times Theatre.** (416) 410-4291, www.ffida.org.

First Night Toronto Festival. Arts, crafts, rides, live musical and dance entertainment, magic, petting zoo, and live comedy for families to celebrate New Year's Eve alcohol-free. $15/person ($10/person in advance). Unlimited ride passes are $10/person. FREE admission and rides for children under 6. Skydome from Dec 25-31. www.firstnight.toronto.com, (416) 362-3692.

IDance Festival. 12,000 young rave fans dance and mill around in **Nathan Phillips Square.** First September weekend. www.idancetornto.com. FREE.

International Auto Show. Canada's largest auto show, with 1,000 cars and trucks, 150 exhibitors, 800,000 sq. ft, and 300,000 visitors. 9 days in mid Feb in the Metro Convention Centre. $15/adult, $6/children 6-12, $30/family for 2 adults and 2 children under 13. (905) 940-2800, www.autoshow.ca.

International Festival of Authors. 10 days in late October. 2,500 authors including 11 Nobel Laureates and J.K. Rowling (who read from her Harry Potter book in 2000) have read at this festival. $8/person. Harbourfront. (416 973-3000, www.harbourfront.on.ca.

International Home Show. Early October. 250,000 sq. ft. of home and garden products and services, how-to advice, and future products. International Centre. 6900 Airport Rd.

Milk International Children's Festival of the Arts. Victoria Day weekend and the following weekend. Lots of "on-site activities" for children of all ages, including glass blowing, crafts, and metalworking. $7.50/person. $12/person gets you an extra show and $15/person gets two extra shows. **Harbourfront**.

Molson Indy. Held in the Canadian National Exhibition grounds in mid July. Lots of pre-race events and activities. (416) 870-8000, www.molsonindy.com.

North American International Motorcycle Show. Held at the International Centre at 6900 Airport Rd, near Pearson International Airport. 400 exhibitors, 1,000 motorcycles, stage shows, celebrity racers, information kiosks, and a daily leather fashion show are offered. $12/adult, $5/child 6-12, and FREE for children under 6. FREE parking. (905) 655-5403, www.supershowevents.com.

Pet Show Exhibition Place. Late October. Pet products and services, breeders, petting zoo, and performing dogs. www.canadianpetexpo.com.

Pride Toronto. Second last week of June. Now THIS you don't see everyday. Approximately 750,000 gather to watch this celebration of Gay Pride and Toronto diversity in Toronto's "Village". www.the519.org. FREE.

Roncesvalles Street Festival. A harvest celebration held the Saturday of the Thanksgiving weekend (Oct). Activities include Polish and other music, horse and wagon rides, a petting zoo, face painting, and more. Open 10 am – 5 pm on Roncesvalles Ave at Wright Ave. FREE admission. (416) 535-1169.

Royal Agricultural Winter Fair and Royal Horse Show over 10 days in early November. Garden exhibits, farm animals, petting farm, horse shows and activities, dog shows and activities, food exhibits and shows, and antiques. National Trade Centre, Canadian National Exhibition grounds. $15/adult, $10/seniors over 60, $9/children 5-17, and FREE for children under 5. Family pass for 2 adults/2 children is $34. Two for one admission Mon-Fri after 5 pm. Open Mon-Sat 9 am - 9 pm, Sun 9 am - 8 pm, last Sun 9 am - 6 pm. (416) 263-3400, www.royalfair.org.

Santa Claus Parade. 2001 saw the 97th version of the world's largest Santa Claus/Christmas parade. Almost 50 floats and marching bands, and 1,500 costumed paraders. The 3rd Sunday of November. Parade heads down University Ave from Bloor St West to Queen St West, then down Yonge St. Stands at University Ave and Bloor St and at Queen St in Nathan Phillips Square. Get there 2 hours before the parade in order to get front row seating along the curb. www.santaclausparade.org. FREE.

Santo Cristo. The 5th Sunday after Easter features a parade along Adelaide St West to **St. Mary's Roman Catholic Church** in Portugal Square. A mass and other activities are held in and around St. Mary's. FREE.

Snow Jam. Rock bands, BMX bike tricks, skateboarding tricks, in-line skating, snowboarding, and freeskiing. Sat and Sun of the third week in September. Exhibition Place, on CNE grounds. $20/person.

St. Patrick's Day Parade. The green of Ireland is celebrated in part each year with a parade down Yonge St, south of Bloor St. 2,000 marchers, 30 floats, and 14 bands. The first Sunday after March 17. FREE.

Swedish Fair. Swedish dancing, foods, baked goods, crafts, glogg (mulled wine), and more. One weekend in late November. Harbourfront, in the York Quay Centre at 235 Queen's Quay West. (416) 973-3000. FREE.

Symphony of Fire Fireworks Festival in late June/early July. Different countries competing with fireworks over Lake Ontario. Harbourfront or nearby lakefront venue such as **Clarke Beach Park**. FREE.

Taste of the Danforth Festival. The street is closed to traffic and becomes a mile-long street party with Greek food, shops, and entertainment. Second weekend of August. FREE admission. www.tasteofthedanforth.com.

Toronto Boat Show. Held for 9 days in mid January at the National Trade Centre on **Canadian National Exhibition** grounds. Canada's largest boat show. Boats, fashion shows, safety information, fishing at a live trout pond, and more. $11/adult, $9/seniors, $7/child 5-15, FREE for children under 5. (416) 203-3934, www.torontoboatshow.com.

Toronto Downtown Jazz Festival. Last 9 days of June and July 1. FREE.

Toronto Fall Home Show. 4 days in late Sept held at The National Trade Centre on **Canadian National Exhibition** grounds. 300 exhibits. $8/adult, $6/senior, $6/youth (13-17), FREE for children under 13. www.dmgworldmedia.com/consumer-exhibitions/.

 The Toronto Street Festival. Busy Yonge St is closed for a weekend of free entertainment at four of Yonge St's main intersections: Bloor St, St. Clair St, Eglinton Ave, and Lawrence Ave. The entertainment includes 1,200 performers, 100 musical groups, 57 dance performances, and 102 cirque performances! One year there was a motorcyclist on a high wire! Food concessions. Early July: Sat from 11 am – 11 pm and Sun from 11 am – 7 pm. Over 800,000 people partake. (416) 338-0338, www.city.toronto.on.ca/special_events. FREE admission.

Toronto Fringe Festival. Over 100 performing art companies from all over the world performing more unusual live theatre. 11 days in early July. Maybe you'd like to be a volunteer for the Festival and really become part of the Toronto art community fabric! (416) 966-1062, www.fringetoronto.com.

Toronto International Dragon Boat Race. Over 200 teams race in decorated boats as part of a Chinese tradition since the 4th century. Late June. Toronto Islands. (416) 598-8945, www.dragonboats.com.

128

Toronto International Film Festival. See "Hollywood North".

Toronto Outdoor Art Exhibition. Paintings, drawings, sculptures, jewelry, ceramics, and metal/glass works from over 500 artists. **Nathan Phillips Square**. (416) 408-2754. FREE.

Toronto Ski and Snowboard Show. 4 days in mid October. $12/adult, $8/seniors and youth (6-15), children under 6 FREE. Automotive Building in the **Canadian National Exhibition**. www.sportsmenshows.com/skishow/, (416) 695-0311.

Toronto Winterfest. Feb 8-10 (2002). Music, ice-carvings, skating and dance shows, comedy, and skating. www.city.toronto.on.ca/special_events. (416) 338-0338. FREE.

Toronto's Word on the Street Festival. A celebration of books, with 250 exhibitors. Includes readings from authors and a number of musical acts. Almost 150,000 people attend. Queen St West and side streets are closed and become a pedestrian mall. Last Sunday in Sept. (416) 504-7241, www.thewordonthestreet.ca. FREE.

Ukrainian Fest. Food, music, a parade, midway rides, and street dance along colorful Bloor St West (between High Park and Jane St). 2nd last Saturday in Sept. (416) 410-9965.

Vegetarian Food Fair. Over 75 exhibits, food samples, cooking demos, and workshops. Harbourfront, 235 Queen's Quay West. (416) 973-4600.

Whole Life Expo. 2nd last weekend in November. Exhibits, demos, products for natural health and alternative medicine. $5/person. Metro Convention Centre at 255 Front St West. (416) 515-1330, www.wholelifecanada.com.

World Leaders, A Festival of Creative Genius. Last week of Sept and all October. A celebration of 10-15 people's ability to drive world culture through their creative innovations. Admission to each "Hommage" for each person is $175 plus tax, including dinner. Most Special Events (panel discussions, photo exhibitions, lectures) are free. (416) 973-3000, www.worldleaderfestival.com.

Other Festivals/Events

AIDS Walk. 3rd weekend of Sept. 15,000 people walk the 5.2 mile (8.5 km) route through **Queen's Park** and The Village before returning to **Nathan Phillips Square**. Raises money for services to those affected with HIV/AIDS.

ArtsWeek. Concerts, and a visual arts display and sale. Last week of Sept in Nathan Phillips Square. www.artstoronto.com. FREE.

Black Creek Pioneer Village hosted an American Civil War re-enactment for the first time on July 14/15, 2001. Up to 50,000 Canadians fought in the Civil War and 29 were awarded the Congressional Medal of Honor for bravery. (416) 736-1733.

Dragon Party. 100 performers on two stages celebrating Chinese culture in Chinatown East. On Gerrard St East between Broadview and Logan. 2nd last Saturday in September.

Festival of Dance on Film and Video. 5 days of films about dance. $8/person at the door. Harbourfront and three other downtown venues. (416) 961-5424, www.movingpicturesfestival.com.

Harvestfest. Held late Oct in Market Lane Park, beside St. Lawrence Market (North). Ontario grown 600 and 700 lb pumpkins, pumpkin carving, German beer and sausages, a petting zoo, and carnival games. FREE.

Magical Arts Festival. Magic, illusion, and conjuring art performances. The Glenn Gould Theatre, and The Charlotte Room and Big Daddy's bar lounges. Last week of September. $29/person week pass or $10 per show. (416) 201-6992, www.magical.com.

Movies for Mommies. Films for mom, dad, and infants under 12 months old. $8.50/adult price includes change tables, bottle warming, and free wipes. In January. Regent Cinema at 551 Mt Pleasant. www.movies4mommies.com.

The Harbourfront Reading Series. Readings from books, including by some world famous authors (like Salman Rushdie and John Irving in 2001). Various venues. (416) 973-3000.

Women's Health Matters. Held mid January. 40 forums and speakers on various health topics of interest, and 130 exhibits of products, services, and information. $10/adult and seniors/full time students FREE. Metro Convention Centre (South Building). (416) 323-6000, www.womenshealthmatters.ca.

World Youth Day. This event, organized by the Catholic Church, is meant to bring young people together to share their spiritual and cultural experiences and to learn about the Catholic religion. It is expected to draw 750,000 delegates to Toronto, and even more for the Papal Mass. July 22-28, 2002. (416) 971-5353, www.wyd2002.org.

Military and Police

Tours 7 and 10 have most of the military and police items noted below.

Admiral Yeo's monument. On the northeast corner of Front and Jarvis Streets is a bas relief monument to the War of 1812 Admiral, *Sir James Yeo's and his flagship "St. Lawrence"*, erected at the original waterfront. FREE.

Cannons. Two cannons from the French warship "Le Prudent, captured at Louisbourg by the British in 1758, are displayed at Whitney Block at Queen's Park. Queen's Park Circle, north of Grosvenor St. There are two cannons from Louisbourg at Wellesley St and Hart House Circle. FREE.

Coronation Park. A *World War II Monument* near the large flagpole and Canadian flag about 50 yards south of the trail. A most intriguing metal relief map of the Atlantic shows where individually identified Canadian ships and German U-boats were sunk! There is also another relief map providing further information on Canadian participation in World War II (1,081,865 of Canada's 11,300,000 enlisted, of which 700,000 were under 21 years old). All of the trees here were planted in 1937 to commemorate the Canadian Expeditionary Force in 1914-18, the Veterans of the Fenian Raids in 1866, Northwest Rebellion of 1885, and Boer War of 1898-1902. This is also where the Americans invaded Toronto for a second time on July 31, 1813. FREE.

First Burying Ground in Toronto. It contains the remains of Captain Neal McNeale, killed in the Battle of York on April 27, 1813, as well as other War of 1812 veterans. Located a few blocks northeast of the Fort York at Niagara and Portland Streets (northeast of Bathurst and Front Streets). FREE.

Fort York. Established in 1793 by Lt. Governor John Graves Simcoe as the founding part of Toronto, Fort York has Canada's largest collection of original War of 1812 buildings. The Fort was originally on the shore of Lake Ontario, before years of landfilling. $5/adult, $3.25 for seniors and children 13-18, and $3 for children 6-12, and FREE for children 5 and under. 100 Garrison Rd, north east of Strachan Ave. and Lakeshore Blvd. Take TTC Streetcar 511 (ask driver for drop-off point) or drive (FREE parking). Open daily 10 am – 5 pm. (416) 392-6907, or email fortyork@city.toronto.on.ca.

Fort York was built by the Queen's Rangers, a Regiment initially comprised of Americans from New York, Connecticut, New Jersey, Rhode Island, and Virginia. The Queen's Rangers had fought on the British side in the American Revolution. Fort York and Toronto weres invaded by Americans on April 27,1813.

Fort Rouille. Commonly known as Fort Toronto, Fort Rouillè was built in 1750-51 by order of Marquis de la Jonquière to strengthen French control of the Great Lakes. While it was destroyed in 1759, there is a concrete wall base along the ground that shows the Fort's exterior walls. A plaque shows the locations of the Fort's interior buildings. There are three cannons (two from 1843 and one from 1856) guarding the site. Take the pedestrian path that runs just north of Lakeshore Blvd West and west of Ontario Dr on **Canadian National Exhibition** grounds. FREE (when CNE is not on in August).

HMCS Haida Naval Museum. This World War II destroyer participated in the D-day invasion of Normandy and sank more enemy ship tonnage than any Canadian ship in history (9 solo, 5 assists). FREE exhibits include mines, a sonar dome from under the ship, a torpedo, and a radar antenna. $5 per person, $3/senior 55+, FREE for children under 3. $10/family for twoadults and three children. Ontario Place. (416) 314-9755. You can get a virtual tour on www3.sympatico.ca/hrc/haida. The ship is moving to Hamilton in 2003.

Marine Museum. See "ATTRACTIONS, General". FREE.

Michael Sweet Avenue. This street was dedicated to the Toronto police officer killed on duty while responding to an armed robbery on March 14/80.

Old City Hall. Several WWI and WWII plaques and a monument, the most noteworthy being the one naming the first casualties of enemy action in World War II from Ontario: R.T. Knox, L.E. Sword, and J.F. Bailey. FREE.

Provincial Parliament Buildings. See "ATTRACTIONS, General". FREE.

Ontario Police Memorial. A wall of names commemorating fallen Ontario police officers. Queen's Park Circle, 50 yards north of Grosvenor St. FREE.

Peace Garden. Then Prime Minister Pierre Trudeau turned the sod in 1984 and Pope John Paul II kindled an eternal flame with an ember from Peace Memorial Park in Hiroshima. FREE.

Queen's Park. See "ATTRACTIONS, General". FREE.

Queen's Own Rifles monument. Honoring those killed in action at Limeridge on June 2, 1866. FREE.

Queen's Rangers Plaque. Tucked away to the left of Ontario Place west bridge is a plaque honoring the Queen's Rangers, the first British regiment raised in Britain specifically for service to Ontario. FREE.

Royal Canadian Military Institute. The building was built in 1912. Two "9 pounder guns", the type used at the Battle of Waterloo and the 1853-56 Crimean War, stand by its entrance. 426 University Ave, south of Dundas.

Shrine Peace Memorial. Gifted in 1930 to commemorate "the peaceful relationships existing for over a half century between Canada and the U.S." It is surrounded by a lovely rose garden overlooking Lake Ontario and Ontario Place, yards away. FREE.

Soldiers' Tower. Built in 1924, it lists the names of University of Toronto attendees who died in service during World Wars I and II. FREE.

Toronto Police Headquarters and the **Toronto Police Museum.** Admission is free although donations via a donation box are appreciated. Lots of great stuff here, including the holding cell that will give your kids an idea of what it might be like to be incarcerated even for a few minutes. 40 College St. FREE.

War Monument. The monument identifies the 7 Canadians from Ontario who were awarded the prestigious Victoria Cross in World Wars I and II. In the traffic island along University Ave on the south side of Dundas St West. FREE.

Yorkville Constable (Policeman) House. This 1867 built home was part of the original Village of Yorkville founded in 1830. 77 Yorkville Ave. FREE.

The following military points of interest are just off the QEW highway on your way into Toronto through Buffalo/Fort Erie:

Lundy's Lane Museum (War of 1812). In Niagara Falls at 5810 Ferry St, near Lundy's Lane and Main St. $1.60/adult, $1/senior and student, $0.50/child 6-12, and FREE for children under 6. (905) 358-5082.

Canadian Warplane Heritage Museum. World War I and II planes. 9280 Airport Rd, Mount Hope (just southwest of Hamilton) near Hwys 53 and 6. Mon-Sun 9am-5pm (8pm on Thurs). $10/adult, $8 seniors and children. Children under 8 FREE. Family pass for two adults and two kids is $30. (905) 679-4183, www.warplane.com.

DINING

Toronto offers the world of cuisine – pretty well anything you could ask for is served somewhere in Toronto in thousands of restaurants. The Bloor-Yorkville district alone has over 100 restaurants to choose from. I've listed *a few notable examples*, almost all in the downtown core.

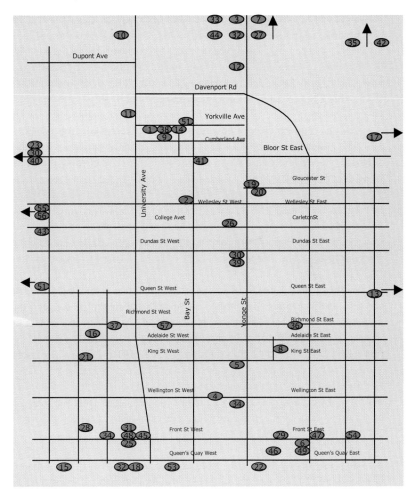

The price range noted for each restaurant is the dinner price. Lunch prices, and sometimes menu selection, are normally less. Please note that Toronto has a no-smoking by-law for all restaurants. Some have gotten around this by technically qualifying as a bar. Unfortunately, children are not allowed into "bars" even during the day.

Fine Dining

1. Bellini's. Hollywood stars often dine here. Entrees $17-$37. Mains include veal, fish, lamb, beef, chicken, risotto, and pasta. 101 Yorkville Ave. (416) 929-9111. Italian.

2. Bistro 990. Hollywood stars frequently dine here. Entrees $14-40. Mains include steak, seafood, chicken, lamb, duck, game, pasta, and veal. 990 Bay St. (416) 921-9990. French.

3. Centro. Entrees $28-$43. Mains include caribou, rabbit, seafood, lamb, veal, steak, and duck. Valet parking. 2472 Yonge St, north of Eglinton Ave. (416) 483-2211. Italian & Contemporary European.

4. Canoe. Superb view of downtown Toronto from 54 floors up. Entrees $24-39. Mains include Alberta beef and deer, pork, lamb, veal, fish and seafood. 66 Wellington St West, 54th floor of the TD Centre. (416) 364-0054, www.canoerestaurant.com. Canadian.

5. Jump Café and Bar. Very popular with the business lunch crowd. Entrees $16-30. Mains include steak, seafood, veal, chicken, lamb, and pasta. Commerce Court East at King and Yonge Streets. (416) 363-3400, www.jumpcafe.com. American.

6. Le Papillon. Superb cheesy French onion soup – our favourite! Entrees $8-$20. Mains include filet, steak, salmon, Quebecois meat pie, and chicken, and stuffed crepes. 16 Church St, just south of Front St in the fabulous St. Lawrence neighbourhood. Several times voted the favourite French restaurant by the Toronto Sun Readers Choice. (416) 363-3773. French.

7. North 44°. A very popular uptown fine dining restaurant, along with nearby Centro. Entrees $21-$47. Mains include pasta, seafood, beef, rabbit, lamb, duck, and steak. Valet parking. 2537 Yonge St, a few blocks north of Eglinton Ave. (416) 487-4897. Contemporary.

8. Rosewater Supper Club. Hollywood stars like to dine here. Exquisite interior with 22 foot ceilings, waterfall, and marble floors. Entrees $25-$39. Mains include lamb, beef, shellfish, and cannelloni. 19 Toronto St, near Yonge St and King St East, in a beautiful 1888 Italianate building. (416) 214-5888.

9. Sassafraz. One of the three most popular spots for Hollywood and other stars to dine (see their website under "Celebrities"). Autographed pictures of Hollywood stars adorn one wall. Lovely setting and location. Entrees $20-40.

Mains include seafood, chicken, veal, lamb, and pasta. 100 Cumberland St in trendy Yorkville, northwest of Bloor and Bay Streets. (416) 964-2222, www.cafesassafraz.com. American, Continental.

10. Scaramouche. Long standing and premier restaurant. Entrees $26-$40. Mains include beef, chicken, venison, seafood, lamb, and pasta. Renovated in early 2002. 1 Benvenuto Place, just west off Avenue Rd on Edmund, north of Dupont St. Entrance is in the far left corner of an apartment complex. (416) 961-8011. French.

11. Sotto Sotto Trattoria. One of the three favourite spots for Hollywood stars to dine. Entrees mostly $17-$32. Mains include seafood, pasta, veal, chicken, lamb, steak, and quail. 116-A Avenue Rd, north of Bloor St West, in fashionable Yorkville. (416) 961-8011. Italian.

12. Thai Magic. Entrees $10-20. Mains include chicken, Thai curries, and seafood. 1118 Yonge St at Roxborough Ave. (416) 968-7366. Thai.

13. Whitlocks. In a beautiful 1891 building in the bustling Beaches neighbourhood. Entrées $14-36. Mains include vegetarian meals, pasta, stirfrys, seafood, steak, lamb, chicken, and ribs. 1961 Queen St East, east of Woodbine Ave. (416) 691-8784.

14. Yamato's Japanese Steak House. Includes 10 tables at which chefs prepare your food in front of you. Entrees $9-22. Mains include sushi, steak, seafood, and chicken. 24 Bellair St, in Yorkville. (416) 927-0077. Japanese.

15. 360° Restaurant. The world's highest revolving restaurant. Superlative views over Toronto and Lake Ontario. No cost to ride up, if you're eating at the restaurant. Entrees $27-55. Mains include chicken, ribs, lamb, beef, bison, salmon, bison, marlin, pasta, and portabello mushroom. Top of the CN Tower, south of Front St at John St. (416) 362-5411. www.cntower.ca.

Middle of the Road

16. Alice Fazooli's Italian Crabshack. Very pleasant ambiance. Entrees from $10-$27. Mains include seafood, chicken, steaks, pizza, pasta, and salads. 294 Adelaide St West, west of John St. (416) 979-1910. Italian.

17. Astoria. A Greektown favourite. Entrees $9-19. Mains include chicken, pork, and beef souvlaki, moussaka, quail, lamb, steak, seafood, and vegetarian plates. 390 Danforth Ave, at Chester Ave. (416) 463-2838, www.astoriashishkebob.com. Greek.

18. Boathouse Bar & Grill. A wide variety of choices including soups, pastas, burgers, salads, pizzas, sandwiches, BBQ chicken and ribs, seafood, and steak. Partial view of Toronto Harbour. Entrees $8-19. Queen's Quay Terminal (Harbourfront Centre) at 207 Queen's Quay West. (416) 203-6300.

19. Boccone Deli and Pizza Bar. Very good Italian food at reasonable prices. Pick your food, pay, and take a seat at the restaurant style seating. $3-6 for salads, Italian sandwiches (excellent!), pizza, and soup. 1378 Yonge St, one block south of St. Clair Ave. (416) 960-6419. Italian.

20. Brownstone. Lovely interior brick walls and view of Yonge St people traffic. The friendly owner is often there to greet people. Best seat for a killer view onto Yonge St is the southwest corner. Summer patio facing south. Entrees $7-13. Mains include salads, pastas, pizza, chicken, salmon, and steak. 603 Yonge St, north of Wellesley St, in the beautiful 1888 Masonic Hall building. (416) 920-6288.

21. Bumpkins. Entrees $11-$22. Mains include lamb, chicken, duck, beef, seafood, and pasta. 21 Gloucester St, just east of Yonge St. (416) 922-8655.

22. Canadian Bar & Grill. Entrees $7-$13 for lunch ($13-$30 for dinner). Dinner mains have wonderful Canadian cuisine offerings such as salmon, trout, French pea soup, Alberta beef, wild rice, and Newfoundland clam chowder. Mains for lunch include pasta, stir-fry, pizza, sandwiches. All you can eat breakfast buffet for $10.95. 370 King St West, in the Holiday Inn Hotel. (416) 595-2525, www.hoik.com/dining/canadian.htm. Canadian.

23. Captain John's. Entrees $11.75-$40.95. Mains include seafood (including shark steak), steak, stroganoff, tortellini, soups, salads, and surf'n'turf. Located on a converted, small ocean liner now docked at the foot of Yonge St. (416) 363-6062. Seafood.

24. Country Style Restaurant. Very plain décor, but huge schnitzels and strudels to die for. Voted "Favourite Cabbage Rolls" in 2001 by Toronto Life Magazine. Mains include cabbage rolls, schnitzels, and goulash. Entrees $3.50-$11.50 tax included. 450 Bloor St West, just east of Bathurst St. (416) 537-1745. Hungarian.

25. Dessert Sensation Café. Cosy little café with south and west facing windows overlooking an outdoor patio. Salads, quiche, fancy sandwiches, and chicken based entrees. Entrees $5.50-$11. 26 Baldwin St, north of Dundas St West and west of University Ave. (416) 348-0731.

26. East Side Mario's. Entrees $7-16. Mains include pasta, salad, pizza, chicken, salmon, veal, and steak. 151 Front St West, just west of University Ave in the Entertainment District. (416) 360-1917. Italian.

27. Fran's Restaurant. Plain, reliable, and open 24 hours every day. Entrees $7-14. Mains include burgers, wraps, pasta, steak, salmon, and sole. Feature all day breakfasts. 20 College St. (416) 923-9867. American.

28. Grazie. There are often line-ups for this popular North Toronto eatery and its great food. Entrees $9-16. Mains include pizzas, pastas, veal, salmon, and chicken. 2373 Yonge St, north of Eglinton. (416) 488-0822, www.grazie.net. Italian.

29. Gretzky's. Lots of hockey memorabilia to gaze at while dining. Rooftop patio and a sports bar. The Gordie Howe Room houses Gordie's original 1947 Detroit Red Wings rookie sweater. Entrees $8-$25. Mains include perogies, ribs, pork, chicken, burgers, sandwiches, pizzas, salads, pasta, steaks, and seafood. 99 Blue Jays Way, just north of Front St West and the Skydome. (416) 979-PUCK, www.gretzkys.com.

30. Hernando's Hideaway. Voted #1 Mexican Restaurant by NOW Magazine in 1999. Entrees $7-30 (most under $15). Mains include nachos, salads, chili, burgers, sandwiches, tamales, quesadillas, fajitas, enchiladas, and wraps. 52 Wellington St East. (416) 366-6394. Mexican.

31. JJ Muggs. Entrees $7- 14. Very wide range of mains that's great for families with diverse tastes. Good spot for families. 500 Bloor St West at Bathurst St, (416) 531-8888, and 1 Dundas St West at Yonge St (in the Eaton Centre), (416) 598-4700.

32. Joe Badali's. Great interior brick walls, humungous ceiling height, and wood floors make for an endearing ambience. Entrees $7-26. Mains include salads, seafood, pasta, pizza, steak, pork, lamb, veal, and chicken. 156 Front St West. (416) 977-3064, www.joebadalis.com. Italian.

33. Il Fornello. Excellent $8.95 buffet lunch, although the choices are relatively limited. Mostly pizzas, pastas, salads. Other mains include seafood, chicken, veal, lamb, and steak. Voted best Italian Restaurant by Eye Magazine readers in 1998. Entrees $9-$18, except the $30 Angus Beef steak. 1560 Yonge St, a block north of St. Clair Ave (416 920-7347), 1968 Queen St West, east of Woodbine (416 691-8377), **Queen's Quay Terminal**, and 576 Danforth Ave (Greektown, 416 466-2931). General number (416) 861-1028, www.ilfornello.com. Italian.

34. Il Passione Italiana. Part restaurant, part market. Good Italian food at reasonable prices. Entrees $7-26. Kids' meal (under 10) is $5.50-6.95. Mains include salads, pizza, pastas, gnocchi, sandwiches, steak, and seafood. Take-out counter. 1423 Yonge St, just south of St. Clair Ave. (416) 966-3999. Italian.

35. Marche. Take a tray and wander the market for your dinner. Pick sumptuous foods from various stations in the amounts you want and they'll be prepared as you wait but moments. No entrees per se, as you mix and match your meal. Kids will love this place, as will you. Prices very reasonable: $7 for a bowl of Indonesian noodles and veggies, for example. Mains include spicy noodle dishes, pasta, seafood, pizzas, sausages, salads, and sushi. Wellington and Yonge St in the BCE Place. (416) 366-8986. A similar Marche is at the northeast corner of Front St West and John St in the Entertainment District.

36. McSorley's Wonderful Saloon. Outdoor patio. Stock-full of sports memorabilia. Eat peanuts and toss the husked shells on the floor for fun. Entrees $7-8, except steak ($17). Mains include chicken, salmon, stir frys, pastas, pork, shrimp, burgers, and salads. Great value. 1544 Bayview Ave, north of Davisville Ave. (416) 932-0655.

37. McVeigh's Irish Pub. They show all Celtic and Irish soccer games live via satellite ($15 for non-members, $10 for members). Entrees $7. Mains include Irish pub food and Thai food. 124 Church St. (416) 364-9698. Irish.

38. Montana's. Rustic cowboy interior. In the heart of the Entertainment District. Entrees $7-24. Mains include pizza, sandwiches, wraps, pasta, chicken, salmon, steak, and ribs. 145 John St, at Richmond south of Queen St. (416) 595-5949.

39. Movenpick. Bright and cheery ambience. Good food with large portions at reasonable prices. Quick and attentive service, with meals served piping hot even when busy. The fried eggs and bacon are served in a frying pan! Entrees $7-14. Mains include pasta, salads, burgers, beef dishes, seafood, sandwiches, omelettes, schnitzels, and rosti dishes. Delectable sweets menu including waffles with a huge bowl of fruit, crepes, torts, and tarts. 133 Yorkville Ave. (416) 926-9545. Swiss-Continental.

40. Mr. Greenjean's. Family restaurant with a view over Trinity Square. Salads come in a flower pot and servings are generally large. Entrees $8-19 and the kids menu only costs $5/meal with drink. Mains include salads, burgers, sandwiches, pastas, ribs, and steaks. Eaton Centre (Yonge and Dundas Streets). (416) 979-1212. American.

41. Nataraj Indian Restaurant. Voted best Indian restaurant in 2001 by Eye Magazine. Entrees from $7.50-$12.95 (one at $18.95). Mains include Tandoori dishes, lamb/chicken/beef dishes, shrimp dishes, rice dishes, and vegetable dishes. 394 Bloor St West. (416) 928-2925. East Indian.

42. Panorama. On the 51st floor of the Manulife Centre, providing a superb view south and north. Voted "Best Cocktails and Best View" by the Toronto Sun Newspaper and "Best Spot for a Romantic Date" by Now Magazine. Entrees $9-15. Mains include Thai beef satay, jumbo shrimp, salmon, nachos, pizza, and spring rolls. 55 Bloor St West, 51st floor. (416) 967-0000.

43. Penrose Fish & Chips. Pacific halibut only, and potatoes from PEI and Ontario. The décor is from the 50s, but so are the prices almost. Fish'n'chips go for $6.45, pop costs $1, and a slice of pie is $1.95. Black and white photos of Toronto in earlier years. Several times voted best in the city and district. Closed Sunday and Monday. 600 Mount Pleasant Rd. (416) 483-6800.

44. Saigon Palace Restaurant. Plain décor, but fast service and good food. Entrees $5-8. Mains include vermicelli and rice dishes, satay, and spring rolls. 454 Spadina Ave at the north end of Chinatown, just south of College St. (416) 968-1623. Vietnamese.

45. St. Louis Bar & Grill. Voted best wings in Toronto in 2001 by Now Magazine. Very popular, especially on ½ price wings Tuesday night. Kids can only eat on the outside patio, due to liquor licensing restrictions. Live entertainment at night. Entrees $7-$12. Regular daily Specials like 36 wings, fries, and 60 oz of beer for $22.95. Mains include wings, ribs, finger foods, chicken and beef sandwiches, and ribs. Live music every Thursday to Saturday. 2050 Yonge St at Lola Rd 3 blocks north of Davisville subway station. (416) 480-0202.

46. The Fish House. On the site of the now gone "Strachan Palace", where government troops amassed before setting off to quell the 1837 Rebellion. Entrees $7-23. Mains include salads, sandwiches, steaks, chicken, jambalaya, and of course all kinds of seafood. $6/child 11 and under for an entrée, drink, and ice cream. Kids also get a FREE pirate hat and tattoo. 144 Front St West at University Ave, just west of the Royal York Hotel. (416) 595-5051.

47. The Old Spaghetti Factory. Superb family restaurant, with lots of "eye candy" to keep the kids amused, including the shell of a streetcar. Entrees $9-$15. Mains include steak, pasta, chicken, seafood, and salads. Meal deals for $15-$17 include salad, bread, entrée, tiramisu dessert, and coffee/tea. The meal deal for kids 11 and under is $5.29-$6.99 and includes milk or pop and ice cream. 54 The Esplanade, southeast of Yonge St and Front St East. (416) 864-9761. Italian.

48. The Hot House Café. The Sunday brunch was voted the best in Toronto and it is indeed magnificent! $15/person, $7.50/children 5-10, and FREE for under 5. 35 Church St on Front St. (416) 366-7800.

49. The Loose Moose. Entrees $8-13. Mains include pizza, pasta, chicken, sandwiches, and shrimp. 146 Front St West, west of University Ave. (416) 977-8840.

50. The Keg Steakhouse. Dark, but pleasing décor. Dinner only. Entrees $17-30. Mains include steaks, ribs, chicken, fajitas, and seafood. 12 Church St (near the hopping Esplanade and St. Lawrence Neighbourhood) and 515 Jarvis St (in the historic Euclid Hall known as the "Mansion"). (416) 367-0685 (Church St), (416) 964-6609 (Jarvis St), www.kegsteakhouse.com.

51. The Sultan's Tent. Be entertained by a Moroccan belly-dancer while eating Moroccan food at this long-standing restaurant. A 4 course meal, including soup or salad, entrée, dessert, and coffee or tea costs $35.95 on Fri/Sat. Entrees include lamb, veal, and chicken. 1280 Bay St, north of Bloor St West, in Yorkville. (416) 961-0601. Moroccan.

For Breakfast

52. Senator Restaurant. This real 50s diner style restaurant complete with stools has been serving patrons since 1948. For $4.95, you get a bagel or toast with nice jam, small glass of real orange juice, and coffee/tea (with one free refill). For $8.95, you get bacon and eggs, toast/bagel, home fries, and coffee/tea for $8.95. Three blueberry pancakes with compote and maple syrup cost $9.25. A la carte breakfast choices include cereals and yogurt. Not inexpensive, but a great location just east of the Eaton Centre. 249 Victoria St, south of Dundas St East. (416) 364-7517.

53. PATH System. At Union Station where there is both a subway station and a train station, there are several spots to grab a coffee and bun, or other fast food: Cinnabon, mmmuffins, McDonald's, Second Cup, Country Style, The Bagel Stop, The Croissant Tree, Michel's Baguette, and Jugo Juice.

54. Golden Griddle. All Day Breakfasts from $4-7.50, or try the Weekday Morning Special. You get two eggs, large juice, bottomless coffee/tea, two strips of bacon or sausage or ham, two pancakes or hash browns, and Texas toast for $6.89. Breakfast options include omelettes, Belgian waffles, crepes, French toast, Benedicts, pancakes. Also serves lunch and dinner. Discount of 10% for over 55. FREE Kids Meal on Wednesdays. Open 24 hours. 11 Jarvis, at Front St kitty corner to the St. Lawrence Market. (416) 865-1263, www.goldengriddlecorp.com.

55. Maggie's. All day breakfast of 2 eggs, fries, toast, ham or sausage or bacon, and unlimited coffee and tea - $5.95. 400 College St, east of Bathurst St near Kensington Market. (416) 323-3248.

56. KOS. Named after a small Greek island, this aging 50s diner offers a "Super Special Breakfast" of 2 eggs, bacon or ham or sausage, home fries, and toast for $4. A refillable coffee is $1. Cereals with milk cost $2.25. 434 College St near Kensington Market. (416) 923-1868.

57. Jenzer's Deli. All day breakfast of 2 eggs, bacon, toast, small coffee/tea for $3.75 plus tax in the Sheraton Centre's underground food court (southwest corner of Bay and Queen St West). (416) 863-9929.

58. Mr. Souvlaki. $3.95 for 2 eggs with ham or sausage, pancake or toast, with home fries, juice, or coffee. In the Sheraton Centre's underground food court (southwest corner of Bay and Queen St West).

Fast Food

Basically, all the fast food places are here in Toronto, including: Arby's, Burger King, Harvey's, KFC, McDonald's, Mr. Sub, Subway, Swiss Chalet, Wendy's, and Mega Wrap. Downtown, many are on Yonge St from King to Bloor St.

Coffee Bistros/Shops

 The **Café Deli** is a pleasant spot offering deli sandwiches, pizza, salads, and bagels all under $6. It offers Breyer's ice cream during the summer and Reunion Island coffees via two separate parts of the store. **Queen's Quay Terminal**, Harbourfront.

A small sample of coffee bistros and shops include Coffee, Tea, or Me; Just Desserts; Second Cup; Starbucks; Tim Horton's; Timothy's; The Joy of Java, and Lettieri's. Most of these have many locations throughout Toronto. My favourite is Second Cup for its breadth of coffees (especially flavoured coffees) and in-store décor/furnishings (try the cozy one at the corner of Front St East and Church St in the beautiful St Lawrence neighbourhood).

ACCOMMODATIONS

The hotels below were chosen because of their fantastic downtown locations.
Rates are approximate and are for a room, single or double occupancy. Rates
vary significantly due to high vs. low season, promotions, number of beds,
need for pull-outs and/or cots, inclusion of breakfast or not, and so on. The
information below will give you a good preliminary sense of each hotel – it is
recommended that you then follow-up directly with the hotel. Remember, you
will be additionally charged 5% room tax and 7% GST tax on room charges
for all stays less than 30 days. Parking normally costs extra: $8-15/day.

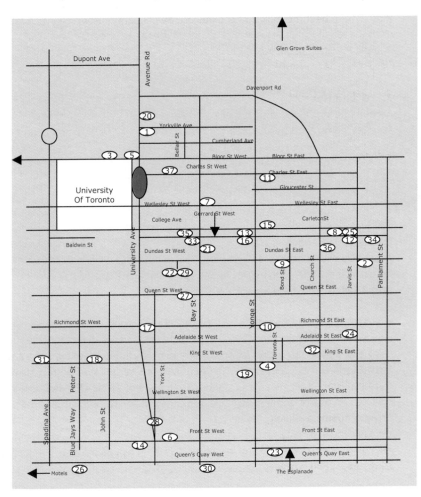

"Higher-end in-room services" means that a room generally includes an iron and ironing board, a hairdryer, AM/FM clock, color TV with remote control, telephone, one or two double/Queen/King beds, and ensuite three-piece washroom. Some may include bathrobes, FREE newspaper, computer data ports, more cable stations on the TV, and a sitting couch.

High-End

1. **Four Seasons.** Toronto's only CAA 5 diamond rated hotel. 380 rooms and suites on 32 floors. Hollywood stars routinely stay here. Anchors the west end of the upscale Yorkville area. Amenities are top-end, including "Just For Kids" where bedtime milk and cookies are available just from asking, health club, indoor/outdoor pool with sundeck, whirlpool, saunas, 2 restaurants, and 2 lounges. From $350/night. 21 Avenue Rd, just north of Bloor St West. (416) 964-0411, (800) 819-5053, www.fourseasons.com.

2. **Grand Hotel.** 177 rooms and suites, a 50' indoor pool, rooftop patio garden and whirlpool with city view, and a 5,000 sq. ft. fitness centre. Grand Deluxe Rooms are $149-$169/night and include a kitchenette and continental breakfast. The large sometimes two story Ambassador Suites are $499-$599 per night and include a full granite kitchen and complimentary breakfast. 225 Jarvis St. (877) 324-7263, www.grandhoteltoronto.com.

3. **Hotel Inter-Continental.** 208 rooms. Amenities include the usual high-end in-room amenities, marbled bathrooms, on-site restaurant and lounge, fitness centre, spa, and lap pool on the top floor with a south facing exterior pool patio with a great view. Rated number 1 out of all Inter-Continental hotels in the world. From $279/night. 220 Bloor St West. (416) 960-5200, http://hotels.toronto.interconti.com.

4. **King Edward/Meridien.** Built in 1903 by Toronto's richest man, George Gooderham of Gooderham & Worts Company, this venerable and elegant hotel has hosted overnight stays for many high profile people including John and Yoko Lennon, The Beatles, Pierre Trudeau, Jean Claude Van Damme, Richard Burton, Elizabeth Taylor, Rudyard Kipling, and Mark Twain. The hotel was selected as one of Conde Neste's 2001 Annual Gold List of Hotels. A wide array of rooms available. Amenities include high-end in-room services, spa, fitness centre, on-site restaurant and bar, but no pool. From $390/night, including a deluxe continental breakfast. 37 King St East, east of Yonge St. (416) 863-0888, www.lemeridien-kingedward.com.

5. **Park Hyatt (Regency).** 18 floors with 346 rooms averaging 500 sq. ft. Superb location near Yorkville and the ROM. On-site fitness centre and use of

its Bally Fitness Centre. A 10,000 sq. ft. Stillwater spa. Kosher kitchen available as a guest service. Popular with Hollywood stars during the **Toronto International Film Festival**. Great top floor lounge with view south over Toronto, but expensive. From $240/night. 4 Avenue Rd at Bloor St West. (866) 333-8881, www.hyatt.com/canada/toronto/hotels/hotel_torph.html.

6. The Fairmont Royal York. 1,365 rooms, though lower end rooms are smallish at 200 sq. ft. Amenities include high-end in-room services, fitness centre, spa, indoor lap pool and children's wading pool, saunas and steam rooms, on-site medical centre, small shopping plaza of 26 shops and services, on-site restaurants and bar, and connectivity with the **PATH** system (see Tour 2), **Union Station**, and the TTC subway system. The tallest building in Toronto until the 1960s. From $239/night. 100 Front St West, just west of Bay St. (416) 368-2511, www.fairmont.com.

7. **Sutton Place Hotel.** 294 rooms and suites on 33 floors. Amenities are high-end in-room services, an indoor pool, outdoor sundeck, sauna, fitness room, bar, restaurant, and beauty salon. Suites available for longer term stays. Popular with Hollywood stars during the **Toronto International Film** Festival. From $169/night. Fantastic discount with an Entertainment Card. Fee for parking. 955 Bay St at Wellesley St West. (800) 268-3790, www.suttonplace.com.

Moderate

8. **Best Western Primrose Hotel.** 341 recently renovated rooms, each about 300 sq. ft. Amenities include higher end in-room services, a seasonal heated outdoor pool, sauna, fitness centre, and complimentary newspaper. 111 Carleton St. From $99/night, including continental breakfast. Parking underground is $15/day. (416) 977-8000, www.torontoprimrosehotel.com.

9. **Bond Place Hotel.** 286 rooms, recently refurbished, and steps to the Eaton Centre (but no pool or fitness centre). Parking off site steps away. From $85/night. 65 Dundas St East. (416) 362-6061.

10. **Cambridge Suites Hotel.** 240 2-room suites on 20 floors. Amenities include in-room microwave and refrigerator, complimentary deluxe continental breakfast, a health club, use of a nearby club and racquetball facility, and an underground connection to the Eaton Centre and **PATH** system. From $160/night. 15 Richmond St East, near Yonge. (800) 463-1990, www.cambridgesuiteshotel.com.

11. **Comfort Hotel.** 108 rooms, newly renovated. Amenities include higher end in-room services (with fridges and microwave ovens in some rooms), but

no pool. From $99/night single/double occupancy, $10/night for each extra person, and $15/day for parking. 15 Charles St East, near Yonge and Bloor Streets. (800) 228-5150, www.choicehotels.com.

12. **Comfort Suites**. 151 suites on 7 floors. Amenities include higher end in-room services (with fridges and microwaves), indoor pool and whirlpool spa, fitness centre, and on-site restaurant and lounge. 200 Dundas St East at Jarvis St. (877) 316-9951, (416) 362-7700, www.toronto.com/comfortsuites.

13. **Courtyard by Marriott**. 575 rooms on 17 floors. Amenities include higher end in-room services, free coffee in the lobby, free newspaper, on-site lounge and restaurant, indoor pool, whirlpool, and exercise room. From $125/night. 475 Yonge St at College. (416) 924-0611, (800) 847-5075, www.courtyard.com/yyzcy.

14. **Crowne Plaza.** 586 rooms on 25 floors. Amenities include an on-site lounge and 2 restaurants, Canadian Duck down duvets, exercise room, pool, whirlpool, sauna, and spa. Kids' swim hours are limited to Mon-Fri 3 pm - 5 pm, and Sat/Sun 7 – 9 am. On-site parking is $30. A block away from the CN Tower, Skydome, and the Harbourfront. 225 Front St West, west of York St. From $159/night, including continental breakfast. (416) 597-1400, (800) 422-7969, www.sixcontinentshotels.com/crowneplaza.

15. **Days Inn.** 538 rooms recently refurbished, with small pool, sauna, and mini-fridges. From $110/night. Pets allowed at $20/day, with restrictions. $15 parking. 30 Carleton St, just east of Yonge St. (416) 977-6655 or www.daysinn.com. There are several Days Inn hotels in the Toronto area. The 50 room Days Inn at 1684 Queen St East is 3.5 miles to downtown and on the western border of The Beaches district. From $110/night, plus free parking. (416) 694-1177, www.daysinn.com/canada.

16. **Delta Chelsea.** 1590 rooms (43 with kitchenettes), pool, whirlpool, sauna, health club for guests 19 and over, laundry facilities, and babysitting services. Signature rooms from $169, and 2 bedroom suites from $505 and include full breakfast and parking. 33 Gerrard St West (just west of Yonge St). (800) 268-1133, www.deltahotels.com, www.deltachelsea.ca.

17. **Hilton.** 32 stories and 601 rooms facing north and south. Amenities include higher end in-room services, a part indoor/part outdoor pool, hot tub, sauna, fitness room, several restaurants and bars, and an underground connection to the **PATH** system. Best views from upper floors and rooms facing north. The west bank glass window elevators, almost hidden in the far northwest corner of the hotel, provide a superb view of the CN Tower, west harbour, Skydome, CNE grounds, and the Entertainment District. From

$139/night, including buffet breakfast (superb, but expensive at $18 if you had to pay separately). Parking costs $12 for 24 hours with in/out privileges if you have the hotel validate your parking stub. 145 Richmond St West, at University Ave. (416) 869-3456, (800) 445-8667, www.hilton.com.

18. **Holiday Inn on King.** 425 rooms. Nicely furnished rooms with the usual high-end in-room amenities. The **Canadian Bar and Grill** is on-site. Nice view of Lake Ontario from the south rooms on higher floors. From $150/night. 370 King St West. (800) 263-6364, www.hiok.com.

19. **Hotel Victoria**. 48 newly renovated rooms on 8 floors. Amenities include higher end in-room services, a pass to a local health club, and complimentary continental breakfast. From $105/night. 56 Yonge St. (800) 363-8228, www.toronto.com/hotelvictoria.

20. **Howard Johnson** (Yorkville). 69 rooms. Complimentary continental breakfast and newspaper and free parking but no pool. Check-in of 4 pm is later than most. From $129/night. 89 Avenue Rd, just north of Bloor St West and Yorkville. (416) 964-1220, (800) 654-2000, www.the.hojo.com.

21. **Marriott** (Eaton Centre). 459 rooms on 18 floors. Amenities include high-end in-room services, a pool on the top floor, whirlpool, sauna, health club, restaurants, and lounges. 525 Bay St, behind the Eaton Centre. From $149/night. (416) 597-9200, (800) 905-0667, www.marriotteatoncentre.com.

22. **Metropolitan Hotel**. 426 rooms and suites. Amenities include high-end in-room services, indoor pool, fitness centre, and restaurants. From $149/night, including breakfast. 108 Chestnut St, just north of City Hall. (416) 977-5000, (800) 668 –6600, www.metropolitan.com/toronto.

23. **Novotel** (Toronto Centre). 262 rooms. Amenities include higher-end in-room services, indoor pool, on-site restaurant and bar, Jacuzzi, and bike rack facilities. 45 The Esplanade, east of Yonge St, in the south part of the St. Lawrence neighbourhood. From $119/night. Parking is extra. Excellent value. (416) 367-8900, www.novotel.com.

24. **Quality Inn.** 196 rooms. Amenities include higher end in-room services and exercise room (but no pool). 111 Lombard St at Jarvis St. From $98/night, including continental breakfast and parking. (416) 367-5555, www.choicehotels.ca.

25. **Ramada Hotel & Suites**. 102 rooms newly renovated mid 2001, on 10 floors. Amenities include higher-end in-room services, indoor pool, fitness centre, and on-site restaurant and lounge. From $109/night, including

breakfast. 300 Jarvis St, south of Carleton St and across from **Allan Gardens**. (800) 567-2233, (416) 977-4823, www.ramada.ca/tordt.html.

26. **Radisson Plaza Hotel Admiral.** Amenities include higher end in-room services, an outdoor pool overlooking Lake Ontario, nearby squash court and whirlpool, and on-site restaurant and bar. From $119/night. 249 Queen's Quay West. (416) 203-3333, www.radisson.com/torontoca_admiral.

27. **Sheraton Centre.** Our personal favourite downtown hotel. 1,377 rooms with indoor/outdoor pool (in winter, kids just love swimming here when it's 25°F outside and the stars are twinkling above), hot tub, sauna, fitness room, Waterfall Gardens, and connection to the underground PATH system. A lounge on the 43rd floor with a superb view out of the almost floor to ceiling windows. Steps to everything. From $125/night. Parlor suites, Jacuzzi suites, and Presidential suites offer more and cost more. 123 Queen St West. (416) 361-1000, (888) 625-5144, www.sheratontoronto.com.

28. **Strathcona Hotel.** 194 rooms. Contemporary amenities and two restaurants. $75-129/night. 60 York St, north of Front St (and near Union Station). (416) 363-3321, (800) 268-8304, www.thestratchonahotel.com.

29. **Toronto Colony Hotel**. 739 rooms and suites, recently refurbished. Amenities include higher end in-room services, indoor and outdoor pools, fitness room, whirlpool, sauna, restaurants, bar, and dinner theatre. The Airport Express bus has a stop here. 89 Chestnut St, just north of City Hall. From $109/night, including executive breakfast and parking. (800) 387-8687, www.toronto-colony.com.

30. **Westin Harbour Castle**. 980 rooms on 35 floors, refurbished in 1999. Amenities include high-end in-room services, pool, tennis, fitness centre, hot tub, and on-site restaurants and lounges. Great views over Toronto **Harbour**, Islands, and downtown. From $155/night. 1 **Harbour** Square, at Bay St and Queen's Quay. (416) 869-1600, (888) 625-5144, www.starwood.com/westin/.

Budget

31. **Global Village Backpackers Hostel**. What a cool, funky place this is for budget-minded tourists! 185 beds, mostly in shared accommodations. Shared bathrooms, licensed "guests-only" bar and outdoor patio, a comfortable common area lounge, a kitchen available to all, and games room. From $23.50/night

in a dorm, $26/night for a quad, and $60/night for a private room. The weekly rate for any shared accommodation is $130! Discounts for people with a ISIC or HI card. 460 King St West at Spadina Ave. (416) 703-8540, www.globalbackpackers.com.

32. **Hostelling International.** 185 beds (family accommodations available). $25/night for non-members. 76 Church St, between King St East and Adelaide St East. (416) 971-4440, (877) 848-8737, www.hihostels.ca/hostels/Ontario/.

33. **The Bay Hotel.** Small budget hotel with 29 small rooms. Shared hallway bathroom with showers. In-room amenities are TV, hot and cold water sink, and central air conditioning. Needs refurbishment, but is conveniently located. Rooms are $60/night/single or $80/night/double, taxes included. Lower rates for week-long stays. 650 Bay St at Elm St. (416) 971-8383, www.baystreethotel.com.

34. **The Pembroke Guest House.** 50 rooms of shared accommodations near **Allan Gardens**. Fully furnished rooms with phones/TVs, microwave, fridge and ensuite bathroom. $100/week for students. 117 Pembroke St, south of Gerrard St East and east of Jarvis St. (416) 925-8456.

35. **The Residence.** Over 100 basically furnished rooms: bed, desk, chair, vanity, phone, sink, individual climate control. Each floor has one laundry room, one full kitchen, one TV lounge, and washroom facilities. There is a swimming pool, squash and tennis courts, and a gym. $55/single/night or $325/single/week. $95/double/night or $550/double/week. Parking separate. 90 Gerrard St West, west of Bay St near the Eaton Centre. (416) 351-1010, www.theresidence.net.

36. University of Toronto (On Campus)

Victoria University. Several parts of U of T offer accommodation during the summer from May 13 – August 24, 2002. Victoria University offers single and twin bedded rooms with fresh linen, towels and soap for up to 800 guests. Washrooms are shared and complimentary local telephone calls, laundry facilities and a complete breakfast are provided. An extraordinarily beautiful campus near Yorkville, Queen's Park, and Yonge St. $45/single/night, $65/double/night; $39/students with ID & seniors 65+/night, $57 for a twin. Check in is a late 4 pm. Advance reservations must be made by completing the "summer accommodation application" form (see website) and paying a deposit of one night. 140 Charles St West. (416) 585-4524. Email to accom.Victoria@utoronto.ca, or see www.vicu.utoronto.ca/accommodation/summer.htm. A map of the downtown U of T campus is available on www.osm.utoronto.ca/map/.

University of St. Michael's College. Rooms are available May 13 – August 17, 2002 in three dorms and four Victorian "Century" houses. Take the Victorian houses if you can. The whole campus is gorgeous and includes St. Basil's Church built in 1855. No air-conditioning. On-site "all you can eat" cafeteria offers meals from July 1- August 17. Rates are $22/single/night, $40/double/night, and for students/seniors with ID, $20/single/night and $34/double/night. The Sorbara Residence offers A/C and an in-room sink for an extra $5/night. $125 of deposits required with advance reservation (see website). Minimum 7 days, payment due in full at arrival. Parking separate. 81 Saint Mary St, west of Bay St south of Yorkville. (416) 926-7296, www.utoronto.ca/stmikes/sumres/.

Loretto College. Located in the north part of St. Michael's Campus, single and double dormitory style rooms are available during the summer. Single rooms have a sink in room but use common washrooms. Double rooms have a bathroom facilities attached. Lounges on the 3rd and 5th floors have a common use fridge. The lounge on the 4th floor has a common use fridge, TV, and VCR. No air-conditioning. 3 meals/day included in the rates, as are taxes. $250/single/week, $200/person for a double (shared) room/week for non students. $220/single/week, $175/person (double)/week for students with ID. Deposits of $225 due in advance, and the balance of payment due upon arrival. Reservations are made in advance by sending a completed "Summer Occupancy Agreement" and application (available on-line at their website), and deposit. All applicants must be 18 yrs old or older. No credit cards. Check in is 3–7 pm. 70 St. Mary St, south of Bloor St West, west of Bay St. (416) 925-2833, www.web.net/~loretto/index.html, and/or email to loreto.summer@utoronto.ca.

University College. University College offers summer accommodation for students and staff of colleges and universities. A beautiful campus with a free art gallery and minutes from Yorkville, the Eaton Centre, or the Entertainment District. "Spartan, but clean and comfortable study bedrooms" with a bed, chair, desk/dresser, bookcase, study lamp, and closet. Shared co-ed washrooms. $145/week for a single, $250/week for two. 73 and 85 St. George St. (416) 978-2530, www.utoronto.ca/ucres/,

Camping

Glen Rouge Campground. 87 serviced sites with 15 or 30 amp electrical and water, 27 unserviced sites, and 11 backpacker sites operated by the City of

Toronto. Full washrooms with showers. Service sites are $30/day, $189/week, and $718/month. Unserviced sites are $22/day, $138/week, and $526/month. Backpacker sites are $14/day. Kingston Rd east of the Port Union/Sheppard exit from Highway 401 in the Rouge Park. Open from Victoria Day to Labour Day. Call (416) 392-2541 for reservations, or www.city.toronto.on.ca/parks/.

Bed & Breakfasts

I've stayed in B&Bs around the world, but so far not in Toronto – just never got around to it! The Bed and Breakfast Association of Canada offers a superb website at www.bedsandbreakfests.ca with links to the websites of their members. Several are located in **Cabbagetown** and **The Village** in magnificent Victorian century homes minutes from the downtown epicentre. The 9-room Banting House, for example, is $85-110/night (an additional person is $15-20) and parking is free.

Motels

The following motels are right beside each other yards away from Lake Ontario and the Martin Goodman Trail, about 4 miles west of downtown.

Beach Motel. $75-115/night, double occupancy. 40 rooms. No swimming pool or restaurant on-site. 2183 Lakeshore Blvd West. (800) 830-8508, (416) 259-3296, www.ctdmotels.com/beach/.

Hillcrest Motel. $77-88/night, double occupancy. 45 rooms. No swimming pool or restaurant on-site. 2143 Lakeshore Blvd West. (416) 255-7711, www.kawartha.com/motels/hillcrest_motel.

North American Motel. $55-85/night, double occupancy. 35 rooms. No swimming pool or restaurant on-site. 2147 Lakeshore Blvd West. (877) 445-5273, (416) 255-1127, www.ctdmotels.com/northamerican/.

Other motels along this strip of Lakeshore Blvd West include Shore Breeze Motel [at 2175, (416) 251-9613)], Silver Moon Motel [at 2157, (416) 252-5051)], and Casa Mendoza Inn [at 2161, (416) 259-3756)].

Longer Term Stays

Glen Grove Suites. Furnished rooms and suites from $2,300 monthly. Daily and weekly stays available. Several locations including 7 King St West and 2837 Yonge St, two blocks south of Lawrence Ave. (800) 565-3024, www.glengrove.com.

SHOPPING

(approximate number of stores, restaurants, cafes, and services are identified in parentheses).

Downtown

Bloordale Village (100). See Tour 18. Bloor St West between Lansdowne Ave and Dufferin St.

Bloorcourt Village (150). See Tour 18. Bloor St West between Ossington Ave and Christie St.

Bloor St in the Annex (100). See Tour 18. Bloor St W between Spadina and Bathurst St. One of the most "happening" street scenes in Toronto.

Bloor West Village (200). See Tour 8. Bloor St West from High Park to South Kingsway. www.bloorwestvillage.com.

Bloor-Yorkville (300). See Tour 9. Toronto's "Rodeo Drive" with lots of fashionable, upscale stores. Bloor St from Yonge to Avenue Rd; Manulife Centre, Yorkville Ave, **Hazelton Lanes**, Cumberland Ave and the Cumberland Terraces, and the Holt Renfrew Centre. Superb lighting during winter, especially near the Christmas holidays. www.bloor-yorkville.com.

Chinatown East (75). See Tour 15. At the corner of Gerrard St East and Broadview Ave. www.riverdaletoronto.com.

Chinatown West (500). See Tour 3. Dundas St West from Beverly to Spadina Ave, and Spadina Ave from Queen to College Streets. Looks like a scene from Hong Kong – vibrant, colorful, busy, and full of Far East goodies like Durian fruit, lychees, and Peking Duck. Unfortunately the area is not as clean as most of downtown Toronto.

Corsa Italia (150). See Tour 18. St. Clair Ave West between Dufferin and Lansdowne. Nice touch with the streetlights and signs.

Eaton Centre (285). See Tour 3. With 50 million visitors per year, the Eaton Centre is considered to be the top tourist spot. A soaring overhead glass galleria with a flock of Canadian geese flying south is worth a look. The Yonge and Dundas Streets corner is a favourite spot for buskers (street performers). Open Mon-Fri 10am-9pm, Sat 9:30am-7pm, and Sun noon-6pm. The website offers a nifty store directory and locator. 220 Yonge St between Queen and Dundas Streets. (416) 598-8700, www.torontoeatoncentre.com.

Fashion District (225). See Tour 4. Spadina Ave from Wellington St to Queen St West. East along Queen St to Peter St, and west along Queen St.

Goodwill. Donated clothes cleaned for resale to raise funds for the Goodwill charity. 234 Adelaide St at Jarvis St. Mon-Fri 9am-6pm, Sat 9am-6pm, and Sun noon-5pm. (416) 366-2083. www.goodwill.on.ca.

Harbourfront Antique Market. 40,000 square feet of a variety of antiques from Royal Doulton to Militaria to Stamps/Coins to home furnishings and more. Open Tue – Sun 10 am – 6 pm year round. 390 Queen's Quay West. (416) 260-2626, www.hfam.com.

Hazelton Lanes (45). See Tour 9. Part of the **Bloor-Yorkville** area, Hazelton Lanes is an upscale boutique mall with primarily fashion and fashion accessory stores, restaurants/cafes, and an outdoor skating rink in winter. Mon-Sat 10am-6pm (Thur 10 am-7 pm), and Sun noon-5 pm (selected stores only). 52 Avenue Rd on Yorkville, north of Bloor St West. (416) 968-8602, www.hazeltonlanes.com.

Hillcrest Village (300). See Tour 18. St. Clair Ave West between Bathurst and Dufferin Streets.

Little India (40). See Tour 15. Gerrard St East between Greenwood and Coxwell. One of North America's largest Indian markets. www.indo.com or www.riverdaletoronto.com.

Kensington Market (150). See Tour 3. Kensington St between Dundas St West and College St. Lots of very small shops packed in a few blocks on narrow streets. Colorful and flavorful. Unfortunately, not as clean as most of downtown Toronto.

Leslieville (100). See Tour 15. Queen St East between Logan and Connaught. Where people from the Hollywood North "Studio District" like to lunch. Look south on Pape Ave to see the entrance to the 9 acre Toronto Film Studios complex that bills itself as Canada's Largest Film Studio Complex. www.riverdaletoronto.com.

Little Italy (200). See Tour 5. College St between Euclid and Shaw Avenues. A major night scene, with the many restaurants and clubs. There are also about 100 stores along College between Kensington Market and Euclid Ave.

Little Korea (125). See Tour 18. Bloor St West between Christie St and Euclid Ave.

Manulife Centre (45). See Tour 9. 55 Bloor St West between Yonge and Bay Streets. Anchor stores include William Ashley, Birks, Indigo Books, and Jacob. Has a Cineplex Odeon (movie) Theatre. Upscale shopping, part of **Bloor-Yorkville**. (416) 923-9525.

Mount Pleasant (75). A lovely ½ mile long strip of stores, restaurants, theatre, and services set among a mid-Toronto residential area. This is antiques central with 14 fine antique stores: Fyfe's at 553, Aklados at 558, WHIM at 561, Nadia's at 581, The Store at 588, Whimsey at 597, McLean Ribbehegge at 604, Sharon O'Dowd at 606, Nastri's at 609, Acanthus at 612, Andrew Richens at 613, Horsefeathers at 630, Bernandi's at 699, and Loreng at 701. Other interesting stores include George's Trains at 510, Quilter's Quarters at 595, T. Bear's Den at 594 for all teddy bear things, The Pottery Place at 602 ($25 +tax to make your own ceramic), and the Little Dollhouse Company at 617. You can grab a bite to eat at the popular Chick'n'Deli at 746 or at **Penrose Fish & Chips** at 595. Mount Pleasant Ave between Davisville Ave and Eglinton Ave East.

North Toronto (500). See Tour 19. Yonge St between Davisville Ave and Blythwood Rd, south of Lawrence Ave. Tons of interesting places including Ten Thousand Villages at 2599 Yonge, a non-profit organization that sells Third World artisan handicrafts and ploughs any profits into food, housing, health care, and education.

PATH (400). See Tour 2, and/or "ATTRACTIONS, General".

Queen's Quay Terminal (upscale touristy). See Tour 6. The original warehouse built in 1926 was designed by New York architects Moore and Dunford in the Art Deco style. It was transformed with $60 million into today's beautiful Queen's Quay Terminal. Almost 40 shops, restaurants, and services including Il Fornello's, Boathouse Bar & Grill, Café Deli, Dollina, Harris Gallery, Premiere Dance Theatre, Toy Terminal, YNK Notables, and First Hand Canadian Crafts. 207 Queen's Quay West, at the foot of York St. Take TTC streetcar 509 or 510 from Union Station or walk down the three blocks. (416) 203-0510, www.queens-quay-terminal.com.

Queen Broadview Village (100). See Tour 15. Queen St East between the Don River and Empire Ave, with the highest concentration at Broadview Ave.

Queen St West (150). See Tour 3. Eclectic, with a lot of fashion stores. Queen St West from University Ave to Spadina Ave. The stores continue west of Spadina Ave in the Fashion District.

The Bay. Part of Canada's oldest corporation, founded in 1670, almost 200 years before the founding of Canada. A shopping mall in one store, with 10 floors of just about everything you can imagine. Also houses the "Don't Miss" **Thomson Gallery**, the **City View Café**, the Bay Street Bar and Grill, and the Arcadian Court Restaurant. 176 Queen St West at Yonge St, directly south of (and interconnected with) the Eaton Centre. (416) 861-9111.

The Beaches (200). See Tour 12. Queen St East from Woodbine Ave to Scarboro Beach Rd. A fabulous street scene all year round, but over the top in summer. www.thebeaches.com.

Yonge-Lawrence Village (250). See Tour 19. Yonge St between Lawrence Ave and Yonge Blvd, the original northern boundary of Toronto city proper.

Yonge-St. Clair (200). See Tour 18. Yonge St between Rosehill Ave and Heath St West.

Yorkville. See **Bloor-Yorkville**.

Large Suburban Shopping Malls (within Toronto)

The parentheses indicate the approximate number of stores, restaurants, services, and the like.

Bayview Village Shopping Centre (100). Sheppard Ave East and Bayview Ave. Anchor stores are Roots, Chapters, and Loblaws. Mon - Sat 9:30 am – 9 pm, Sun 11 am - 6 pm. (416) 226-0404, www.bayviewvillageshops.com.

Centrepoint (100). Yonge St and Steeles Ave West. Anchor stores are The Bay, Loblaws, and Canadian Tire. Mon-Fri 10 am-9 pm, Sat 9:30 am-6 pm, and Sun noon - 5 pm. (416) 222-6255, www.centrepointshops.com.

Don Mills Centre (120). Anchor stores include Sears and Dominion. Don Mills Rd and Lawrence Ave East. Mon-Fri 10 am – 9 pm, Sat 9:30 am-6 pm, and Sun noon - 5 pm. (416) 447-5511, www.donmillscentre.ca.

Eglinton Square (85). Anchor stores are The Bay, Dominion, and Shoppers Drug Mart. Eglinton Ave East and Victoria Park Ave. Mon-Fri 10am-9pm, Sat 9:30am-6pm, and Sun noon-5pm. (416) 757-3762, www.eglintonsquare.ca.

Fairview Mall (270). Anchor stores are Sears and The Bay. Sheppard Ave East and Don Mills Rd. Mon-Fri 10 am – 9 pm, Sat 9:30 am – 6 pm, and Sun 11 am – 6 pm. (416) 491-0151, www.fairviewmall.com.

Scarborough Town Centre (230). Anchor stores are The Bay, Wal-Mart, Sears, Old Navy, and Famous Players Theatres. Hwy 401 between Brimley and Progress Avenues. Mon-Sat 10 am - 9 pm, Sun 11 am - 6 pm. www.scarboroughtowncentre.com.

Yonge-Eglinton Centre (60). Anchor stores are HMV, Indigo, and Dominion. Northwest corner of Yonge St and Eglinton Ave West. There is also a Famous Players Silver City Theatres (movies) and food court. Connected underground to the Yonge subway line. Mon-Fri 10 am - 9 pm, Sat 9:30 am - 6 pm, and Sun noon - 5 pm. (416) 489-2300, www.yongeeglintoncentre.com.

Yorkdale Shopping Centre (200). Almost 1.9 million sq. ft. of stores! Anchor stores are The Bay, Holt Renfrew, Eaton's, Sears, and Harry Rosen. 3401 Dufferin at Allen Expressway and Hwy 401. Mon-Fri 10 am - 9 pm, Sat 9:30 am -9 pm, and Sun 11 am-6 pm. (416) 789-3261, www.yorkdale.com.

Other

If you're looking for computer stores, there are 11 on one block of College Ave, from Spadina Ave to Augusta Ave.

If you're looking for antiques, try **Mount Pleasant** with its 11 antique stores over a few blocks, or Yonge St between Marlborough and Woodlawn Avenues (see Tour 19) with 6 antique stores over a few blocks.

SPORTS and ACTIVITIES

Beaches

Most large urban centres aren't blessed with super beaches, notwithstanding Honolulu, Los Angeles, and a few others. Toronto has several beaches with fair to good sand and good to excellent amenities. Most people don't swim in the water because it is too cold. Periodically, swimming is forbidden due to high bacteria counts. All beaches are FREE.

Eastern Beaches

Rouge Beach Park has very good clean and firm sand that at one point is 80 yards wide. The relatively shallow Rouge River empties into Lake Ontario at the eastern end of the Beach. Washroom facilities, a water fountain, and parking by the nearby marsh (good for bird-watching). If you take the pedestrian bridge over the river, you come to a boardwalk-like path that travels under a rail bridge. It is quite a sensation to stand there and see the undercarriage of the GO and VIA trains zooming by 10 feet overhead. The approximately 30 feet elevation also provides a better bird's eye view of the beach and marsh. Take the Don Valley north to Hwy 401 east to Port Union Rd south to the end of Lawrence Ave East.

Woodbine Beach Park and Ashbridge's Bay beaches have good to very good golden sand and superb facilities. Outstanding beach volleyball, playground for kids, food concessions, covered picnic areas, boardwalk, paved biking and rollerblading path, BBQs (bring your own charcoal), and tons of mature trees and grassy areas. A lovely paved path can be taken to a scenic lookout over Lake Ontario and by the Ashbridge's Bay Yacht Club marina. My favourite beach. Along Lakeshore Blvd East between Coxwell and Woodbine Avenues.

Beaches Park also has superb facilities like Woodbine Beach Park, but the sand is more pebbly. Instead of beach volleyball, Beaches Park has the Summerville outdoor pool. Eastward extension of Woodbine Beach Park, at the foot of Woodbine Ave and Lakeshore Blvd East.

Kew Gardens is my favourite! Not for the beach, but for the park and amenities. The eastward extension of Beaches Park, running south from Queen St East between Lee and Waverley Streets. See Tour 12.

Harbour Beaches

Hanlon's beach, on the western end of Toronto Islands, is a "clothing optional" beach. Not the greatest sand or beach but fairly private behind a sand dune covered by woods. Good view of Ontario Place, the western beaches, and of the many small aircraft taking off and landing at Toronto Island airport. Take the ferry to Hanlon's Point, walk south a few hundred yards, and look for the unmarked paths through the wooded sand dunes to your right.

Toronto Island Pier beach. Fair sand, with the swim area protected by break walls. Unencumbered view looking south over Lake Ontario. Nearby amenities include food, lockers, bike rentals, a water fountain, a lookout pier, and lots of grassy areas with mature trees and picnic facilities.

Clarke Beach Park is commonly known as Cherry Beach Park as it is at the southern end of Cherry St in the Port of Toronto lands south of Lakeshore Blvd East. The beach is a large, wide expanse of fair to good sand overlooking the Outer **Harbour** Channel and its myriad of sailboats and windsurfers. A good view of the Leslie St Spit and Tommy Thompson Park that is based entirely on landfill from downtown and other construction excavations. A fast food truck, washrooms, water fountain, and FREE parking are the amenities.

Clarke Beach

Western Beaches

Sunnyside Park. Fair sand, with the swim area protected by breakwalls. The Sunnyside Pavilion and outdoor pool here is a better choice. Amenities include a boardwalk, paved biking/rollerblading path, the Sunnyside Pavilion courtyard, a restaurant and nearby food concession, and lots of grassy areas and mature trees for picnics. A scene from the Whoopi Goldberg movie, "What Makes a Family", was shot here.

Swimming

Toronto has 72 indoor and 53 outdoor public swimming pools, and many outdoor saucer style wading pools for kids. My favourite outdoor pools include **Summerville** on Lakeshore at Woodbine Ave (for its view over the Beaches), Riverdale Park on Broadview south of Danforth Ave (great for families), and Gus Ryder Sunnyside on Lakeshore Ave West at Parkside (right by the beach). Call the general pool hotline (mid June to Labour Day) at (416) 392-1111 or see www.city.toronto.on.ca/parks/recreation_facilities/swimming/.

Professional Sports

Toronto is very well represented in professional sports with the Toronto Maple Leafs, Toronto Raptors, Toronto Blue Jays, Toronto Argonauts (football), Toronto Rock (lacrosse), and the Toronto Lynx (soccer). The Leafs, Raptors, and Rock play at the Air Canada Centre. The Blue Jays and Argos play at the Skydome. The Lynx play at Centennial Stadium.

Your chances of getting Leaf hockey tickets without going to a ticket scalper are slim, but you can try www.ticketmaster.ca. You may have more luck in getting Raptor tickets by calling 416-366-DUNK (3865) or www.raptors.com. Tickets to the Argonauts, once the home of Doug Flutie and Joe Theisman, can be more readily obtained at $12-42 for adults, and $8-37 for seniors and students. (416) 489-ARGO (2746), www.argonauts.ca. Rock tickets cost $18-$40/seat or $50 for a family of 2 adults/2 children under 17. (416) 872-5000, www.torontorock.com. Lynx tickets cost $5-15 per seat and children 6 years and under are FREE. (416) 251-4625, ext. 31, www.lynxsoccer.com.

Recreational Biking, Walking, and Rollerblading

On-street biking is relatively common in Toronto. The City has added many bike-only lanes on several major roads and over 7,000 "post-and-ring" bike parking posts. See www.city.toronto.on.ca/cycling/bikeplan.htm for the expansion plan and latest progress. The most pleasant place to leisurely bike is on the Toronto Islands. You can rent a bike at Toronto Island Bicycle Rental. (416) 203-0009.

Toronto has many walks (see the "Tours" section), several trails for biking, and two major trails for rollerblading. If you're going to take your bike on the TTC, please note that the TTC allows bikes on their subways, buses, and streetcars in the non rush hours between 9:30 am - 3:30 pm and then again after 8 pm. All trails are FREE.

1. Martin Goodman Trail West. Start at Yonge and Queen's Quay West. The trail goes west about 10 miles to Mississauga (and then onward). The west trail is not great for rollerblading between Yonge and Bathurst Streets. The west trail goes past **Harbourfront**, the **Music Garden**, Coronation Park, the **Canadian National Exhibition**, the **HMCS Haida**, **Ontario Place**, Marilyn Bell Park, the Boulevard Club (where the Americans landed before their attack on Fort York), **Sunnyside Park** and **Pavilion**, Sir Casimir Gzowski Park, **High Park**, the Sheldon Lookout and *Palace Pier Monument*, Colonel Samuel Smith Park, and Marie Curtis Park before reaching Mississauga. The trail from the Lakefront Promenade Park (Lakeshore Road, east of Cawthra Rd) to Port Credit is outstandingly beautiful! FREE.

2. Martin Goodman Trail East. The trail goes east about 6.5 miles to Balmy Beach. It goes by the **Redpath Sugar Museum**, *Bill Wyland mural*, "tent city", **The Docks**, **Clarke Beach Park** (windsurfing heaven),

Ashbridge's Bay, **Woodbine Beach**, the boardwalk, **Summerville Pool**, **Beaches Park**, **Kew Gardens**, Balmy Beach, and Queen St East in the Beaches. Even though this stretch tends to go through industrial lands that were to be redeveloped as part of Toronto's 2008 Olympic bid, the trail is very popular especially from Ashbridge's Bay eastward. It also facilitates hooking up with the Don Valley Path, noted below, and doing the Leslie St Spit trail in Tommy Thompson Park. FREE.

3. Leslie Spit/Tommy Thompson Park. At the southern end of Leslie St, south of Lakeshore Blvd East. A park and bird sanctuary built on landfill from downtown and other construction excavations. Basically a road, it is very flat and about 4 miles return. Weekends only. FREE.

4. Don Valley Path. You can walk, bike, or rollerblade this path from the foot of Cherry St on Lakeshore Blvd about 5 miles north until you reach Seton Park/Taylor Creek Park. The whole way is a lovely 8-10 foot wide pavement and virtually flat. The Don River, named in 1793 after the Don of Yorkshire, England, is near or adjacent to the path. You'll pass by several unused bridges, the **Don Jail**, **Riverdale Farm**, the Bloor St viaduct (subway), the **Don Valley Brickworks**, Crothers' Woods for mountain-biking/hiking, the Toronto Police Dog Training Centre, the Leaside bridge, lots of wooded areas and meadows, and, lastly, the "Elevated Wetlands", several 20 foot high containers of shredded tires and plastics supporting wetland plants. See "Toronto Adventure Trail" under Mountain Biking/Hiking below if you want to continue on; otherwise, retrace your steps and return to the starting point. FREE.

5. German Mills Settlers Park Trail (Easy). A nice 1.8 mile return trip ride through the East Don River valley and parks. Starts on John St, 100 yards west of Don Mills Rd, and ends at the top of Leslie St. If you follow Leslie St south for 0.6 miles, you'll reach the trailhead of the Betty Sutherland Trail (see Trail #7). FREE.

6. German Mills Creek Trail (Easy). About 8 scenic miles in the East Don River valley and parks, with 8-10 foot wide pavement the whole way. Take the subway up to Finch station and transfer to the eastbound Steeles Ave East TTC bus 53 to Leslie St (about 45-60 minutes trip). The trailhead starts about 0.3 miles south of Steeles Ave East on the west side of Leslie St, and heads mostly south until you reach the intersection of Sheppard Ave East and Leslie St. FREE.

7. Betty Sutherland Trail (Easy). You'll see the hospital on the southeast corner. Cross over to this corner and follow Sheppard Ave East for about 50 yards and turn right or south back onto the trail. It goes under the 16

lane mega Hwy 401. Other than the first 50 yards or so, it's a paved path through parkland along the Don River. You'll end at Duncan Mills Rd – a few yards to your left (east) is Don Mills Rd. Take southbound TTC bus 25 to York Mills and transfer to the westbound TTC bus 95 to the York Mills Subway Station. Take a southbound train back downtown. Or backtrack and return to your starting point. FREE.

8. The Belt Line Trail (Easy going southbound). About 9.6 miles return trip, but I would suggest just going one way. Start at the north end of Old Park Road, east 2 blocks of the Eglinton Subway Station on Eglinton Ave West. Follow the trail east, then southeast. The trail is wide and firm and runs through Eglinton Way, upper Forest Hill, Mount Pleasant Cemetery, Moore Park, and just past the Don Valley Brickworks Park. At this point, you can join the Don Valley path (see Trail #4) or ride up the hill to Bloor St and the Castle Frank Subway Station (about 0.3 miles) and take the westbound Bloor train to the Bloor-Yonge Subway Station and transfer to the southbound train back to Queen St. FREE.

9. Taylor Creek Park Trail. (Easy). About 7 miles return trip. Start at the trailhead on Don Mills Rd, on the first right north of the Don Valley Parkway. Follow the road on the right under the Don Valley Parkway to a parking lot and the trailhead is off to the left. When you get to Victoria Park Ave, turn left or north to Donside Rd. Follow Donside east to Pharmacy Ave, then right or left to Prairie Drive Park. The trail winds north through Warden Woods Park: turn around before you each St. Clair Ave East. Return to your starting point or grab the westbound train at Victoria Park Subway Station just to the south. FREE.

10. The Rosedale/Moore Park Trail (easy going southbound). About 3.4 miles return, but I suggest taking the trail one way. Start at Yonge and St. Clair Subway Station. Go east to Avoca Ave and turn south to David Balfour Park. The trail starts a few hundred yards south at the edge of the woods. It is a beautiful, wooded ravine trail that goes through Moore Park and Rosedale. At this point, you can join up with the Don Valley Path (see Trail #4) or turn right to Craigleigh Park and cycle south 0.4 miles through very upscale Rosedale to the Sherbourne Subway station. FREE.

11. The Rosedale Valley/Cedarville Trail (easy). About 3 miles return. Start at Yonge St and Collier Park Rd, two blocks north of Bloor-Yonge Subway Station. Follow the trail along the wooded Rosedale Valley Rd to Bayview Ave where it ends. To your right on the hill is the **Necropolis Cemetery** where some of Toronto's most influential people are buried. FREE.

12. <u>Ivan Forrest Gardens Trail (Easy)</u>. About 1.3 miles return trip in the Beaches district. A narrow strip of valley greenery with lovely homes on the tablelands. Start at Queen St East at Glen Manor Dr where the trail starts with lovely flower gardens and a small waterfall. Walk north, under the wooden pedestrian bridge, across and north along Glen Manor Dr East until you reach the "Nature Trail" sign. This trail winds its way through grand old red oak, black cherry, witch hazel, American Beech, white pines and sugar maple trees. Log benches provide resting spots. The most northerly part of the trail has a steep climb up to Kingston Rd. FREE.

Mountain Biking and Hiking

The best and most rugged trails in Toronto are in the heavily wooded **Rouge Park**. It is North America's largest urban park at over 11,600 acres –New York City's famous Central Park is 843 acres by contrast. The Don Valley trails are the next best. Call The Ontario Cycling Association at (416) 426-7416 to check out trails outside of the Toronto area.

The Rouge Park Trail

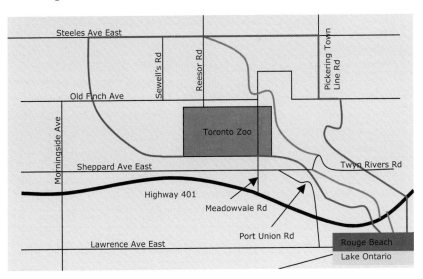

A trail, or technically a few trails pieced together, goes from Steeles Ave East (Toronto's northern city limit) down to within 100 yards of the shore of Lake Ontario. I've separately identified each part of the trail for those who may wish to do the trail in parts over time, or who only want to do part of the trail.

Part I (about 2 miles one way – moderate to difficult)
Start at Woodlands Park at Steeles Ave West and Reesor Rd. Park your car and look for the trail along the river. This is true mountain-biking territory as the trail wanders in and out through thick forest and bush, mostly along the riverside (see picture). The trail will come to a rail overpass, which you will have to carry your bike under. NOT for families or beginners. Bring water and a cell phone with you in case you get lost, as there are very few houses or businesses in the vicinity until you reach Meadowvale Rd.

Part II (about 2 miles one way - moderate)
Most people will want to start here or at Part III. Park on the side of the road near the fairly noticeable trailhead on Meadowvale Rd, 1 mile north of the entrance to the Toronto Zoo. This trail is called the Orchard Trail and runs south from Meadowvale Rd. If you mountain biked Part I, the trailhead will be on your left, past the bridge once you "surface" from the previous trail.

This trail is much easier to follow, in spite of several lateral trails. You will soon come to dirt stairs up the side of the valley to the tablelands. Continue on the tablelands (there'll be a farmer's field off to your left some of the way) until you reach a spot with a log seat. Follow the trail down and over the small creek and back up the other side to a large meadow area with a railroad track and hill off to your left. This "hill" used to be Toronto's garbage dump!

Follow the trail to your right as it is now a dirt access road sandwiched between the meadow and the edge of the forest. You will come to a paved road, which is the Beare Landfill Access Rd. That building off to your left is an electricity plant that uses methane gas emanating from the dump! Cross the road and continue on the trail to the right (or west side) of the small pond and dam and back into the forest. This is a lovely part of the trail, as it descends back down into the valley and along the meandering Little Rouge River. You will come out onto a major paved road known as Twyn Rivers Rd. If you want out, turn right and follow the road for about 1 mile to Sheppard Ave East, catch westbound TTC bus 85 to McCowan, transfer to southbound TTC bus 129 to the McCowan LRT station, and take the LRT/subway to Bloor-Yonge.

Part III [about 1.5 miles one way – easy (two moderate climbs)]
When you come out on Twyn Rivers Rd, turn right for about 0.2 miles and you'll see the Riverside trailhead off to the left in the elbow of the road as it makes a sharp right turn. This part of the trail is technically for hikers only (you can walk your bike), as it climbs to a ridge covered in old growth forest. The 7 foot wide, fairly flat trail ends at the Glen Rouge Park parking lot just north of Kingston Rd and Hwy 401. If you came by car and want to start the trail at Part III, you can park on the side of the road near the trailhead and/or at the park parking lot about 0.5 miles further east along Twyn Rivers Rd.

Part IV (about 1 mile one way –mostly easy. Hiking only)
The trailhead is at the most southeastern corner of the Glen Rouge Park parking lot, near the large bridge. The trail goes under the Kingston Rd bridge and the Hwy 401 bridges along an access road to a storm pond. Look for a two-foot wide footpath off to the left of the access road near the western end of the storm pond. The first few hundred yards are relatively difficult to hike, especially after a rain, due to the steep cross-grade of the hill. Follow the path through heavily wooded bush along the beautiful Rouge River and you can imagine the Indians who once canoed along here. This path ends in a marsh of cattails beside the river, just 50 feet of shallow water away from the lovely Rouge Beach Park, one of Toronto's nicest beaches.

Rouge Park Trail

The Don Valley Trails

1. Crothers Woods (moderate; some difficult spots)
One of the best trails (1.5 miles return) in Toronto starts at the foot of Pottery
Rd at Bayview Ave, less than 4 miles from Yonge and Queen Streets. Drive on
Queen St East to Bayview Ave and turn north to Pottery Rd. An unmarked
driveway by the railroad tracks leads to a grass clearing where you can park
FREE. Clubs use this trail frequently during summer weekends. The trail

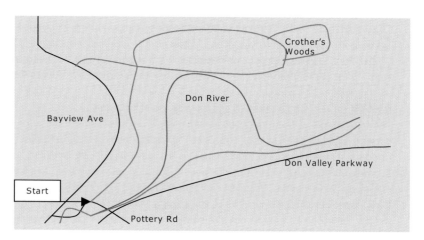

starts with a fork: take the right trail as it is more scenic and avoids a short
but very steep uphill climb. Both trails join again. Follow the trail, staying on
the left, past 100 year old white and red oaks, sugar maples, crabapple, green
ash, sumac, and basswood trees. Negotiate the bike ladder and 10 foot high
embankment before reaching a pea gravel/dirt path. Turn right for a few
yards and then turn left along a smaller pea gravel/dirt path. Follow this for
about 150 yards, keeping your eye open for a barely noticeable gap in the
bush on your left. A few logs laid in the muck to help cross a seasonal creek
confirm you have the right spot. Go up through this and you'll reach a
noticeable trail. Turn right and follow it until you reach an intersection of
paths anchored by a sign warning bikers of "Steep Hills – Use at Own Risk".
Take the middle path and stay on the right when you come to forks. You'll
shortly come back to the pea gravel/dirt path. As it is basically a circle, you
can take it right or left, but left is shorter and runs along the Don River.

As always, wear protective gear and take care! Try a different trail if you're
with the family or just walk it. My kids, aged 10 and 12, found parts too
difficult and I completely snapped my collarbone in half on this trail.

If you're itching for more nearby, you can 1) take the left fork at the trail intersection mentioned above; 2) join the Don Valley bike path just past the bridge on Pottery Rd, maybe 50 yards away from you parked; or 3) cycle down Bayview Ave for 0.3 miles to the **Don Valley Brick Works** on your right. Besides the very short Brick Works trails, you can connect with several miles of trails that run north and south called the Belt Line Trail.

2. The Belt Line Trail (easy to moderate). This 8.5 mile return trip trail goes through the valley, Mount Pleasant Cemetery, over Yonge St, and northwest to Eglinton Ave along a converted railway track. A wide, mostly flat, packed earth trail that is quite popular.

Crother's Woods

3. Toronto Adventure Trail (about 10 miles one way – moderate).

I call this trail, or rather a series of contiguous trails I've pieced together, "adventure" for the reasons that 1) you may lose the trail in several spots; 2) some parts of the trail are vigorous; and 3) the trail is fairly long. A regular bike will work, but I recommend a mountain bike. Start at Yonge and Queen Streets and travel to the foot of Yonge St. Note the sidewalk inscription honoring Yonge St, the longest street in the world, and a plaque honoring "Captain John" and his floating restaurant. The Toronto Star, Toronto's largest circulation newspaper, is headquartered on the northeast corner. Turn left or east along Queen's Quay East and follow the **Martin Goodman Trail** (identified with markings on the street) past the **Redpath Sugar Museum** and factory, and the *Bill Wyland Mural*, to Lakeshore Blvd. Turn right for 0.3 miles to Cherry St. On the northeast corner of Lakeshore Blvd and Cherry St is the start/end of the Don Valley trail as it meets the Martin Goodman Trail. Follow the Don Valley trail as it heads north along side the Don River past several defunct bridges from the 1900s, the **Don Jail**, the **Riverdale Farm**, and the Rosedale Viaduct at Bloor St. Watch a subway crossing under the viaduct's road surface every few minutes. Soon you'll pass the eastern edge of the tony Rosedale and Moore Park neighbourhoods, **Don Valley Brickworks**, the historic **Todmorden Mills Heritage Museum** site, and Crother's Woods area (see Mountain-Biking). Next, you'll cross *under* a bridge and see the **Elevated Wetlands**. Stay on your left and cross *over* another bridge, and traverse to the far end of a small parking lot. This path heads slightly uphill for a short distance until you reach a pedestrian bridge.

Cross the bridge and follow the left path to the bottom of the short hill and then turn right into the parking lot. You've just covered about 5 miles from the Cherry St start. Continue on northward along the road through Seton Park and you'll join up again with the walking/biking path. You'll pass very wooded areas and the **Ontario Science** Centre, until you reach another parking lot with a very steep hill to the road (Eglinton Ave East). Don't climb the stairs... continue on westward to the other end of the parking lot and a road will take you under Eglinton Ave East (easier than climbing up and then down) into Serena Gundy Park. Follow this road and turn right or north at the second right onto a 10 foot paved path at the confluence of two rivers. Follow this path north until you reach the key point, a small path heading off to the left. You can tell for sure if you follow this path and come to a small bridge over the Don River within moments. If you can't find it, retrace your path back to the Sunnybrook Park road (the only one), and follow it west until you reach the Central Don or Sunnybrook Riding Stables (i.e. the shortcut).

You now have three choices from the key point: a) the west path to Yonge St and Lawrence Ave; b) the north path to Bayview Ave and York Mills Rd; or c) the northwest path to York University's Glendon College and the Granite Club.

a)   West Path to Yonge St and Lawrence Ave East (about 10 miles one way – moderate difficulty).

Cross over the bridge and follow the now dirt path uphill to a gorgeous picnic spot and table among tall sugar maples and pines. When you're done, follow the path uphill through a forest dominated by oak, maple, beech, ironwood, witch hazel, and trillium and wild ginger flowers. Ignore the many smaller side trails and you'll come to an "intersection" with a park sign. Follow the path now known as "The Thomas H. Tomson Nature Trail" left (not straight ahead – you'll know you took this path if you come to a point where you can see the backs on some houses) that terminates at the 8th parking stall of a FREE parking lot. Exit the parking lot and follow the road for about 0.6 miles past the rugby fields to the Central Don or **Sunnybrook Riding Stables**.

The first right past the stables takes you over a bridge into a very small parking lot for maybe 10 cars. The path picks up to the left through a "dog-run-free-zone" for about 150 yards. Don't follow the road up the hill, but rather, look for an opening in the forest to your right just near a small marsh area with bulrushes. Follow this dirt path through another beautiful forest, along a tributary to the Don River, past the Sunnybrook Hospital and Canadian National Institute for the Blind way up on the cliff-tops, until you come to a steep embankment and Bayview Ave. Cross this busy 4 lane roadway and you'll spot the well marked path trailhead on the other side. If you want out, take southbound TTC bus 11 on Bayview Ave back to the Davisville Subway Station via "South Bayview" (see Tours) and a 15 minute subway ride back downtown. Otherwise, delve back into the 100 acre forest known as Sherwood Park and you'll shortly come to a boardwalk over some sloppy wet areas. It will take about 30 minutes to get through Sherwood Park and you'll see black walnut, mulberry, weeping willow, hemlock, white pine, sumac, oak, ash, beech, ironwoods, maples, and many other tree species. You'll also see lots of joggers and people walking their dogs, and glimpses of some pretty nice homes and properties abutting the park. Stay on your right throughout and you'll come to a nature trail (!) amid 100 year old oaks that is about 100 feet above the main trail and abuts some of Toronto's richest properties. The nature trail runs parallel to, and eventually joins, the main trail. Note that the main trail is a dogs-run-free zone, complete with doggie drinking fountains! Cross Blythwood Rd and follow the path off to the left. You'll skirt by Lawrence Park, another well-to-do Toronto neighbourhood, before it veers off to the left and under the Mt. Pleasant Ave bridge. You can stay on the main path out in the open, or you can take the parallel path a few yards to the right through the woods. Either way you'll pass the Lawrence Park Lawn Bowling and Tennis Clubs before reaching the exquisite landscaped Alexander Muir Gardens. Benches and a drinking fountain provide a good resting spot after the long walk or bike ride, while you watch the many wedding couples taking their photos here. Yards west is Yonge St, south of Lawrence Ave. Walk north one block and you'll reach the Lawrence Subway Station for a quick 20 minute ride to downtown. Or, if you have energy and time left, there is fantastic shopping, window-shopping, restaurants, pubs, cafes, stores, and people watching to be done on Yonge St south to Eglinton Ave (see Tour 19).

b)   North path to York Mills Ave and Bayview Ave (2.5 miles one way – easy).

Instead of turning left at the key point, continue on the main path until you reach popular Edwards Gardens. Take the trail right to come out in the Edwards Gardens parking lot. But it is easy to spend some time (walking only) in Edwards Gardens that is immediately to your left and down the small hillside. An extraordinarily landscaped oasis of trees, flowers, geese and duck ponds, dam and waterfall, rock gardens, water fountains, greenhouse, and the Teaching Garden.

Cycle to the north exit of the parking lot. Crossover Lawrence Ave East, follow Banbury Rd to Post Rd, and turn left. The trail starts at the end of this very short road. Follow this heavily wooded trail (don't worry about the side trails – this is a narrow strip of park and the side trails mostly all rejoin with the main trail) and you'll pop out into the groomed and grassy Windfields Park. Continue on this path, past the workout stations and enormous homes, turn left at the bridge, and you'll shortly come to York Mills Arena and the York Mills/Bayview intersection.

If you're tired, take westbound TTC bus 95 back to York Mills Subway Station at Yonge St, and take a southbound subway back downtown. The TTC will allow bikes on the subway, buses, and streetcars from 9:30 am – 3:30 pm and after 8 pm when it's not rush hour. If you are up for a little more (about 1.8 miles return), bike a couple of hundred yards north on Bayview Ave to a parkette on your left. Cycle over the grass … it looks like the parkette ends by the fence, but there is a 15 foot wide path that enters St. Andrew's Park at the northwest end. Follow the path through St. Andrew's Park and you will surface on Toba Dr, only 0.3 miles from Hwy 401! Take TTC bus 78 back to York Mills Subway Station or cycle north on Toba Dr, west on Montressor Rd to Lord Seaton Dr to Upper Canada Dr, and south on Upper Canada Dr to **Saint John Cemetery**.

Buried here is Joseph Shepard, a Loyalist who came to Canada in 1774 and was one of the earliest settlers in Lansing (Yonge St and Sheppard Ave). His home built in 1835 still stands at *90 Burndale Ave*. It is one of the last buildings associated with the Rebellion of 1837 that is still standing. Also buried in Saint John's are William Mercer, a Loyalist and one of the earliest settlers in the York Mills area (Yonge St and York Mills Rd, and James Hogg, another early York Mills area settler).

Continue south (Upper Canada changes names to Old Yonge St) until you reach York Mills Rd. The York Mills Subway Station is (downhill) 0.3 miles to the west. Take the southbound subway back to your starting point.

c)   North path to Bayview and Lawrence Avenues (about 0.7 miles one-way – moderate).

From the key point, follow the same trail to Sunnybrook Stables as mentioned in option a) above. From the Sunnybrook Stables, cross the bridge just to the west, go through the small parking lot and look on your right for a narrow trial heading north along the grass. This part of the trail is technically "no bikes". I've either walked my bike or just carried it the short 0.7 miles. This shortly becomes a formal 8 foot wide trail along the beautiful West Don River valley and up to York University's Glendon College. You'll know you're at Glendon College when you see a bridge over the river. Follow the path all the way and you'll reach a parking lot and a clump of College buildings within a very wooded valley. A few yards north and you'll reach Lawrence Ave East (no, it doesn't cross Bayview Ave to the west). Adventurers might be inclined to try the trail that starts at the very western end of Lawrence Ave East. This part of the trail goes west and northwest under the Bayview Ave bridge into heavily wooded land. Only about 0.7 miles return, but you won't know you're in Toronto!

BMXing and Skateboarding

Cummer Skateboarding Park. A great "park" just for skateboarding, BMXing, and trick rollerblading. Includes a half-pipe, bowl, jumps, climbs, and grind poles. Southwest corner of Cummer Ave and Leslie St. FREE.

Helicopter Rides

Helicopters are lots of fun to ride and provide unprecedented bird's eye views. I believe they are best to use in seeing difficult to reach or inaccessible spots like in Hawaii. Toronto is a relatively flat and easily accessible urban area with a number of vantage points from tall buildings, including the CN Tower. For those of you who still wish to fly:

The Helicopter Company Inc. Toronto Island Airport. $85/person for a group of four for the "City Tour 1" (flight time of 6-8 minutes). Rates are higher for a smaller group booking and/or for the longer "City Tour 2". Take TTC streetcar 509 from Union Station to Bathurst St, and walk south one block. You'll have to take the ferry across the 100 yard wide channel - the price includes the cost of the ferry to the Island Airport (normally $30/car). Open year round during daylight hours. (416) 203-3280, toll free from the US at (888) 445-8542, www.helitours.ca.

Rock Climbing

Joe Rockhead's Climbing Gym. Indoor simulated rock climbing using contoured high walls with finger-grips. Experienced rock climbers can test their skill on the overhangs and across the ceiling. Another great spot for both kids and adults. Rates are $14/adult, $11.50/student with ID, $8 for kids 10 years and under. 29 Fraser Ave, near Dufferin and King Streets. (416) 538-7670, www.joerockheads.com.

Toronto Climbing Academy. Indoor simulated rock climbing using contoured high walls with finger grips. Caves, overhangs, and more for the adventuresome or experienced. 100-A Broadway Ave near Queen St.

$12/adult, $10/student with ID, $8/child under 12 years. $5/day to rent harness equipment and shoes. (416) 406-5900, www.climbingacademy.com.

Boat Cruises

Toronto is blessed to be located on Lake Ontario and to have an excellent and scenic harbour. The water is relatively clean and smell-free. The boarding dock for the following cruises is on the promenade south of **Harbourfront**, a few yards west of the **Queen's Quay Terminal**. As they are basically beside each other, it may be just as easy to just show up and pick the cruise boat that's to your liking and budget. Excellent views of the skyline, harbour, and islands. Take westbound TTC streetcar 509 or 510 from Union Station.

Toronto Boat Cruises. Take a sail through the harbour and Toronto Islands aboard the 165 foot tall ship Kajama. In June, the ship boards at 3 pm and returns at 5 pm. In Jul, Aug, and the first few days of Sept until Labour Day, the ship boards at 11:30 am, 1:30 pm, and 3:30 pm, returning at 1:30 pm, 3:30 pm, and 5:30 pm respectively. $18.95/adult, $16.95/senior, and $10.95/child. (416) 203-2322, www.greatlakesschooner.com.

Toronto Tours Ltd. 1 hour cruise of the harbour and Toronto Islands. $23.75/adult, $19.75/seniors, $9.75/child 2-12. Open Apr–Nov. 145 Queen's Quay West, at the foot of York St. (416) 868-0400, www.harbourtours.com.

Mariposa. 1 hour cruise of the harbour and Toronto Islands. $15.50/adult, $14/seniors 65+ and students, and $10.50/child 4-12. Plus tax. May 15 - Sep 30. (416) 203-0178.

Seaflight Hydrofoils. Boarding at the quay just past Radisson Plaza Hotel Admiral or at the end of Polson St near **The Docks** entertainment complex. (416) 504-8825, (877) 504-8825, www.seaflight2000.com.

Other boat cruises include City View Cruise Lines (416-573-2162), Musique Aquatique Cruise Lines (416-410-0536), and Jubilee Queen Cruises (416-203-7245).

Fishing and Ice Fishing

Canadian Trophy Fishing. Lake Ontario is a popular fishing spot for salmon, especially during the $1,000,000 Great Ontario Salmon Derby held in July and August. They also take people out on the water to view the International Air Show and/or the **Symphony of Fire Fireworks Festival**, and ice fishing trips to Lake Simcoe. Harbour boat slip S15 at Bluffers' Park. Kingston Rd and Brimley Rd. (416) 386-0084, www.cdntrophyfishing.com.

Canning's Fish Hut Company (Outside Toronto). 1hour from Toronto on Lake Simcoe. Open 7 days a week when the ice is safely frozen. $25/person, except on Saturday when it's $30/person. ½ price for kids. Minets Point, Barrie. (705) 721-8500.

Burd's Trout Fishing (Trout Pond Fishing Outside Toronto). 45 minutes from Toronto. RR2, 13077 Hwy 48, Stouffville. Pay by the pound for fresh trout caught. (905) 460-2928.

See www.fishontario.com for additional information on fishing and ice-fishing.

Windsurfing

Windsurfing at Clarke Beach. Bring your own windsurfer, park for FREE, walk across 200 feet of sand beach, and put your board in the water. This is a favourite spot for windsurfers, as well as sail-surfers. At the foot of Cherry St, south of Lakeshore Blvd. Washroom facilities and a food truck available on site. Bring and use all required safety gear, including lifejackets.

Windsurfing and Kite Surfing
at Clarke Beach

You can try taking an introductory member lesson for $25 at the Toronto Windsurfing Club (board supplied). The end of Regatta Rd, south of Unwin Ave (which runs east off Cherry St). (416) 461-7078.

Canoeing/Kayaking

Harbourfront Canoe and Kayak School. Periodic 5½-hour day trips offered for canoes ($40 plus GST) and kayaks ($75 plus GST). Equipment provided. In and around Toronto Harbour and Islands. You can also rent a 15' or 16' fiberglass canoe for three people for $15/hr or $40/day. 283A Queen's Quay West, just west of the Radisson Plaza Hotel Admiral. (416) 203-2277, (800) 960-8886, www.paddletoronto.com.

Go-Karting

Centennial Park Mini Indy Go-Karts. This outdoor 1.25 mile go-kart track is a great spot for kids and adults. There is a mini track for kids under 10, as well as batting cages. Open 10 am – 10 pm, from spring to the end of Oct. Rates are $4/lap, $16/5 laps, or $25/8 laps. 575 Centennial Park Blvd, near Hwy 427 and Burhamthorpe Rd. (416) 620-6669.

401 Mini-Indy Go-Karts. Short and flat indoor track for Indy-style go-karts. Open Mon - Fri noon – 5 pm, Sat - Sun noon – 10 pm, but call before as they sometimes close for corporate functions. Membership is $5/person. Rates for 10-15 year olds are $8 for 10 laps or $15 for 20 laps. Rates for adults are $13.50 for 10 laps and $20 for 20 laps. Children must be >54" and 10 years old. Amenities include a games room and small food concession. 37 Stoffel Dr near Hwy 401 and Martin Grove Rd, south of Dixon Rd. (416) 614-6789.

Skiing, Snowboarding, and Snowtubing

Uplands Golf & Country Club & Ski Centre (Public). 9-hole golf course, downhill skiing, cross-country skiing, snowboarding, and nature trail. This spot is popular with beginners as the vertical is only 110 feet. Six slopes. Tobogganing and the nature trail are FREE. $17/day/adult Tues-Fri, $25/day/adult during weekends and holidays. Downhill and snowboarding equipment rentals are available and are $15/day on Tues-Fri ($16/day for snowboarding) and $22.50/day on weekends and holidays. You can't beat the $39 tax included snowboarding or skiing lesson with a three-hour lift ticket and rental equipment included. Open Tues-Sun. The City of Vaughan's Winterfest in February is often held here. 46 Uplands Ave, Thornhill, Ontario, just 0.5 miles south of Hwy 407. Take the TTC to Finch Subway Station, transfer to the GO bus station, and take GO bus "C" up Yonge St to Uplands Ave. (905) 889-3291, www.uplandsgolfandski.com.

North York Ski Centre in Earl Bales Park (Public). Skiing/snowboarding on three intermediate slopes, one beginner slope, with a double chair lift and one rope tow. The vertical is 130 feet and the longest run is 800 feet. Equipment rentals and a snack bar on site. Open Dec 15 - Mar 17. Cost is $7/day for a rope tow, or $21/day/adult over 19, $19/day/child 5-18, and $7/child under 5. Family passes available. 4199 Bathurst St, south of Sheppard Ave. Take TTC bus 160 from Wilson Subway Station north along Bathurst St to Raoul Wallenberg Rd and walk east to The Ski Centre. Earl Bales Park. (416) 338-6754, www.city.toronto.on.ca/parks/recreation facilities/skiing.

Centennial Park Ski Hill (Public). Skiing and snowboarding with a lift and tow rope. The vertical is 130 feet and the longest run is 500 feet. Equipment rentals and a snack bar on site. 8 hr rental of complete ski equipment rental is $21. Open Dec 15-Mar 17. $21/day/adult over 19, $19/day/child 5-19, and $6/day/child under 5. 256 Centennial Park Rd. West on the Gardiner Expressway to Hwy 427, north to the Renforth Dr West exit. Follow Renforth Dr north to Centennial Park Gate. By TTC, take the Anglesey 2 or 2A bus via the Royal York Subway Station.

Outside Toronto. For those of you who want to include some more serious skiing, snowboarding, and snowtubing as part of your trip to Toronto, some pretty decent skiing, snowboarding, and snowtubing can be found 1-2 hours north of Toronto in the Barrie and Collingwood areas. Collingwood's Blue Mountain Resort has among the highest verticals in southern Ontario at 720 feet, with the longest run being 4,000 feet. Open Dec 22 - Mar 17. Night lift rates, from 4:30 pm – 10 pm is $29/adult and $22/student or senior with ID. Day lift rates are more expensive. (705) 445-0231, www.bluemountain.ca. Snow Valley just west of Barrie and about 1 hour north of Toronto is a ski resort with fantastic snowtubing for the whole family. Long, more horizontal rides and shorter, straight down rides for the adrenaline junkies who would like the up to 50 mph speed. Cost is $12 for 6 rides or $3/ride. Kids under 42" can only use the non-lift "mini-tube" area. www.skisnowvalley.com. See www.skiontario.on.ca for other skiing facilities. (705) 721-7669.

Basketball/Volleyball

YMCA. Day passes cost $12-15 for access to basketball/volleyball courts, pool, weight room, and jogging track. 20 Grosvenor St. (416) 928-9622.

The Docks. Indoor volleyball (see "ATTRACTIONS"). 11 Polson St. (416) 469-5655.

Woodbine Beach/Ashbridge's Bay. Great summer volleyball in the sand by the beach. Coxwell Ave and Lakeshore Blvd. Bring a volleyball.

Skating

Toronto is loaded with almost 100 great and mostly FREE skating spots. The following are skating spots you can easily walk to from your downtown hotel. See www.city.toronto.on.ca/parks/recreation_facilities/skating for information on 100 other skating rinks.

Nathan Phillips Square (City Hall). Outdoor skating with skate rentals, washrooms, snack concession, and underground parking. Skating guards on patrol. Spectacular at night when the "10,000" Christmas lights are on. Can get crowded, especially on nights like New Year's Eve. 100 Queen St, west of Yonge St. FREE.

Barbara Ann Scott (College Park). Outdoor skating. Lockers, heated change area, and underground parking available. Skating guards on patrol. Located at College Ave and Yonge St on the south side of College Park. FREE.

Ryerson (Devonian Square). Outdoor skating. Skating guards on patrol. Heated change area. Kids love to skate around the 15 foot high granite rock slabs. 25 Gould St at Victoria St, one block north of Dundas St. FREE.

Natrel Rink (Harbourfront). Perched a few feet away from Lake Ontario, this rink in the Harbourfront Centre offers skate rentals and sharpening, an indoor heated change room, and food/drinks at Lakeside Eats. Open 7 days a week from 10 am – 10 pm. Take TTC streetcar 509 or 510 from Union Station or walk the ten minutes from Union Station. Harbourfront Centre at 235 Queen's Quay West beside the duMaurier Theatre Centre and Power Plant. FREE.

Snowmobiling

Snowmobile Tours offers a 3 hour introductory program as well as 5 hour and full day tours. Machine, snow attire, helmet, gas, and a tour guide are provided. Open 7 days a week during winter. $150/adult plus tax and kids 12 and under ride FREE on the back. Training provided. (800) 298-2979, www.cctours.com. If have your own snowmobile, call the Ontario Federation of Snowmobile Clubs at (705) 739-7669 or see their website www.ofsc.on.ca.

Horse Racing

Woodbine Race Track. Standardbred and Thoroughbred racing, and 1,700 gambling machines. 50% of pari-mutuel wagering in Canada happens here. FREE parking. 555 Rexdale Blvd at Hwy 427, near the Pearson International Airport. (888) 675-7223, (416) 675-7223, www.woodbineentertainment.com.

Running/Long Distance Walking

Runners Choice Runs. This series of runs starts in early April, and has runs on May 5, July 19, September 15, and October 13 in 2002 in Toronto. Runs range from the waterfront marathon to 5 km walk & run. Part of the proceeds are donated to various charities such as the Marvelle Koffler Breast Centre of Mount Sinai Hospital. www.runnerschoice.com, (416) 250-7700, ext 120.

The SuperCities Walk. Held in late April, these 5 km or 10 km walks raise funds for the Multiple Sclerosis Society of Canada. Held in E.T. Seton Park and Taylor Creek Park. www.supercitieswalk.com , (888) 822-8467.

The **Martin Goodman Trail**, the Don Valley trails, and most of the Discovery Walks are also excellent for running and walking.

Golf

Citycore Golf. Open all year. 9-hole 3 par, plus 3 tiered driving range ($0.35 per minute, minimum 20 minutes). 2 Spadina Ave. (416) 640-9888.

Don Valley Golf. Par 71, 6,109 yards. A lovely public course set in the Don Valley is surrounded by lush vegetation and the meandering Don River. $49/adult and $31/seniors during the weekend. About 10% lower on weekdays. William Carson Cr off Yonge St, between York Mills Rd and Hwy 401. (416) 392-2465, www.city.toronto.on.ca/parks/recreation_facilities/. This website provides details on the other 4 public golf courses in Toronto.

Tennis

One of the biggest events in Toronto's tennis world is the Rogers and AT&T Cup (Women) at the National Tennis Centre at York University (on Steeles Ave West, west of Keele St). Mid-August for 9 days every second year (next one in Toronto is in 2003). www.tenniscanada.com for tournament information. If you just want to play with the rackets you brought with you, call the City of Toronto at (416) 392-1111 for information on over 200 public tennis courts.

Horseback Riding

Call the Ontario Equestrian Federation at (416) 426-7232 for information. Within Toronto, Sunnybrook Stables Ltd offers riding lessons in beautiful Sunnybrook Park for people 9 years old and up. Four week introductory courses are $210 plus 7% GST. (416) 444-4044.

Dance

The National Dance of Canada offers a single dance class for only $11 (tax included)! Just walk up and in – no pre-registration or special clothing or shoes required. Classes are for all age groups. Kids aged 9-13 have jazz and hip hop classes just for them every Sunday at 1 pm (also for only $11). 2 Gloucester St, 4th floor, right at Yonge St. Open 7 days/week. (416) 923-2623, www.92dance.com.

Gambling

On the way from Buffalo, you can gamble at Casino Niagara, or at Casino Windsor on your way from Detroit. Must be 19 years of age to even enter the Casinos. Casino Niagara has 135 table games and 2,700 slots and Casino Windsor has 100 table games and 3,000 slots. See www.casinoniagara.com, www.casinowindsor.com, or "**Horseracing**" for further information.

Laser Tag

LaserQuest. Seek and destroy your opposition by shooting a laser gun at their vest and registering the "hit". Played in an indoor facility with obstacles, darkness, music, and strobe lights. Minimum 7 years old. $7.50/person per game. Open Tue-Thur 6pm – 10 pm, Fri 4 pm-midnight, Sat noon-midnight, and Sun noon – 8 pm. 1980 Eglinton Ave East, just east of Warden Ave. (416) 285-1333, www.laserquest.com.

Paintball

Sgt Splatters. Self-billed as Canada's largest indoor paintball arena, this 35,000 sq ft large converted warehouse's play area looks like a bombed out urban area with buildings, abandoned vehicles, walls, 15 tons of sand bunkers to hid in and behind. $29.95/person for up to 4 hours of playtime, a gun, one tank of CO_2 propellant, goggles, arm band, and 100 paintballs. Half-price all day Monday and Tues-Fri 10 am -4 pm. Only $5 if you own your equipment, protective gear, and paintballs! 54 Wingold, west of Dufferin St, 3 stoplights south of Lawrence Ave West. (416) 781-0991. www.sgtsplatters.com.

Paintball City. 20,000 sq. ft. indoor play area. $20 for 1 hour, $25 for 2 hours, and $30 for 3 hours. Rates include goggles, gun, CO_2, 100 paintballs, protective vest, expert instruction, and on-field referee. Coverall rental is an extra $5. Open 7 days, 24 hours with reservations. Sunday night 7 pm –10 pm is no-reservation, walk-in night. 37 Stoffel Rd. Take Hwy 401 to Dixon Rd, go west to Kelfield Dr, turn left, and again left onto Stoffel Rd.

(416) 245-3856, www.paintball-city.com.

Bowling

Newtonbrook Bowlerama. 5 pin and computerized 10 pin scoring, bumper bowling for the kids, shoe rentals, food concession, and games room. 5837 Yonge St just north of Finch Ave. (416) 222-4657, www.bowlerama.com.

HOLLYWOOD NORTH

Movie Locations

Toronto has a bustling movie and television industry. In 2000 alone, there were 238 productions in Toronto. It can be lots of fun visiting spots where parts of movies and television episodes were taped, mostly for FREE! You can check out the favourite restaurants of big Hollywood stars visiting Toronto. In most cases, people have no clue that a certain scene was filmed in Toronto as Toronto is often portrayed to be an American city in the film. Some movies filmed in Toronto, the key star(s), and some location(s) include:

Movie or TV	Key Star(s)	Location
Ararat	Directed by Atom Egoyan	**Clarke Beach Park** east parking lot
Bait		Flatiron building and Berczy Park
Canadian Bacon	John Candy, Alan Alda, Rhea Perleman, Jim Belushi, Dan Ackroyd	**CN Tower**, **Queen's Park**, CNE's Princes' Gates, Leslie Spit
Cheaters	Jeff Daniels	Central Tech High School
Christmas in my Hometown	Tim Matheson, Gordon Pinsent, Travis Tritt	**Gooderham & Worts Distillery**
DeGrassi Junior High	Michelle Goodeve	Centennial College, The Beaches
Fiona (TV)		300 Bond St, near **Eaton Centre**
Foreign Objects	Arsinee Khanjiian	Scarborough bluffs
Full Contact Fighter Show		Florida Jack's at 782 Yonge St
Garbage Picking Field Goal Kicking Philadelphia Phenomenon	Tony Danzi, Chris Berman, Dan Dierdorf	Skydome

Movie or TV	Key Star(s)	Location
Honeyland		Bayview Glen Church (Steeles Ave East at Bayview Ave)
It's Always Something (The Gilda Radner Story)		Toronto St, at Court St
Kahiladiyon Ka Khilad (Indian film)	Various	**Nathan Phillips Square**
King of Kensington	Al Waxman	**Kensington Market**
La Femme Nikita (TV)	Peta Wilson, Roy Dupuis	University of Toronto (The Faculty Club); **Gooderham & Wort Distillery**
Leap Years (TV)		Adelaide St East at Church St, Steele Valley Rd and Arnold Ave in Thornhill
Loser	Jason Biggs	Central Tech High School
Maximum Risk	Jean-Claude Van Damme	Future Shop, Sam the Record Man, Sunrise Records, Zanzibar Strip Club
Moonstruck	Cher	Centro Trattoria & Frommago (1221 St. Clair St West)
Police Academy 4	Steve Guttenberg	Woodbine Centre
Relic Hunter (TV)	Tia Carrera	Philosopher's Walk, **Gooderham & Worts Distillery**
Robocop	Peter Weiler	The Canary Restaurant
Santa Who?	Leslie Nielson	Metro Hall, Woodbine Centre, **RC Harris Water Filtration Plant**
Serendipity	John Cusack, Molly Shannon, Eugene Levy	**Gooderham & Worts Distillery**
Shining Time Station (TV)	Ringo Starr	Union Station
Short Circuit 2	Fisher Stevens, Michael McLean	The World's Biggest Bookstore
Silver Streak	Gene Wilder, Richard Pryor	**Union Station**

Movie or TV	Key Star(s)	Location
Sinkhole		Market St at Front St
Street Legal (TV)	Sonja Smits, Erik Peterson	280 Queen St West
That Old Feeling	Bette Midler	Holy Trinity Church (Thornhill), Campeau Mansion (Post Rd area), **Royal York Hotel**
The Blues Brothers 2000	Dan Ackroyd, John Goodman	The Canary Restaurant
The Defenders	Beau Bridges	Premier's office, **Queen's Park**
The Freshman	Marlon Brando, Matthew Broderick	**Union Station**
The Hurricane	Denzel Washington	**Old City Hall**
The Pretender (TV)		**RC Harris Water Filtration Plant**
The 6th Day	Arnold Schwarzenegger	**Eaton Centre**
The X-Men	Patrick Stewart, Halle Berry	**Gooderham & Worts Distillery**, **Casa Loma**
Tommy Boy	Chris Farley, David Spade, Dan Ackroyd	BCE Place, University of Toronto (University College), **Gooderham & Worts Distillery**
Tuxedo	Jackie Chan	**Skydome**

Other popular filming locations include the **King Edward Hotel** at 37 King St East, **St. Paul's Anglican Church** at 227 Bloor St East, and **Spadina House** at 285 Spadina Rd. You may also catch a glimpse of your favourite star at the following hotels in the Bloor St/Avenue Rd area: The Four Seasons Hotel, The Hyatt Regency, Hotel Intercontinental, and The Windsor Arms Hotel. A significant amount of "on location" and studio filming is done in Leslieville's Studio District by groups like the Barenaked Ladies (see Tour 15).

Some other movies and TV shows at least partly filmed in Toronto include:

Movie or TV	Key Star(s)
Amazon (TV)	Carol Alt, Margot Kidder
American Psycho	Christian Bale, Wilem Dafoe
Ararat	Arsinee Khanjiian
Blues Brothers	John Belushi, Dan Ackroyd
Crash	James Spader, Holly Hunter

Movie or TV	Key Star(s)
Darkman	Liam Neeson
Death to Smoochy	Robin Williams
Death Wish V	Charles Bronson
Due South (TV)	Paul Gross
Earth: The Final Conflict (TV)	Kevin Kilner, Robert Leeshock
E.N.G. (TV)	Sara Botsford, Mark Humphrey
F/X: the Series (TV)	Cameron Daddo
Goosebumps (TV)	R.L. Stine
Kung Fu, The Legend Continues	David Carradine
Ladies Man	Tim Meadows, Will Ferrell
Made in Canada (TV)	Rick Mercer, Peter Keleghan
Moonstruck	Cher, Nicholas Cage
Night Heat (TV)	Scott Hylands, Tony Rosato
Prom Night	Leslie Nielson, Jamie Lee Curtis
Strange Brew	Rick Moranis, Dave Thomas
The Fly	Jeff Goldblum
The Red Green Show (TV)	Steve Smith, Patrick McKenna
The Royal Canadian Air Farce (TV)	Don Ferguson, Luba Goy,
Three Men and a Baby	Tom Selleck, Ted Danson
Traders (TV)	Sonja Smits, Patrick McKenna

Comedians

You might think Canada produces nothing except oil, wood, snow, and comedians! The following is a list of famous Canadian comedians, who were born in Toronto and/or worked a lot in Toronto's comedy venues (The Second City being number one), and a few of their well-known movie/TV credits:

Well-known Movie/TV Credits	Comic's Name
-The Jiminy Glick Show, Father of the Bride, SNL, SCTV	Martin Short
-Austin Powers, Saturday Night Live, Wayne's World, Shrek, Mystery Alaska	Mike Myers
-Honey, I Shrunk the Kids, SCTV, The Flintstones, Little Giants	Rick Moranis
-The Blues Brothers, Sgt Bilko, The Coneheads	Dan Ackroyd
-Grace Under Fire (TV), SCTV, Strange Brew	Dave Thomas

Well-known Movie/TV Credits	Comic's Name
-Canadian Bacon (sheriff), SCTV, Uncle Buck, Planes, Trains, and Automobiles, Cool Runnings	John Candy
-Father of the Bride ("Habib"), SCTV, American Pie, Ladies Man, Almost Heroes	Eugene Levy
-Home Alone (mother), SCTV	Catherine O'Hara
-The Tom Green Show	Tom Green
-Whose Line is It Anyway?, This Hour Has 22 Minutes	Colin Mochrie
-The Mask, Pet Detective, Me, Myself, and I.	Jim Carrey
-Saturday Night Live	Phil Hartman
-Saturday Night Live (Producer), Wayne's World, Superstar, The Coneheads, The Kids in the Hall	Lorne Michaels
-Animal House, Meatballs, Ghostbusters, Beethoven, Kindergarden Cop, Junior, Twins	Ivan Reitman
-That Old Feeling, SCTV	Jayne Eastwood
-Police Academy (TV), SCTV, The Canadian Conspiracy	Joe Flaherty
-The Kids in the Hall	Kevin McDonald, Bruce McCulloch, Dave Foley, Mark McKinney, Scott Thompson
-Made in Canada	Rick Mercer
-The Red Green Show	Steve Smith, Patrick McKenna,
-Exhibit A: Secrets of Forensic Science (narrator), The Red Green Show	Graham Greene
-The Royal Canadian Air Farce Show	Don Ferguson, Luba Goy, Roger Abbott, John Morgan

You can see two of Canada's most popular comedies for FREE at The Canadian Broadcasting Corporation (CBC) Building at 250 Front St West. Free tickets to fall/winter tapings of The Royal Canadian Air Farce and The New Red Green Show can be obtained by calling (416) 205-5050 (www.tickets@airfarce.com) and (905) 631-7450 (www.redgreen.com), respectively. Both are great family entertainment, and the humor is devoid of bad language and explicit sexual content and violence. The New Red Green Show is as popular in the US as it is in Canada and is shown in over 100 PBS stations.

While comedy is clearly a Canadian strong suit, drama is up there too. Consider Canadian drama directors/producers like James Cameron (credits include Titanic, The Terminator, The Terminator 2, Aliens, Rambo: First Blood Part II, The Abyss, True Lies), David Cronenberg (credits include Crash, The Fly, Friday the 13th), and Norman Jewison (credits include Rollerball, Fiddler on the Roof, Moonstruck, Hurricane), and one can begin to appreciate the contribution to Hollywood that Torontonians and Canadians have made!

Toronto International Film Festival

Some consider the Toronto International Film Festival in early September the world's premiere film festival, even ahead of Cannes. The 2001 Toronto International Film Festival showed 326 films from 54 different countries in 9 theatres mostly along Yonge St and in the Bloor-Yorkville area. A great opportunity to see films you would likely never have the chance to see and a chance to see a lot of movie stars and mover-shakers. 2002's is Sept 5-14.

Some of the Hollywood stars that participated included Lou Gossett Jr., Judd Nelson, Heather Graham, Sissy Spacek, William Hurt, Glenn Close, Jennifer Love Hewitt, Denzel Washington, Danny DiVito, Bob Hoskins, Steve Martin, Ben Kingsley, Jason Biggs, Julianne Moore, Eugene Levy, Mick Jagger, David Schwimmer, Christian Slater, and Julia Stiles.

The theatres showing the various films were The Royal Ontario Museum Theatre at 100 Queen's Park, Alliance Atlantis Cumberland Cinemas at 159 Cumberland St, the **Roy Thomson Hall** at 60 Simcoe St, Famous Player's **Uptown** at 764 Yonge St, Cineplex Odeon Varsity Cinemas at 55 Bloor St West, AGO's Jackman Hall at 317 Dundas St West, National Film Board at 150 John St, **Isabel Bader Theatre** at 93 Charles St, and the Visa Screening Room at the Elgin at 189 Yonge St. The Festival's Box Office for tickets and programs is on Level One of the **Eaton Centre** at Yonge and Dundas Streets. See www.e.bell.ca/filmfest/.

Other Television/Film

ChumCity TV offers:
1. FREE tours. (416) 591- 7400, ext 2770.
2. Dance auditions to get on the Electric Circus show (like "Soul Trail" for you parents). Just bring your dance shoes and clothes and head to ChumCity TV on Wednesdays and Thursdays from 4pm-6pm.
3. FREE tickets to the CityLine television show. (416) 591-7400, ext 4900.

The Canadian Film Centre at 2489 Bayview Ave, north of Lawrence Ave East was originally built in 1936 as the home of E.P. Taylor, famous millionaire and owner of the famous racehorse "Northern Dancer". The Centre was founded by Academy Award winner Norman Jewison and is used for training in film, television, and new media.

The **Walk of Fame** recognizes many famous Canadian Hollywood stars.

Sightings of the Stars

With 3,799 location filming permits issued in 2000 alone, there are lots of places to see movie stars and filming in action right on the street. It is hard to miss them, with the usually long procession of big white trucks parked on the side of a street! Just some of the movies recently shot in Toronto include Tuxedo, Chicago, The Farm, Perfect Pie, and Call Me Irresponsible. A small sample of star sightings:

-Air Canada Centre. Jason Priestley, Michael Douglas, Prince.

-Bellini's. Elton John.

-Bistro 990. Christina Ricci, Jason Biggs, Michelle Williams, Jennifer Love Hewitt, Lou Gossett Jr., Colin Mochrie, Jason Priestley, Tia Carrera, Halle Berry, Conan O'Brien, Nicolette Sheriden.

-Sassafraz. Lynn Redgrave, Gordon Pinsent, Joe Flaherty, Bono, Michelle Gellar, Isiah Thomas.

-Sotto Sotto. Michael Jordan, Timothy Hutton, Cheryl Ladd, Ralf Moeller, Danny DeVito, Gene Hackman.

-Rosewater Supper Club. Alan Arkin, Matthew McConaughey, The Backstreet Boys, Pauly Shore.

-Four Seasons Hotel. Keanu Reeves, Mary Steenburgen, Helena Bonham Carter, Leelee Sobieski.

-Joso's. Dan Ackroyd, Paul Newman.

-Marche's (BCE Place): Donny Osmond.

ARCHITECTURE

Toronto has many architectural points of interest. Below are some virtual and real sites to see great architecture:

The **Eric Arthur Gallery** opened November 16, 2001 at 230 College St in the University of Toronto's Faculty of Architecture.

The City of Toronto hosts an annual Architecture & Urban Design Awards contest. The city's website, www.city.toronto.on.ca, provides photos and addresses of the winning buildings by category. A second entertaining website of Toronto architecture is www.geocities/com/architecturewt. Included are bridges, stone buildings, city hall, historic sites, monuments, and several other categories.

The websites of key Toronto architectural firms also provide photos of past and present projects. See www.mtarch.com for the website of high profile Moriyama and Teshima Architects.

The following are just an excerpt of the buildings identified in this guidebook:

Pre-1800

The only building still standing from Toronto's earliest days is the Scadding Cabin, built in 1794. It is located on Canadian National Exhibition grounds (see Tour 7).

1800-1899

-*Old City Hall (1899)*. See Tour 3.
-*Bank of Montreal Building* (circa 1885-86 beaux-arts classicism*)*. See Tour 1.
-*MacDonald-Mowat House* built in 1872 in the French Second Empire style. Home of Canada's first Prime Minister during 1876-78 (Sir John A MacDonald), and of Sir Oliver Mowat during 1888-92. Both men were fathers of Canadian Confederation. 63 St. George St, north of College.
-*house* where later Prime Minister William Lyon Mackenzie King lived with his parents during 1893-96 when he was a student at U of T. 147 Beverly St.
-*Chudleigh House* built in 1871/72. Once used as barracks for the RCMP, it has been the Italian Consulate since 1977. 136 Beverly St.
-*Edward Leadley House* at 25 Augusta Ave built in 1876 (a magnificent century home with elaborate covered porches and gingerbread trim).
-*Pendarvis House* built in 1860 by Frederic Cumberland, the architect of St.

James Cathedral and University College. 33 St. George St.

-**Casa Loma**. This 98-room castle was built by Sir Henry Pellatt in 1911-14 and has been used in films like "The X-Men".

"Modern"

-**Skydome.** It was the world's first dome to open/close.

-**CN Tower**. Most people don't know that the interior of the world's tallest building's shaft is hollow.

Joseph L. Rotman Business School

-*Joseph L. Rotman* Business School (U of T). Very modern, but fits nicely with surrounding historic buildings. 105 St. George St, south of Bloor St West.

-*Robarts Library* (U of T). The connected rare book building has what appears to be a submarine telescope extending from its roof. 130 St. George St, at Harbourd St.

-*Graduate House* (U of T). A large glass sign over 100 feet long and about 10 feet high protrudes from the building over Harbourd St. 60 Harbourd St at Spadina.

-*The Cube House*. Eastern Ave at Sumach St, just west of the Don Valley Parkway.

E.J. Lennox

One of Toronto's most famous and creative architects was E.J. Lennox born in Toronto in 1855. His works included some of the grandest buildings still standing in Toronto:

-**St. Paul's Church** on Bloor (1909-13).

-**King Edward Hotel** (1903).

-**Old City Hall** (1899).

-*Bank of Toronto* (1905) at 205 Yonge St.

-*Excelsior Life building* (1914) at 36 Toronto St (one of his plainest designs).

-*Massey House* (main section, 1883. 519 Jarvis St.

-West wing of **Ontario Legislative building** (Queen's Park) after a fire.

-*Ralph Thornton Town Hall and Cultural Centre* (1913). 765 Queen St East.

-*Stewart building* (1892) at 149 College St.

-**Casa Loma** (1911-14) and stables (1906).

-*E.R. Rundle House* (1889) at 514 Jarvis St.

CLUBS & BARS

Toronto and its Entertainment District are laden with nightclubs. The two best sources for information on the Club scene are www.clubkidunited.com and NOW Magazine. ClubKidUnited's website offers lists of current and defunct clubs, location maps, top 10 listings, DJ/MC names and music styles, and advice on what's in for fashion at the clubs. NOW Magazine can be picked up for FREE throughout downtown. Given this guidebook is predominantly for families, just a <u>few</u> of the clubs and bars are identified below.

On Queen St West

Bamboo. 312 Queen St West. Live Caribbean music. (416) 593-5771.

Horseshoe Tavern. 370 Queen St West. Since 1947. (416) 598-4753.

Rivoli. 332 Queen St West. (416) 596-1908.

On Spadina Ave

El Mocambo. Many greats played here, including Mick Jagger. The building was sold late in 2001 and now it is just a place to reminisce about the rock'n'roll nirvana it once was. 464 Spadina Ave.

Grossman's. 379 Spadina Ave. (416) 977-7000.

Silver Dollar Room. 486 Spadina Rd. (416) 763-9139.

On Bloor St West (Bloor St in the Annex)

Ye Olde Brunswick House. Jazz upstairs; tavern downstairs. Popular spot for U of T students. 481 Bloor St West, west of Spadina. (416) 964-2242.

Lee's Palace. Alternative rock venue. The first floor has live bands. The second floor is the Dance Cave, an alternate dance club. 529 Bloor St West, one block east of Bathurst St. Open Mon-Sun. No cover charge Sun-Thur, $4 on Fri-Sat. (416) 532-1598, www.leespalace.com.

Other

Chick'n'Deli. Very popular gathering spot for young and old. Live bands. 744 Mt. Pleasant Rd. (416) 489-9464.

Guvernment. Popular with the younger set, this huge converted warehouse has several rooms, bars, and a sky patio. 132 Queen's Quay East at Jarvis St. (416) 869-0045.

Montreal Bistro and Jazz Club. 65 Sherbourne St at Adelaide St East. (416) 363-0179.

St. Louis Bar & Grill. Tuesdays are ½ price wings and the place is packed! Large outdoor patio, with heaters for cooler weather. Stand-up bar, food take-out. Live bands in the evenings. More of a middle aged crowd. 2050 Yonge St, just north of Davisville Ave and subway station. (416) 480-0202.

The Joker. Famous for its live to air retro dance parties Saturday nights. Three venues: The Cathedral dance floor, the Joker's Lounge (with 5 pool tables and 4 TVs), and the Joker's Den for serious dancing. 318 Richmond St West at John St in the Entertainment District. (416) 598-1313.

The Courthouse Chamber Lounge. The Lounge has 4 fireplaces, 25 foot ceilings, and hardwood floors. The building was built in 1853 and was once the site of Group of Seven artist meetings. The building still has its original jail cells, complete with a Louis Tussand wax version of the last prisoner (serving 12 years for theft) available for viewing. 57 Adelaide St East. (416) 214-9379.

Whiskey Saigon. 2 dance floors, a patio, and pool tables. Many music styles including hip-hop, techno, progressive, and Euro. 250 Richmond St West. (416) 593-4646, www.home.inforamp.net/~bain03/whisk/.

AFRICAN-CANADIANS

African Canadians have also made significant contributions to Toronto and Southern Ontario. A few items of note:

1. February is Black History Month.
2. The first black male officer in the Toronto Police Services was Lawrence McLarty from Jamaica who joined in 1960 after graduating in the top 5 of his class. The first female black officer was Gloria Bartlett.
3. The first black Toronto police officer killed in the line of duty was PC Percival B. Cummins, on Sep 23, 1981.
4. Anderson Ruffin Abbott (1837-1913), son of Wilson Ruffin Abbot (1801-1876, a Loyalist from Virginia) was the first Canadian born black doctor and was one of eight black doctors to serve in the American Civil War. He is buried in **Necropolis Cemetery**, location VNG-75.

5. Thornton Blackburn, a former slave who came to Canada via the Underground Railway, is buried in **Necropolis Cemetery**, location E-100.
6. William Peyton Hubbard, who served as City Alderman for 14 years and as acting Mayor in 1907 and 1908. He grew up in the Brunswick & Bloor St West area. He is buried in the **Necropolis Cemetery**, location L-27.
7. Delos Rogest Davis was Canada's first black lawyer in 1885.
8. Harriet Tubman, who escaped the US in 1849 and came to Ontario, was the founder of the Underground Railway. She was identified as one of the top 100 people of all time in a documentary by A&E.
9. A company of 30 former black slaves was initiated by black Loyalist Richard Pierpoint. Known as the "Coloured Corps", they fought for Canada at Queenston Heights and Fort George (War of 1812) under Captain Robert Runchey. Some black soldiers fighting for Canada in the War of 1812 are buried in Victoria Memorial Gardens at Niagara and Portland Streets.
10. **Caribana**, one of North America's largest festivals, is held annually in Toronto to celebrate Caribbean culture.
11. There is a concentration of Jerk and Jamaican food places at Eglinton Ave West and Oakwood Ave. The BME Church is nearby at 1828 Eglinton.
12. The Annual Black Film Festival is held in late April. www.getreel.ca.

The Black Secretariat at 590 Jarvis St, 4th floor, provides info on services for the Black community and publishes a directory of Black services, churches, organizations, and media in the city. (416) 924-1104.

DAY TRIPS

Petrolia

If you're coming to Toronto through Detroit or Huron, consider stopping off at the town of Petrolia, argued as the site of North America's *first* oil discovery in 1858. See real oil in the ground and smell the oil aroma in the air. Regional Rd 21, between Hwys 401 and 402. www.timewellspent.ca/oilmusuem.html.

St. Jacobs & Mennonite District

St. Jacobs is a quaint town with lots of historic buildings, almost 100 stores, and nearby attractions such as the very large Farmers' Market, Factory Outlet Mall, The Mennonite Story Visitor Guide, Maple Syrup Museum, St. Jacobs Antique Market, Mill Race and dam, and the last remaining covered bridge in Ontario at West Montrose.

Interesting stores include the Riverworks Shops, Quilt Shop, Stone Crock Bakery, and St. Jacobs Mennonite Quilts. The quaintness is enhanced by the Mennonite people and their horse-drawn black buggies, the horse-drawn trolley that plies the street, and the courtesy umbrellas that are provided for your use in rainy weather and that you can return to any store in St. Jacobs after you're done. The nearby Victorian-era town of Elmira is home to Canada's largest maple syrup festival in early April (1st Saturday).

Niagara Falls

The World Famous Niagara Falls

This honeymoon capital receives over 14,000,000 visitors each year. The magnificent falls and surrounding parklands and town are easily worth a stopover on a trip to Toronto. Points of interest include the American and Horseshoe Falls (i.e. Niagara Falls), Niagara Parks and Gardens, Clifton Hill amusements, the Skylon, the Minolta Tower, Lundy's Lane historic and tourist attractions, a greenhouse, The Butterfly Conservatory (with 2,000 butterflies), Casino Niagara, and the Niagara Spanish Aero Car. Activities include the engaging Maid of the Mist boat ride in the summer or the spectacular Festival of Lights and FREE New Year's Eve concerts (2001's included the artist "Snow") in the winter.

Clifton Hill's amusements include the Guinness World of Records (with its 8'11" tallest man adorning its box office), the Dino Island 3D ride, Ride Over the Falls, and Elvira's Haunted Coaster. These rides cost $Cdn9.95/$US6.50 or $Cdn17.90/$US11.93 for all three rides. The House of Frankenstein costs $3.95/adult and $3.00/child. Ripley's Moving Theatre costs $11.95/adult and $6.95/child. While expensive for a 15 minute ride, you get two exciting action movies with 3D glasses and a seat that moves around in concert with the

Clifton Hill at Night

screen. Not recommended for young children because of view difficulties and possible motion sickness. Check around for tourist coupon brochures (like "Niagara's SuperSaver" or "TravelHost") offering discounts. This stretch is marvelously lit up at nighttime, reminiscent of Las Vegas. Casino Niagara is located very close nearby and its tower can't be missed. Its 100,000 sq. ft with 2,700 slot machines and 144 gaming tables are for adults only.

Lundy's Lane can easily be reached from the top of Clifton Hill, by turning left or south on Victoria St, which turns into Ferry St, which turns into Lundy's Lane (total distance from Clifton Hill is less than 1 mile). You'll first come to the historic Stamford Township Hall built in 1874. This building housed the City of Niagara Falls' civic offices from 1874 to 1970! It now houses Lundy's Lane Museum in the back and hosts the Sylvia Place Marketplace in summer.

Next comes Drummond Hill Cemetery (behind Drummondville Presbyterian Church). Turn left on Drummond Rd from Lundy's Lane, and take the first left (Buchner Pl) to the Cemetery entrance. It is here that the bloody Battle of Lundy's Lane took place. Each side lost about 800 of their 2,800 men.

 There is a trench gravesite for US infantrymen of the Connecticut 25th, the New York 23rd, the Massachusetts 9th and 21st, the Pennsylvania 22nd, and the Vermont 11th. A monument was erected by the American Legion, of Niagara County Committee and Department of New York in 1991. There are also graves of individual American soldiers such as Abraham F. Hull, and a monument to Hull erected by the Niagara Frontier Landmarks Association of Buffalo, New York in 1907.

The largest monument, erected in 1895 by the Canadian government, stands for the Canadian and British soldiers who died (including an inscription of the names of many). A sculpture of General Drummond of the Canadian/British side and his horse also stands nearby, as does a monument to Loyalist Laura Secord and her efforts toward Canada's victory at Beaver Dams.

After passing even more motels, eateries, the deeply chiseled canal that feeds water to a hydro-electric plant, mini-golf places, and the QEW highway, you'll reach the Canada One Factory Outlets Mall. Its about 2 miles from Clifton Hill. Stores include Club Monaco, Polo, Ralph Lauren, Roots, Black & Decker, Liz Claiborne, Levi's, Rockport, Reebok's, Nike, Claire's, and Greb-Kodiak.

Food places abound. The one place to stay clear of is Denny's on Victoria St, near Clifton Hill. While the portions are large, the menu varied, and kids are readily accepted, I find the prices crazily expensive. One breakfast special priced at $21.95 (no, it didn't include steak), was priced at $8.49 at the Lundy's Lane Denny's just 2 miles away. Hamburgers with fries cost $12-$15! A soft drink cost $3.96! There are two All-You-Can-Eat Buffets for $5.99 yards away in the Wedgewood Restaurant (Travelodge Near the Falls Hotel), and Quality Inn. The Ponderosa Restaurant 100 yards away on Victoria St offers a buffet breakfast for $US3.50 from 7 am - noon. The Golden Griddle right on Clifton Hill offers breakfasts from $5-10.49 (with a 5 oz steak). The Pilgrim Restaurant also on Clifton Hill offers eggs, toast and jelly, home fries or 3 pancakes with table syrup for $4.95. Casino Niagara's Market Restaurant offers a buffet breakfast for $6.95. Cupps café in the Canada One Factory Outlets Mall offers breakfasts for $2.99 (bagel, coffee/tea, and 2 eggs).

Lunch and dinner can be obtained at several nice restaurants conveniently located on Victoria St near the top of Clifton Hill. Mama Mia's offers Italian meals. Lunches cost $7-8. Paesano's offers pasta entrees for $8-11, with a

$4-6 kids menu. La Parmigiana offers pasta entrees for $9-12 and has steak, chicken, veal, sole, and other entrees for $13-18. Mama Leone's offers pasta entrees for $8-11 and steak/fish entrees for $17-30. Big Anthony's offers pasta entrees for $9-11 and other entrees such as steak and ribs for $13-18. Antica Pizzeria (restaurant) has pasta entrees for $5-10, including a veal parmagiana special for $9.99. Pho-Mai-Vi Vietnamese Restaurant offers various noodle and vermicelli based meals for $6-10. Yank's Bar & Grill has burgers and sandwiches for $5-7 and pizzas for $10. Baron's Steakhouse at 5019 Centre St a few yards past the top of Clifton Hill offers steak, pasta, and seafood entrees for $10-$26 in a lovely cherry wood paneled, more upscale restaurant environment. Excellent food and service. Lundy's Lane has almost all the fast food restaurants you can think of and more. The Flying Saucer (subs, burgers, sandwiches) is a unique place to get some fast food.

If you choose to stay a night or more, accommodation choices also abound. The Clifton Hill/Victoria St section hotels and motels include Travelodge by the Falls, Courtyard by Marriott, Days Inn, Quality Hotel, Howard Johnson's, Super 8, Comfort Inn, and Imperial Suites. There are many, many more motels and bed & breakfasts on Lundy's Lane and elsewhere in Niagara Falls to choose from. Great deals can be had during the off-season. Deals offered by Howard Johnson for example, for two nights accommodation with two breakfasts and one dinner for $120!!

Continue north on Niagara Parkway and you'll see the Butterfly Conservatory, a golf course, Canadian and US electrical generating plants on the Niagara River, the enormous Floral Clock (FREE), and Queenston Heights Park.

Further information: Niagara Falls Tourism at (800) 563-2557, or www.DiscoverNiagara.com; or www.niagaraparks.com.

Queenston

This sleepy historic village belies the enormous carnage that took place here during the War of 1812. The Americans attacked by crossing the raging Niagara River and scaling the almost vertical gorge walls. Canadian hero General Isaac Brock jumped on his horse and left Fort George with a contingent of men to repulse the American attack. Brock was killed and the Americans were winning the day. Major Roger Scheafe joined the battle later with reinforcements from Fort George, and riding into battle on Brock's horse, and with the help of native Indians, forced the Americans back to the US side of the river. Unfortunately Brock's horse was also killed, and there is a little known monument to Brock and his horse where Brock was killed. It is just yards east off the Niagara Parkway coming down from Queenston Heights (where the Brock Tower Memorial is in a lovely park – try climbing the tower spiral stairs for an impressive view of the Niagara River and Lake Ontario), at Clarence and Queenston Streets. The historic stone William Lyon Mackenzie *Print Shop* is also just yards away.

Accommodations are limited but include The Stone Cottage (built in 1812) at 36A Princess St. (905) 468-5413, or see www.kevan.com/stonecottage/.

Continue north on the Niagara Parkway (which has a fantastic paved trail for biking, rollerblading, and/or walking through wondrous park lands and mature trees) and you'll pass several fruit stands and the *McFarland House* (c.1800) used as a hospital by both sides during the War of 1812 on your way to Niagara-on-the-Lake.

War of 1812 buffs should consider a visit to the *Laura Secord Homestead*. Queenston, near Hwy 405 and the Niagara Parkway. $2/adult, $1.25/child 6-12, FREE for children under 6. (905) 262-4851.

Niagara-on-the-Lake

This wondrously rustic and Victorian town is a hit with tourists and is easily worth a stopover of at least a few hours. It placed first as The Prettiest Town in Canada, and second as The Prettiest Town in the World. It was founded in the 1780s by members of Butler's Rangers and other Loyalists after leaving the US, and was once the capital of Upper Canada. It is steeped in history, arts, and theatre. The still existing Law Society of Upper Canada was established here in 1797 before moving to Osgoode Hall in Toronto in 1832. The Agricultural Society of Upper Canada was founded here in 1792.

The oldest inn in Upper Canada still in operation, the quaint yellow clapboard Olde Angel Inn at Market and Regent Streets, was built in 1816 on the burnt foundations of an Inn destroyed in the War of 1812. The whole town was captured and substantially burned down by the US in the War of 1812.

Coming from Niagara Falls along the Niagara Parkway (which becomes Queen St in town), the first point of interest you'll see is the historic Fort George, which battled with the US's Fort Niagara across the river during the War of 1812. The 869-seat Festival Theatre is next, then a park on Queen St with a children's playground and wading pool, a bandshell, washrooms, gardens, and lots of shaded green space for a picnic, and then the extraordinarily beautiful *Prince of Wales Hotel* (c. 1864).

There is a lovely commercial section of a few blocks on Queen St, with several stores housed in buildings from the 1800s. Angie Strauss Fashions and

Gallery (c. 1860) at 125, Newark Shoes in the Evans Block (c. 1840) at 122 Queen St, the Beau Chapeau Shop of hats (c. 1825), Earth Wares Adventure Apparel in the *Gollop House* (c.1830) at 118, and Victoria Gallery and Tea (c.1812) at 108. Several have beautiful wood floors as well.

Other interesting stores include the Maple Leaf Fudge store for old-fashioned candies and fudge. Niagara Castings and Mastermark Pewter at 106, Art Gallery Signature Works (Canadian art) on Victoria a few yards south of Queen St, the Shaw Café and Wine Bar and its popular outdoor patio (entrees $9-15), Niagara Home Bakery at 66, The Owl and the Pussycat (painted by famous Trisha Romance), Loyalist Village.Com (wood and soapstone carvings and chimes), and The Preservation Fine Art Gallery (featuring art of Trisha Romance within an exquisite building). The Stagecoach Family Restaurant at 45 is not in an attractive building but it offers good value for money meals. Entrees are $5-10 and breakfasts are $3-5. Ham, eggs, and toast cost $3.49.

Interesting buildings include the *Niagara Apothecary Museum* (c.1864) was also painted by Trisha Romance, the stone *Niagara Courthouse* (c.1847) built on the previous site of the *Niagara Library* (c.1800) and containing the visitors centre and public washrooms, the Royal George Theatre, *Grace United Church* (c.1852) on Victoria St and Queen, the *Shaker House* (c.1813) at Queen and DeLader Streets, and the Cenotaph monument to World War I and II.

Accommodations abound. The 108-room Prince of Wales is superb, and rooms generally start at $275/night. The 142 rooms of Queen's Landing start from $220. The historic *Olde Angel Inn* offers 9 rooms from $119. Bed and Breakfast places include *The Rogers-Blake-Harrison House* (rebuilt in 1817 after being burned during the War of 1812) right on Queen St at 157, from from $120 double occupancy [(905) 468-1615, www.rogers-harrison.on.ca]; *The Doctor's House* (built in 1824) right on Queen St at 154, from $99 double occupancy with shared bath [905) 468-5413, www.kevan.com/doctorshouse/.

To get back to the QEW highway to Toronto, follow Queen St west to Mary St and turn left. Follow this road until you come to the humungous bridge overhead and you'll see signs leading you the last mile to the QEW on-ramp. Feel free to stop off at the many wineries and fruit stands along the road.

If you take this trip on your return from Toronto, take Exit 38B/Niagara Stone Rd and follow the signs and Regional Road 55 to Niagara-on-the-Lake. Rd 55 ends at Mary St, about 1 mile south of the main part of the town, but continues north under a different name. Take it until you reach Queen St and turn right. Follow this street, which becomes Niagara Parkway, and it will lead you through Niagara-on-the-Lake and Queenston to Niagara Falls.

INDEX

<u>NOTES</u>

ABOUT THE AUTHOR

First time author Walter Weigel has been a resident of Toronto for 41 years, including almost 9 years in three neighbourhoods downtown. He has had the privilege of having lived briefly in the U.S and having travelled to the U.S, Canada, Europe, South Pacific, Caribbean, Australia, and New Zealand. While he considers there to be many immensely beautiful and liveable cities and areas in the world, Toronto remains his first love and favourite city.

He frequently participates in the many fabulous offerings of Toronto, sometimes in the capacity of a "tourist" complete with family and hotel. It was with his love of Toronto and decades of experiencing its attractions, festivals, trails, shopping, and restaurants that he has written this guidebook.